VOLUPTUOUS HORRORS 2

100 WEIRD MENACE PULP MAGAZINE COVERS 1937-1940

VOLUPTUOUS HORRORS 2

EDITED BY G.H. JANUS
ISBN 978-1-8383595-9-1
PUBLISHED BY BONEFYRE BOOKS 2023
COPYRIGHT © BONEFYRE BOOKS 2023
ALL WORLD RIGHTS RESERVED

FOREWORD

One of the first key waves of populist, or pulp, art created in American cultural history came during the period from 1933 to 1940, when a range of provocative magazines sprang up with exceptionally striking, often startling cover illustrations by some of the most imaginative artists of the time. The most controversial of these publications were those themed around "weird menace" fiction, a genre which coalesced in October 1933 with the inception of **Dime Mystery Magazine**, from Popular Publications. This watershed issue saw the magazine – previously titled **Dime Mystery Book Magazine** – shift its focus from crime to horror, with full-cover artwork by Walter M. Baumhofer showing a hooded killer forcing a woman to cut the rope holding her boyfriend from falling into a vat of flesh-eating acid. The skeleton of a previous victim, stripped clean to the bone, can be seen floating in the foreground. This shift in artwork was accompanied by a similar change in story titles, with the cover featuring "Dance Of the Skeletons". Other titles in this issue included "Monster In The Dark", "The Graveless Dead", and "Gate Of The Two Coffins". This new genre was variously described as "horror", "terror-mystery", and "the weirdest stories ever told" on **Dime Mystery** covers, with the definitive term "weird menace" first appearing on the cover of **Terror Tales** in 1937.

The covers produced for this and similar pulps were mainly centred around images of attractive young women – scantily clad in ripped dresses and underwear, or even naked – being threatened with torture, mutilation and death by an array of hooded cultists, mad doctors and other deranged psychopaths. Regular artists for these publications included Baumhofer, Tom Lovell, Rudolph Belarski, John Newton Howitt, John Drew, and John Walter Scott, all purveyors of prime voluptuous horror. Among the other weird menace pulps were **Terror Tales**, **Horror Stories**, **Mystery Tales**, **Strange Stories**, **Eerie Mysteries**, **Uncanny Tales**, and **Thrilling Mystery**, growing increasingly daring in content[1] until finally, in the early 1940s, a combination of moral backlash and the paper shortage caused by world war saw weird menace slowly disappear from the newsstands.

VOLUPTUOUS HORRORS 2 collects 100 full-page, full-colour weird menace magazine covers from 1937-1940, presenting some of the world's most lurid and often sadistic cover designs from the golden age of pulps.

1. For example, when the February 1940 issue of **Dime Mystery** recycled cover artwork from **Horror Stories**, October 1937, the image was reworked so that the woman in peril was now naked, her modesty only shielded by steam from the vat in which she is being slowly boiled alive.

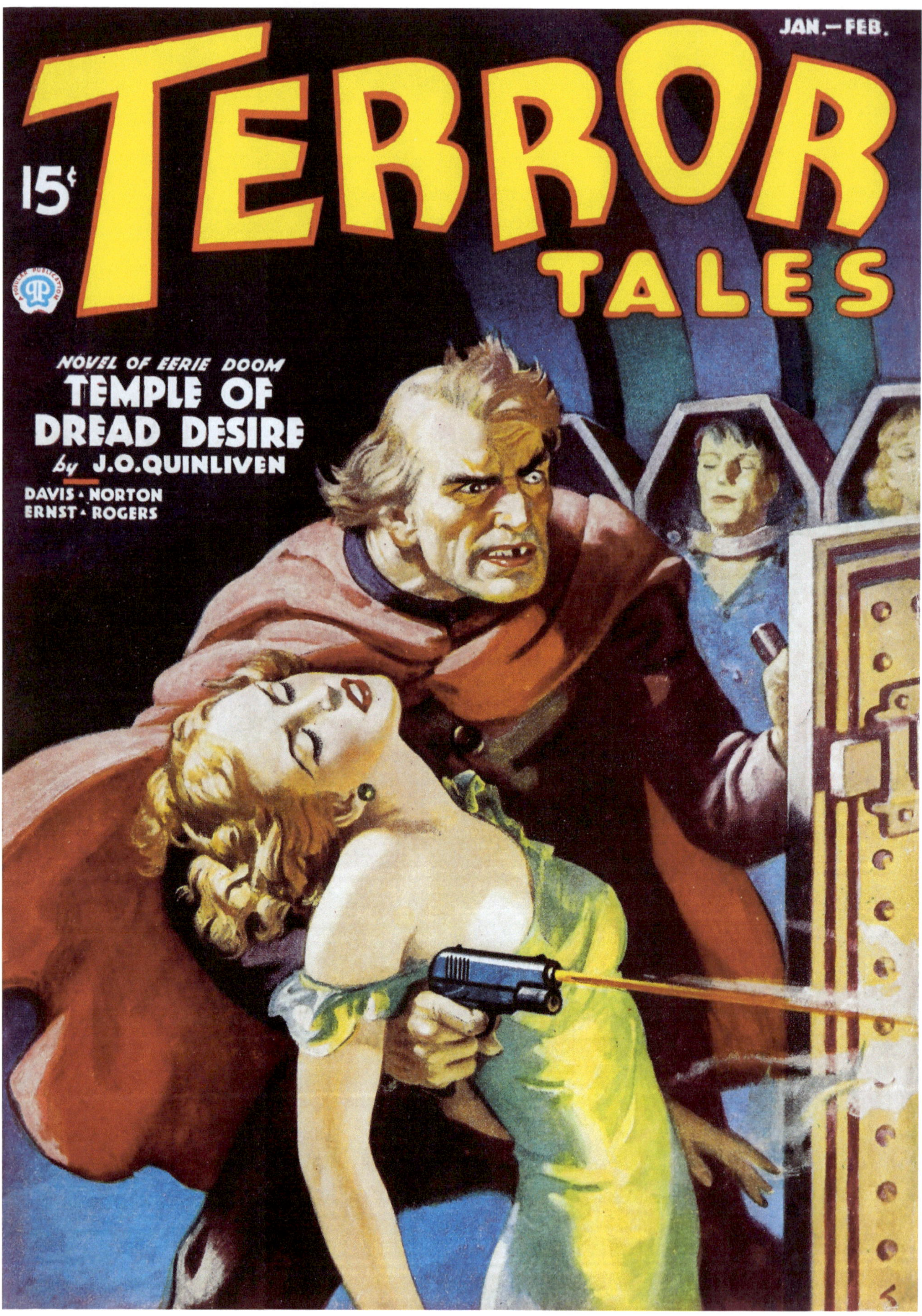

TERROR TALES

JANUARY-FEBRUARY 1937

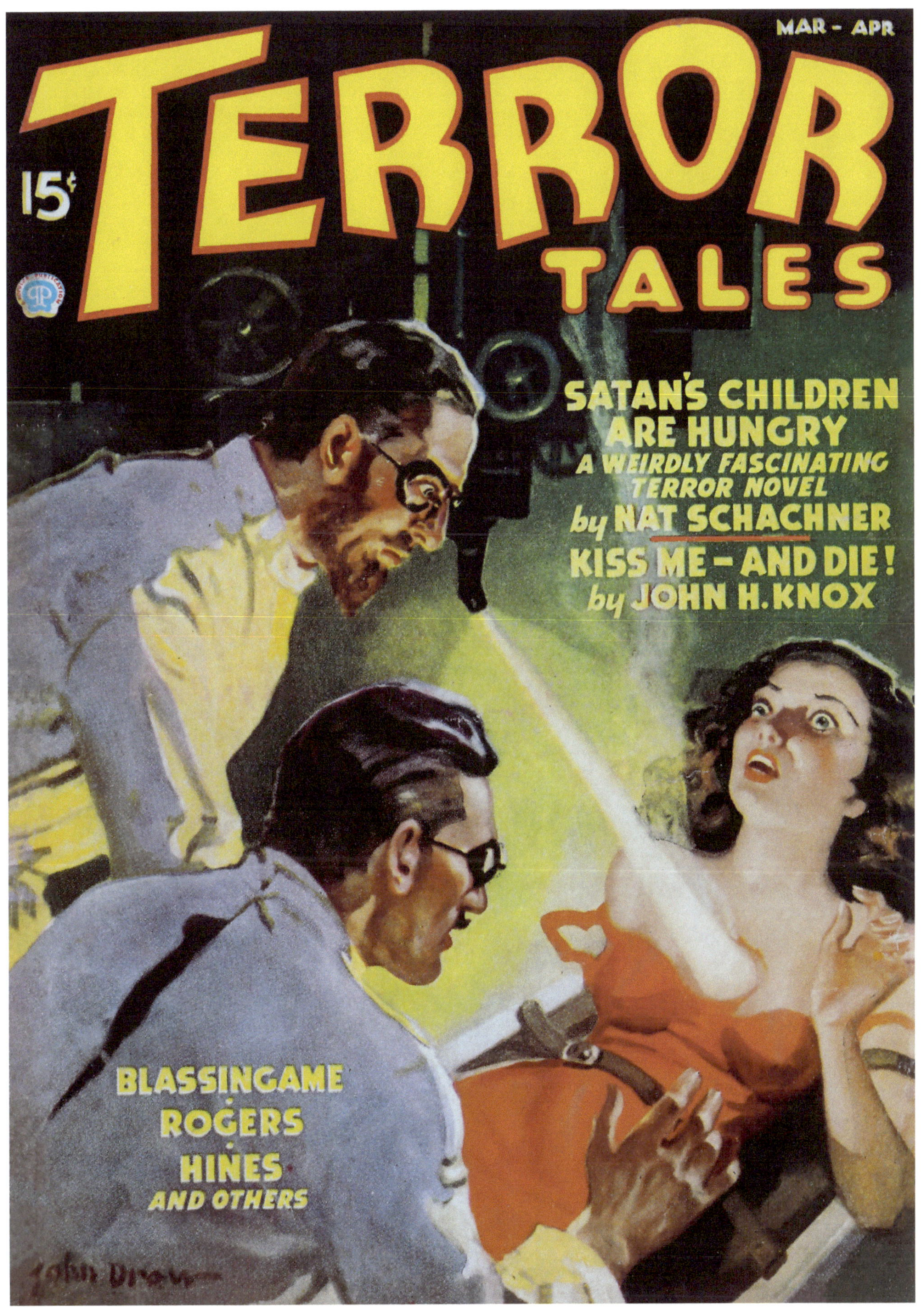

MAR - APR
15¢
TERROR
TALES
SATAN'S CHILDREN ARE HUNGRY
A WEIRDLY FASCINATING TERROR NOVEL
by NAT SCHACHNER
KISS ME — AND DIE!
by JOHN H. KNOX
BLASSINGAME
ROGERS
HINES
AND OTHERS

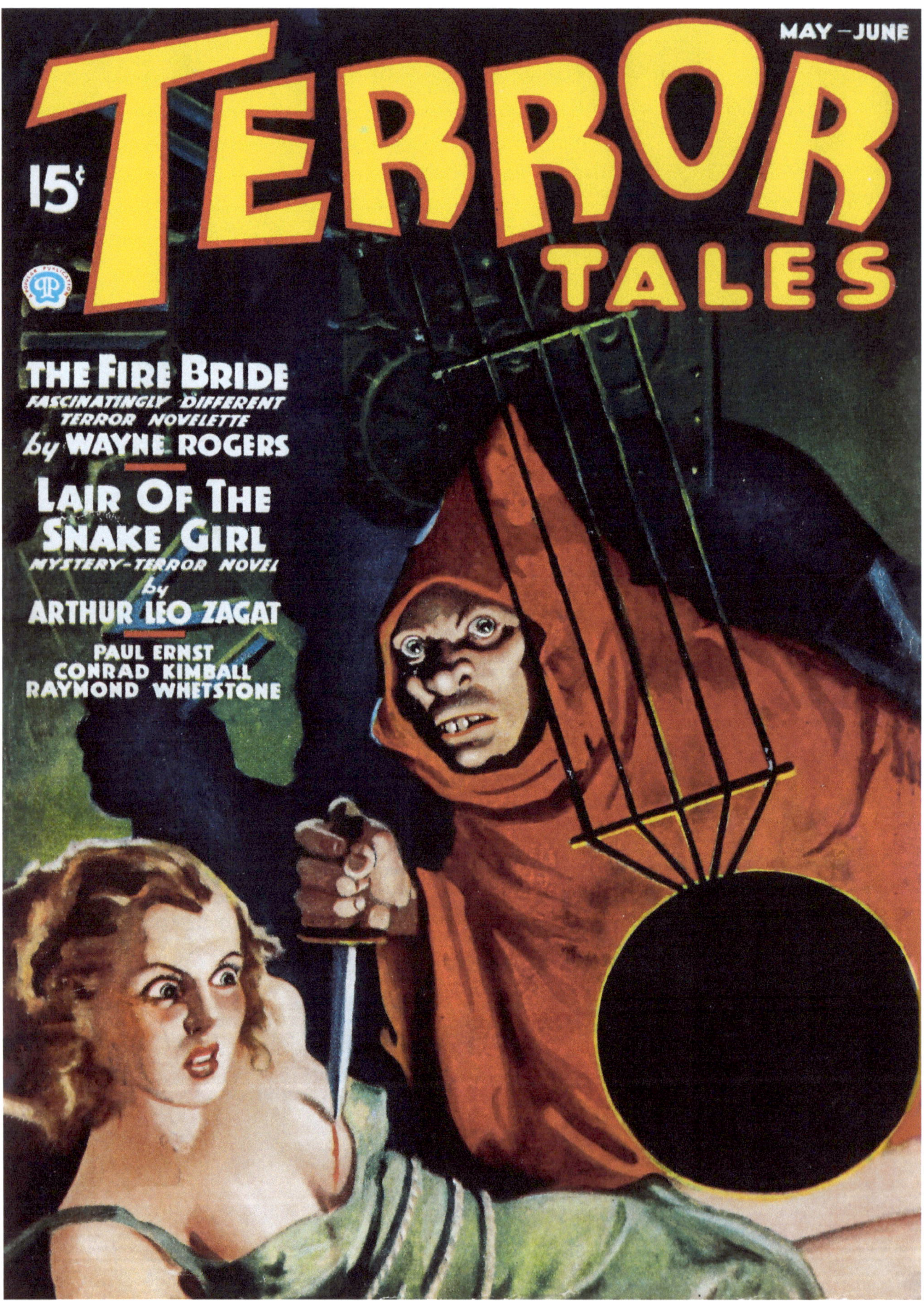

TERROR TALES

MAY-JUNE 1937

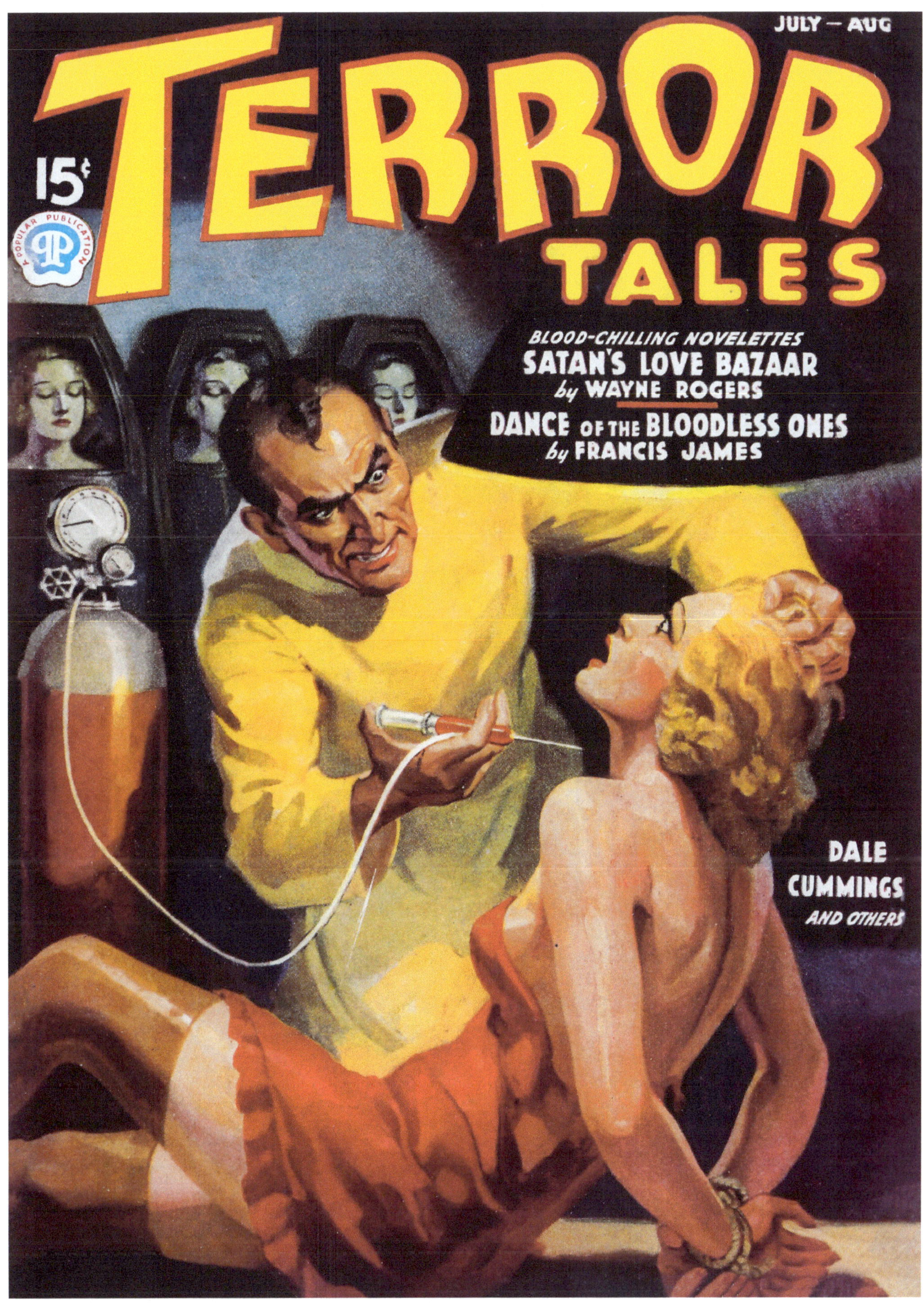

JULY — AUG
15¢
A POPULAR PUBLICATION
TERROR TALES
BLOOD-CHILLING NOVELETTES
SATAN'S LOVE BAZAAR
by WAYNE ROGERS
DANCE of the BLOODLESS ONES
by FRANCIS JAMES
DALE CUMMINGS
AND OTHERS

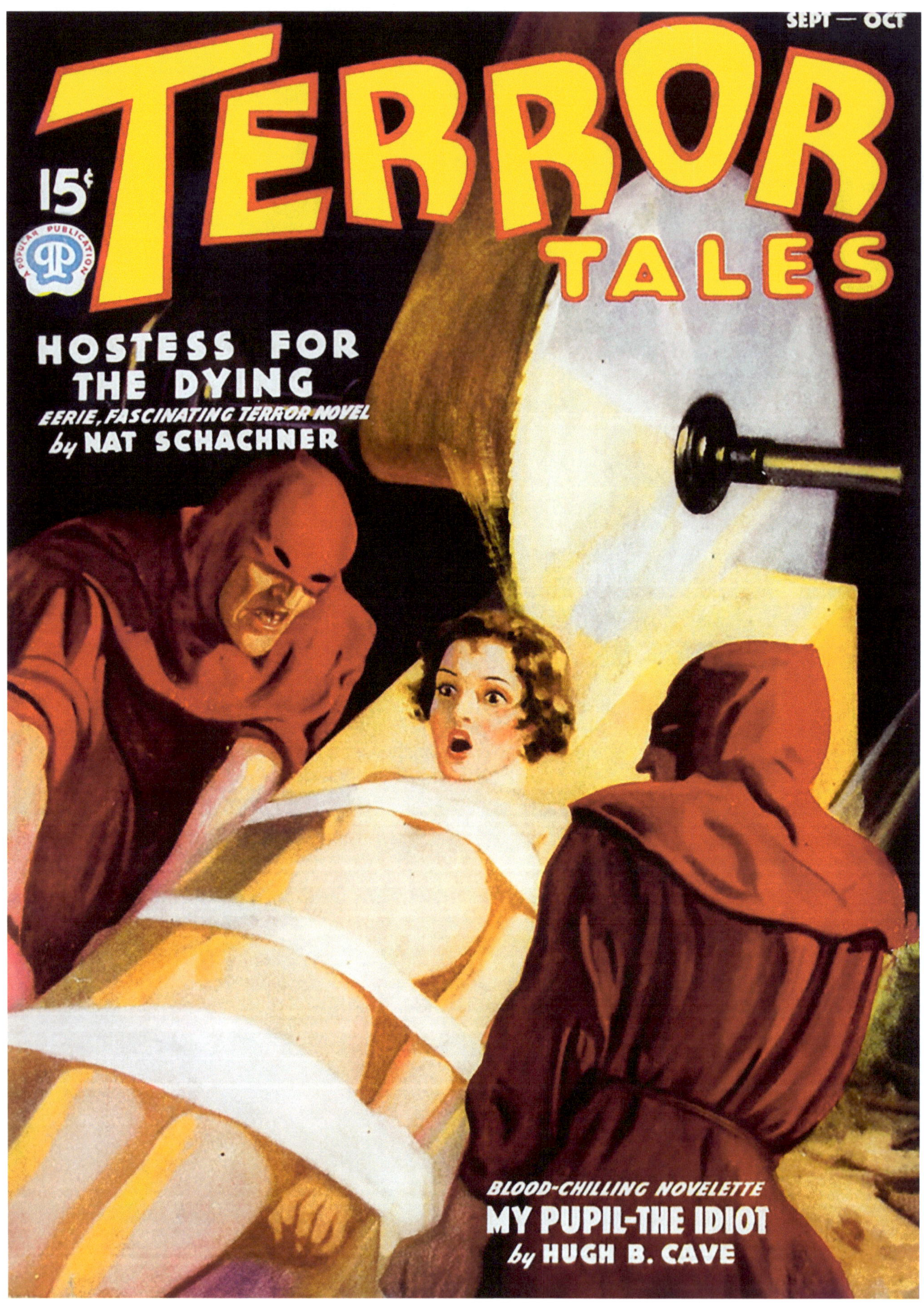

SEPT — OCT
15¢
A POPULAR PUBLICATION
TERROR TALES
HOSTESS FOR THE DYING
EERIE, FASCINATING TERROR NOVEL
by NAT SCHACHNER
BLOOD-CHILLING NOVELETTE
MY PUPIL-THE IDIOT
by HUGH B. CAVE

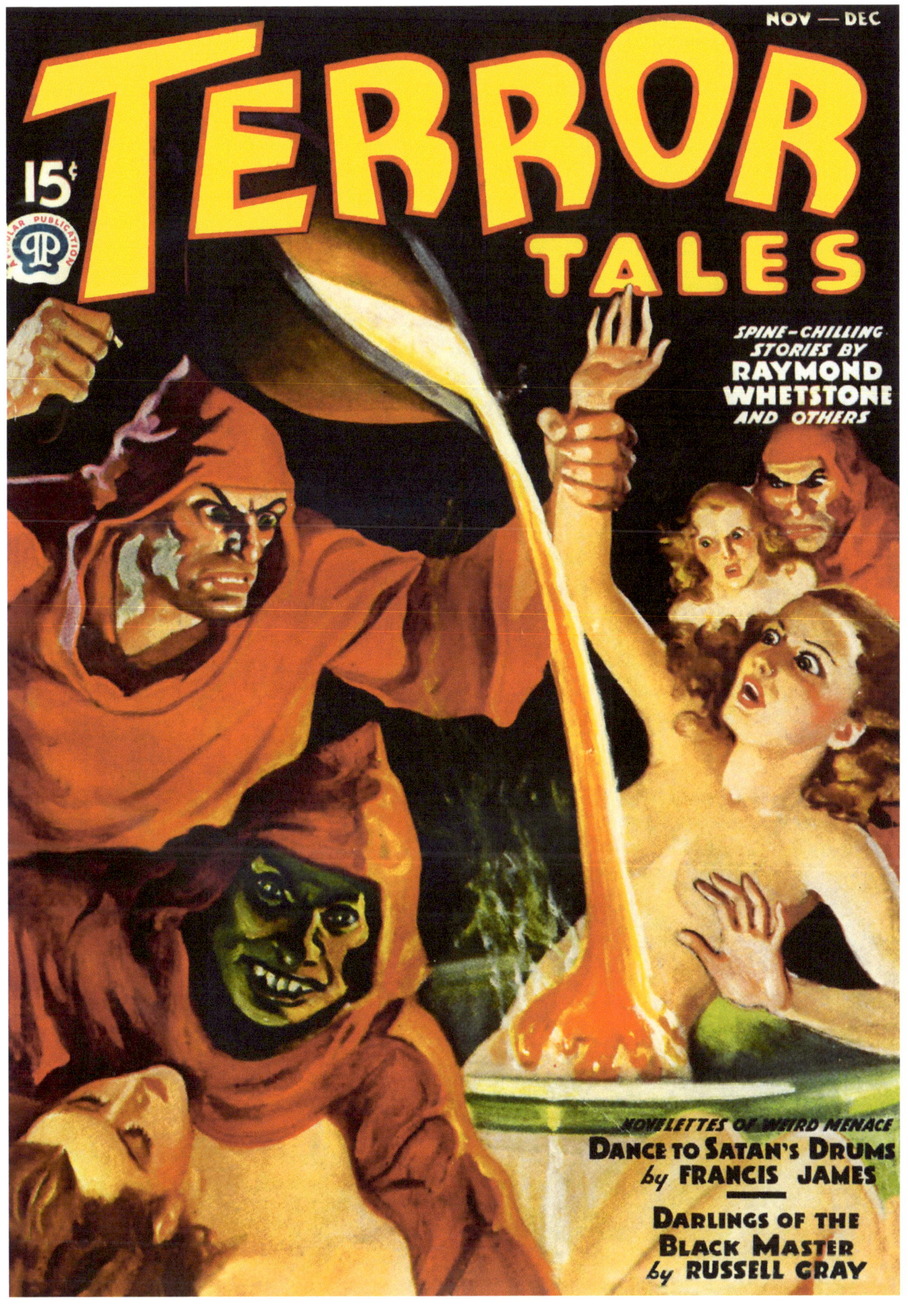

NOV — DEC
15¢
TERROR
TALES
SPINE-CHILLING
STORIES BY
RAYMOND
WHETSTONE
AND OTHERS
NOVELETTES OF WEIRD MENACE
DANCE TO SATAN'S DRUMS
by FRANCIS JAMES
DARLINGS OF THE
BLACK MASTER
by RUSSELL GRAY

9

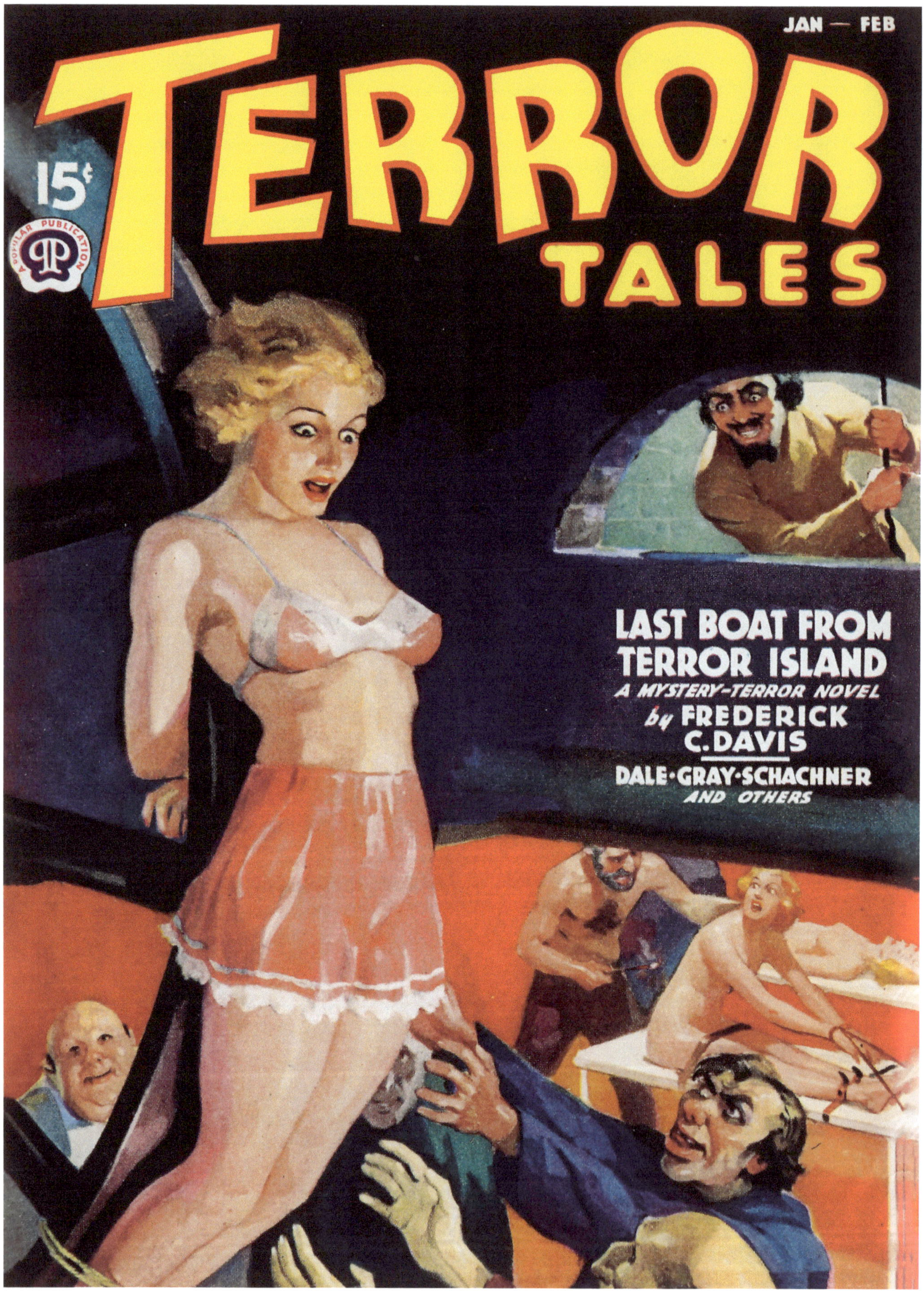

JAN — FEB
15¢
A POPULAR PUBLICATION
TERROR TALES
LAST BOAT FROM TERROR ISLAND
A MYSTERY-TERROR NOVEL
by FREDERICK C. DAVIS
DALE · GRAY · SCHACHNER
AND OTHERS

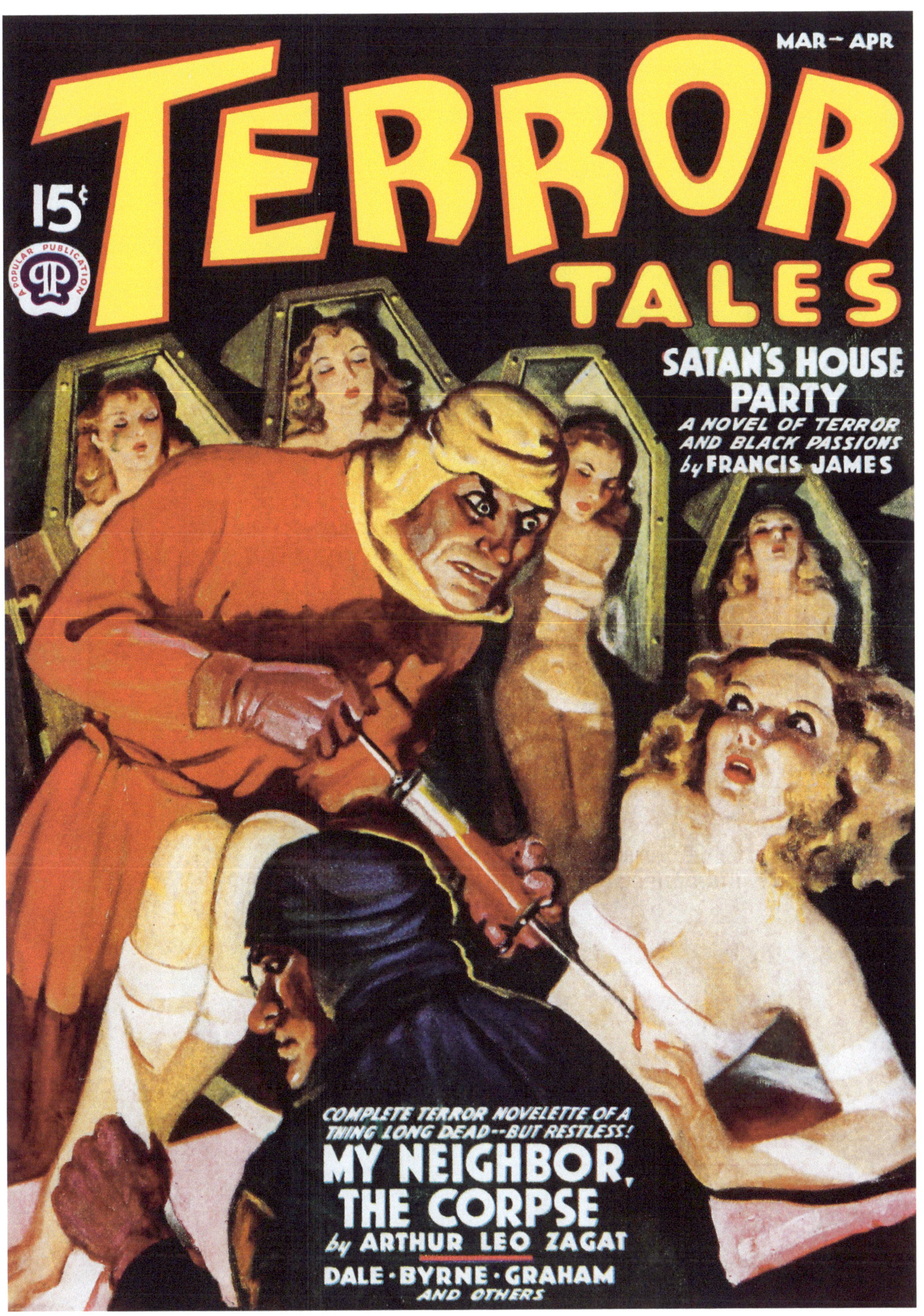

MAR–APR
15¢
A POPULAR PUBLICATION
TERROR TALES
SATAN'S HOUSE PARTY
A NOVEL OF TERROR AND BLACK PASSIONS
by FRANCIS JAMES
COMPLETE TERROR NOVELETTE OF A THING LONG DEAD--BUT RESTLESS!
MY NEIGHBOR, THE CORPSE
by ARTHUR LEO ZAGAT
DALE · BYRNE · GRAHAM
AND OTHERS

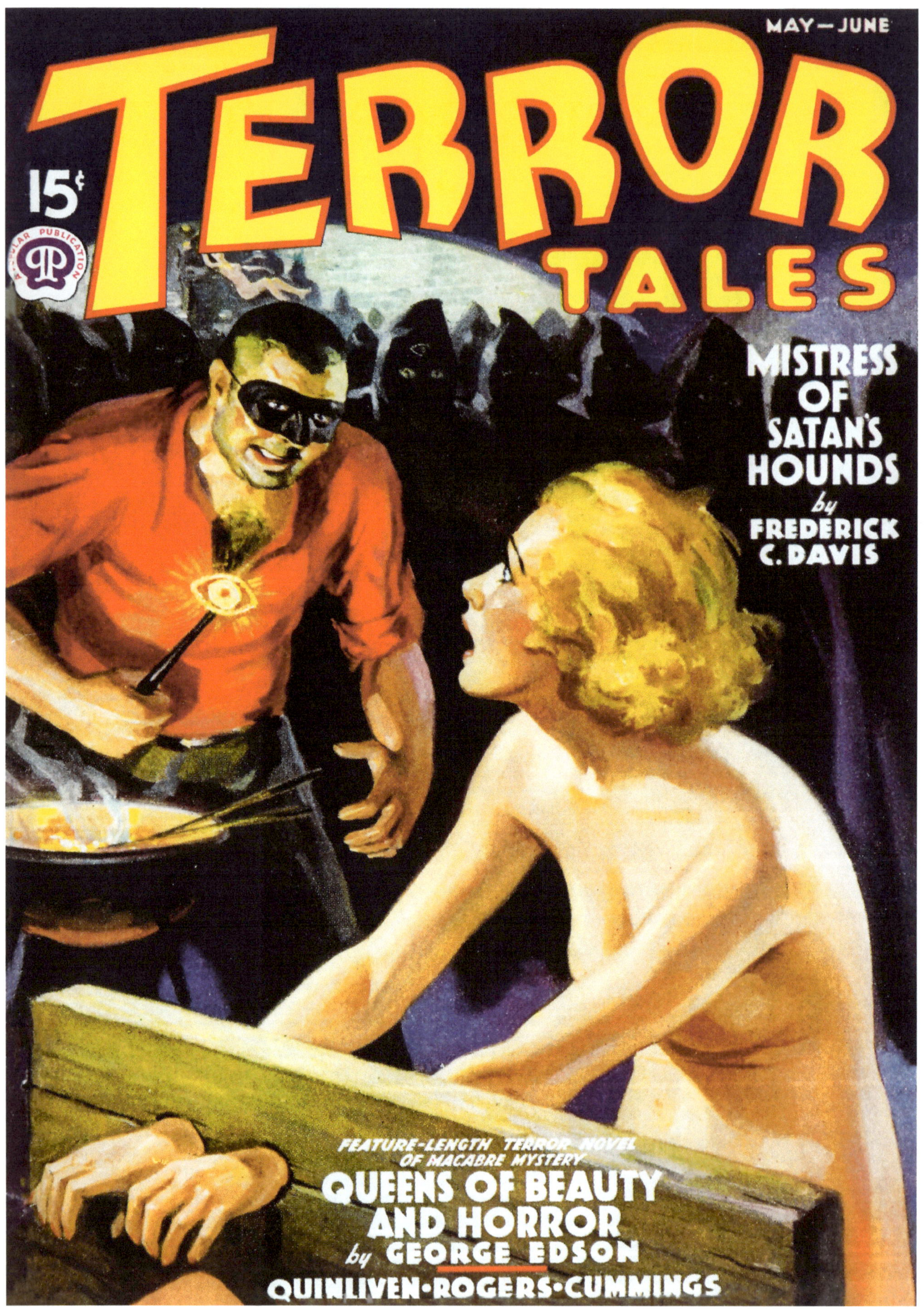

MAY—JUNE
15¢
A POPULAR PUBLICATION
TERROR TALES
MISTRESS OF SATAN'S HOUNDS
by FREDERICK C. DAVIS
FEATURE-LENGTH TERROR NOVEL OF MACABRE MYSTERY
QUEENS OF BEAUTY AND HORROR
by GEORGE EDSON
QUINLIVEN · ROGERS · CUMMINGS

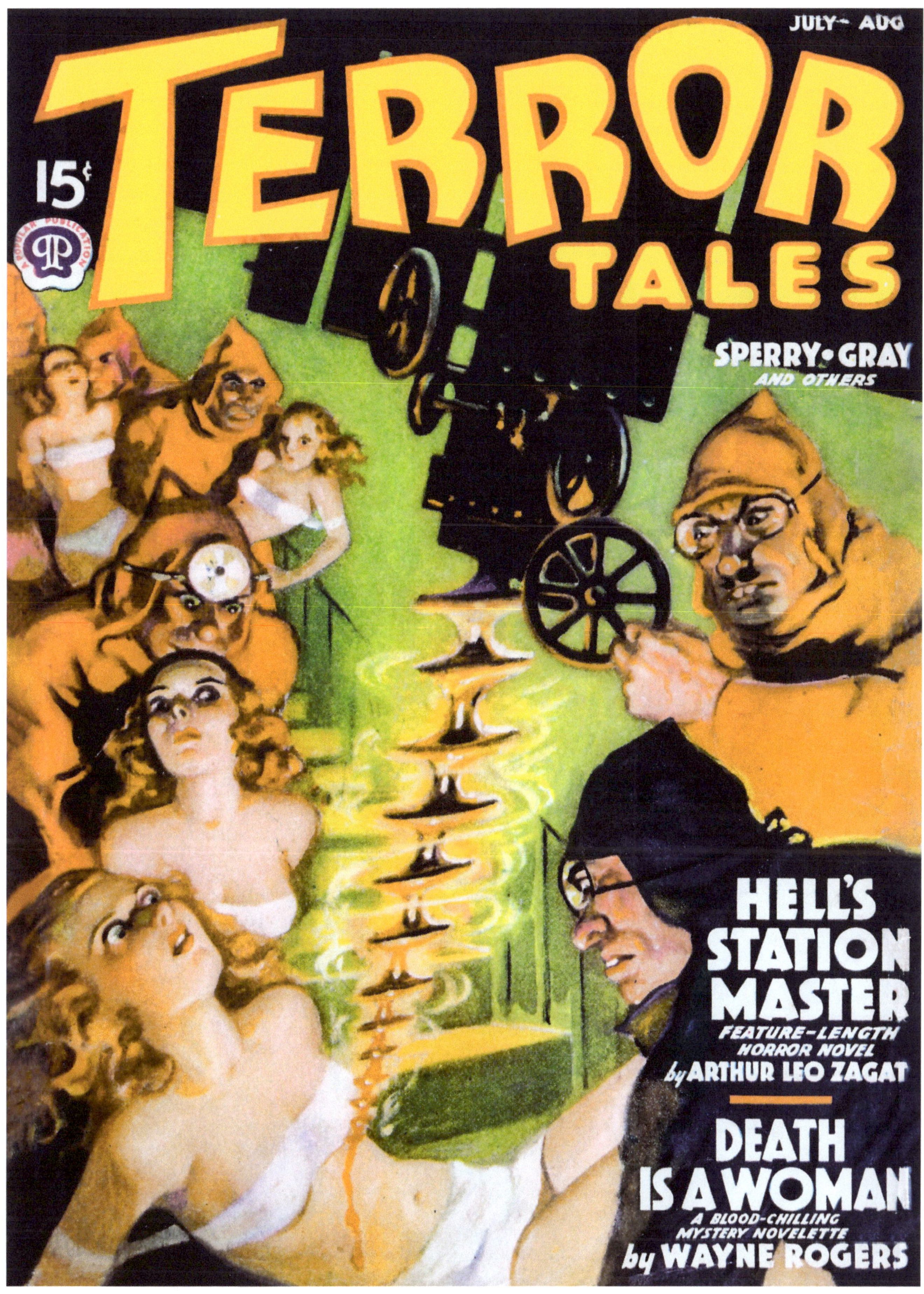

JULY - AUG
15¢
A POPULAR PUBLICATION
TERROR TALES
SPERRY · GRAY
AND OTHERS
HELL'S STATION MASTER
FEATURE-LENGTH HORROR NOVEL
by ARTHUR LEO ZAGAT
DEATH IS A WOMAN
A BLOOD-CHILLING MYSTERY NOVELETTE
by WAYNE ROGERS

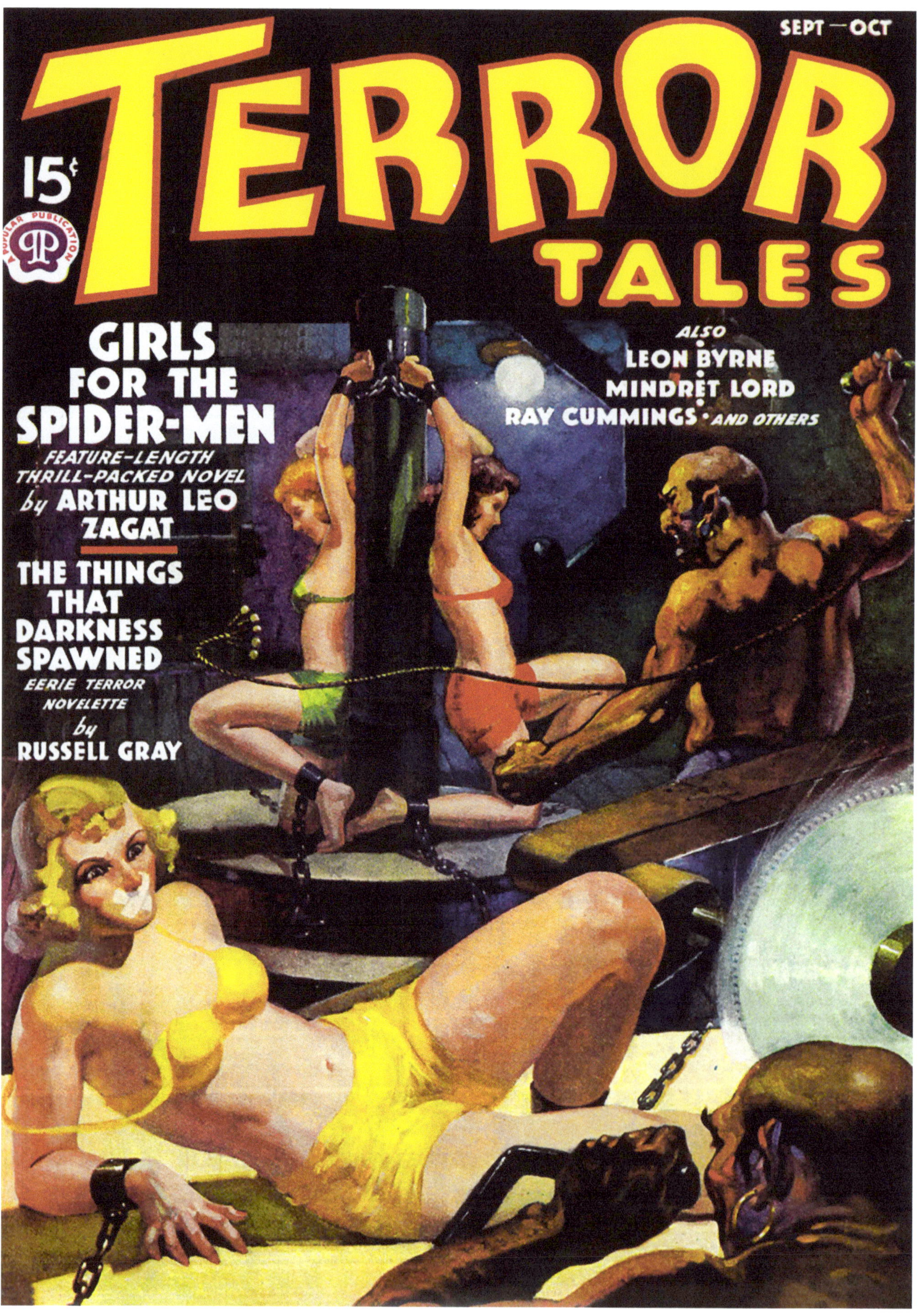

SEPT—OCT
15¢
A POPULAR PUBLICATION
TERROR TALES
GIRLS FOR THE SPIDER-MEN
FEATURE-LENGTH THRILL-PACKED NOVEL
by ARTHUR LEO ZAGAT
THE THINGS THAT DARKNESS SPAWNED
EERIE TERROR NOVELETTE
by RUSSELL GRAY
ALSO
LEON BYRNE
MINDRET LORD
RAY CUMMINGS · AND OTHERS

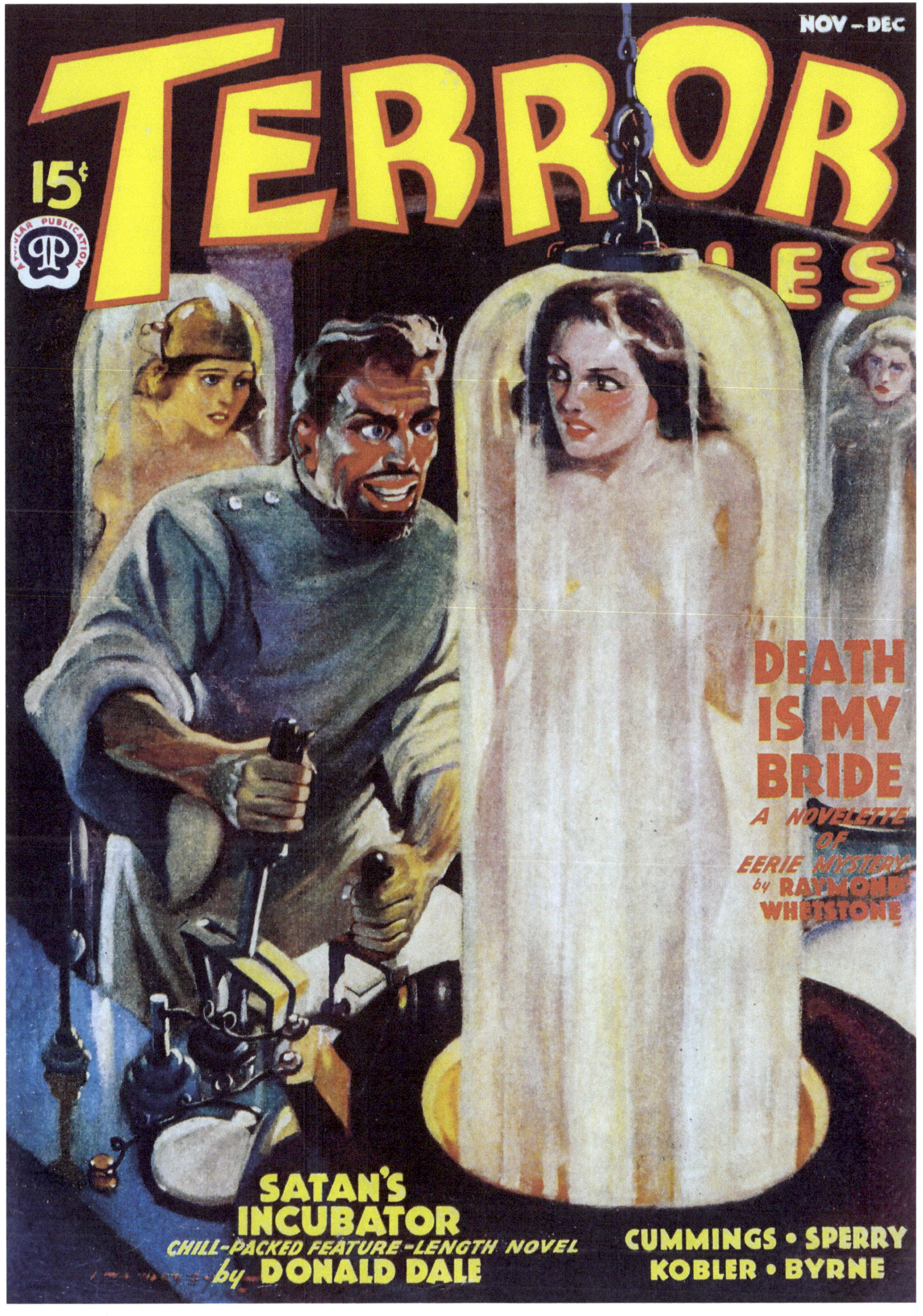

NOV – DEC
15¢
A POPULAR PUBLICATION
TERROR TALES
DEATH IS MY BRIDE
A NOVELETTE OF EERIE MYSTERY by RAYMOND WHETSTONE
SATAN'S INCUBATOR
CHILL-PACKED FEATURE-LENGTH NOVEL by DONALD DALE
CUMMINGS • SPERRY
KOBLER • BYRNE

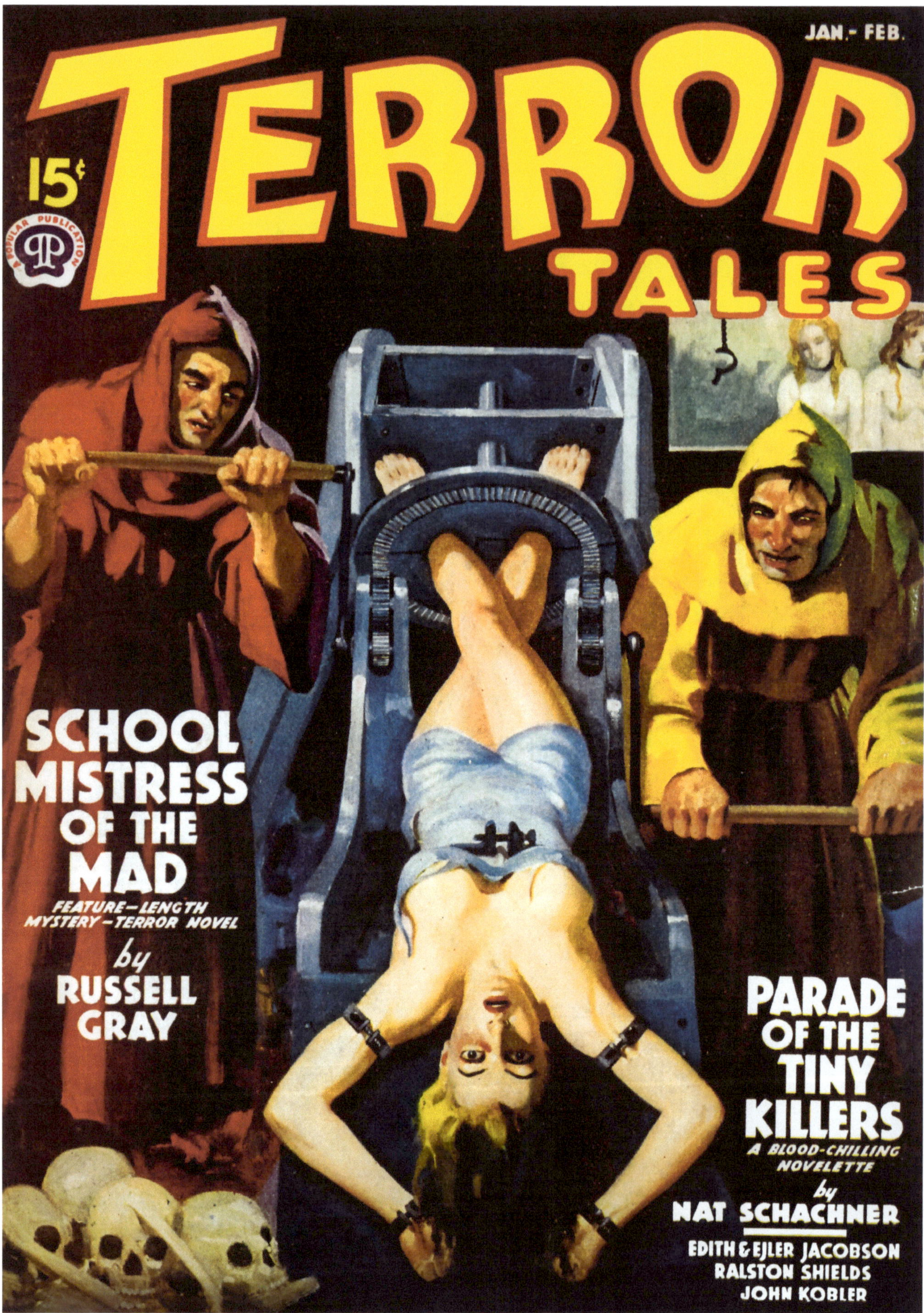
JAN.- FEB.
15¢
TERROR
TALES
SCHOOL MISTRESS OF THE MAD
FEATURE-LENGTH MYSTERY-TERROR NOVEL
by RUSSELL GRAY
PARADE OF THE TINY KILLERS
A BLOOD-CHILLING NOVELETTE
by NAT SCHACHNER
EDITH & EJLER JACOBSON
RALSTON SHIELDS
JOHN KOBLER

16

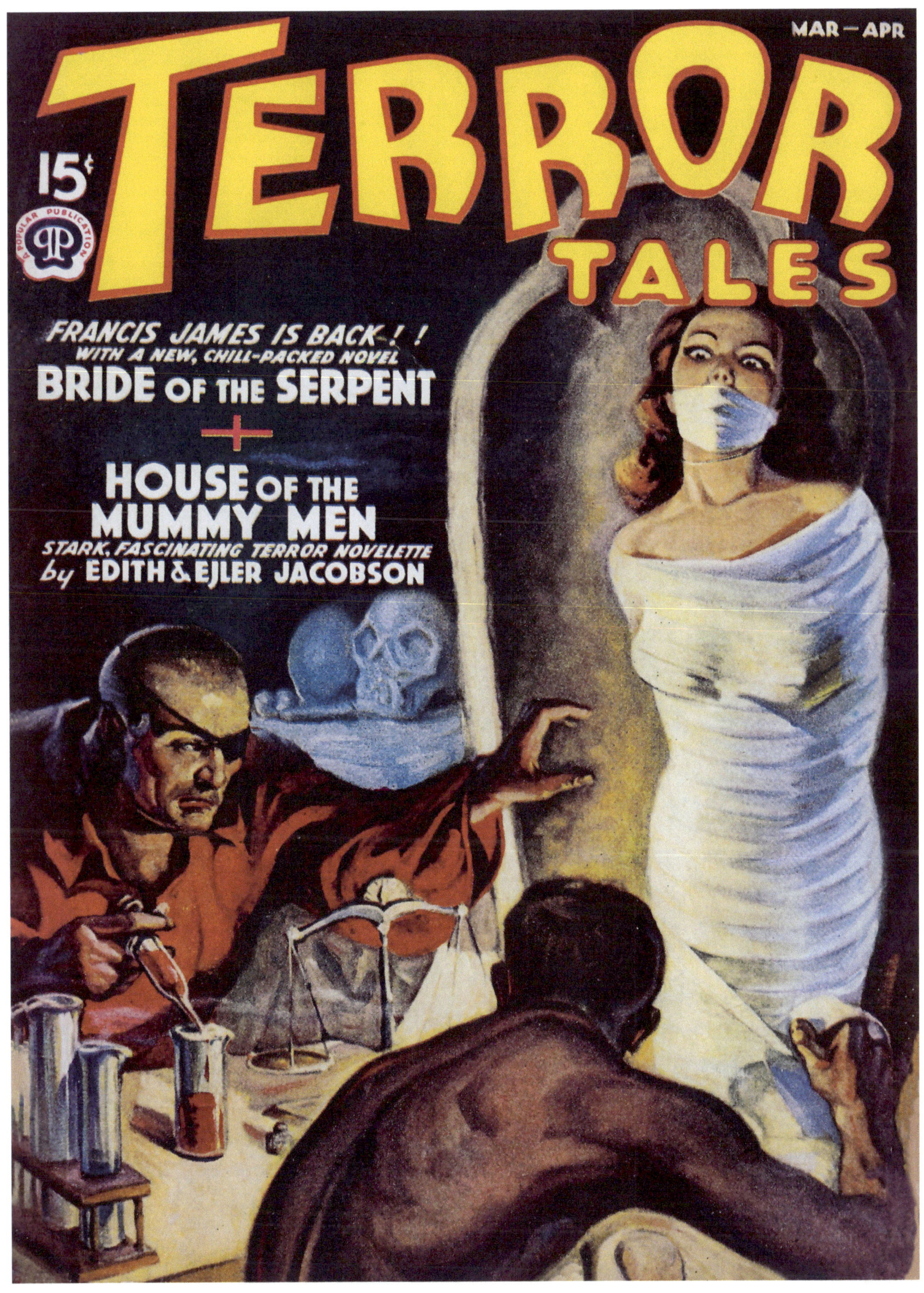

MAR — APR
15¢
A POPULAR PUBLICATION
TERROR TALES
FRANCIS JAMES IS BACK-!!
WITH A NEW, CHILL-PACKED NOVEL
BRIDE OF THE SERPENT
+
HOUSE OF THE MUMMY MEN
STARK, FASCINATING TERROR NOVELETTE
by EDITH & EJLER JACOBSON

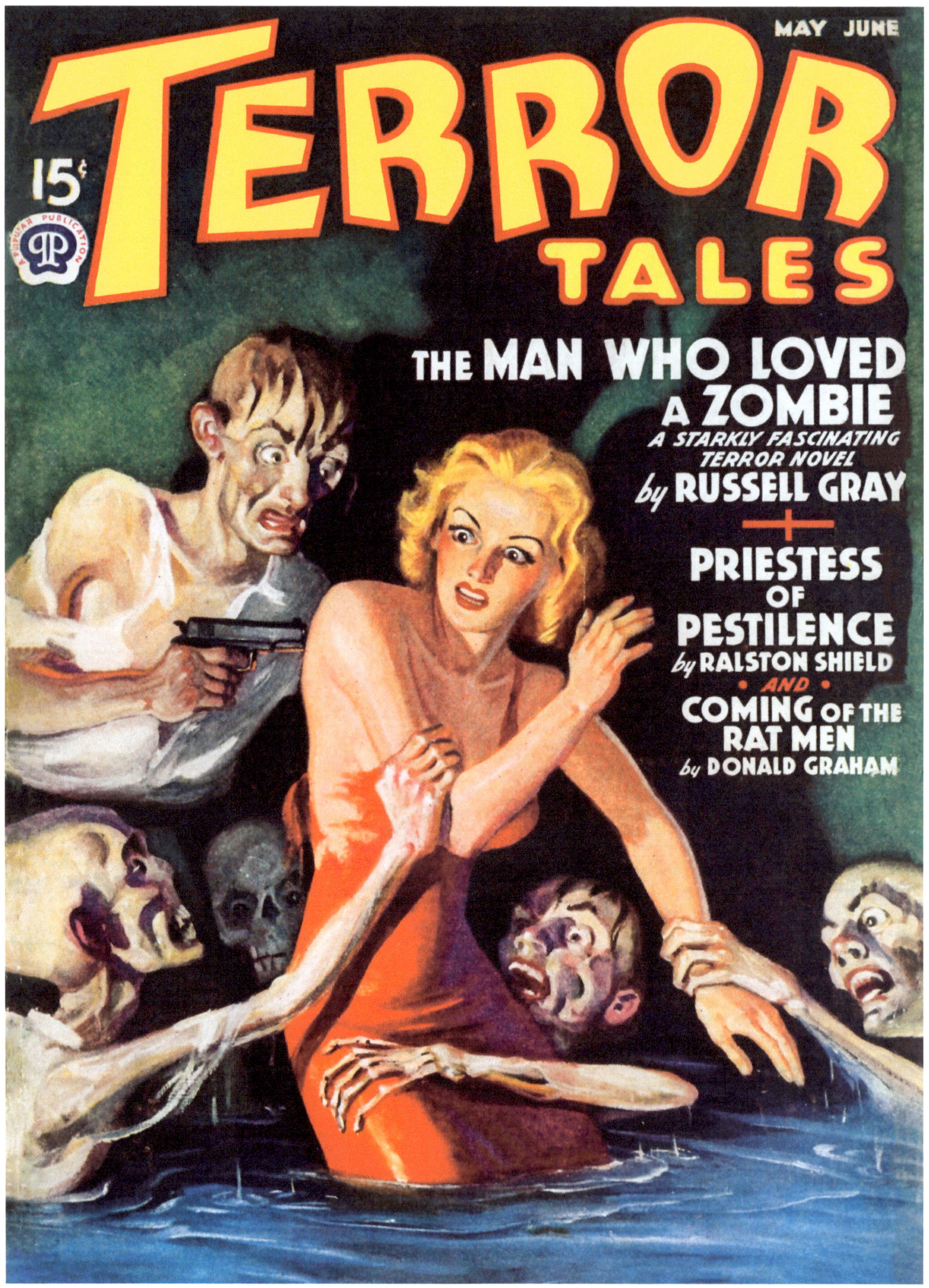

MAY JUNE
TERROR TALES
15¢
A POPULAR PUBLICATION
THE MAN WHO LOVED A ZOMBIE
A STARKLY FASCINATING TERROR NOVEL
by RUSSELL GRAY
PRIESTESS OF PESTILENCE
by RALSTON SHIELD
AND
COMING OF THE RAT MEN
by DONALD GRAHAM

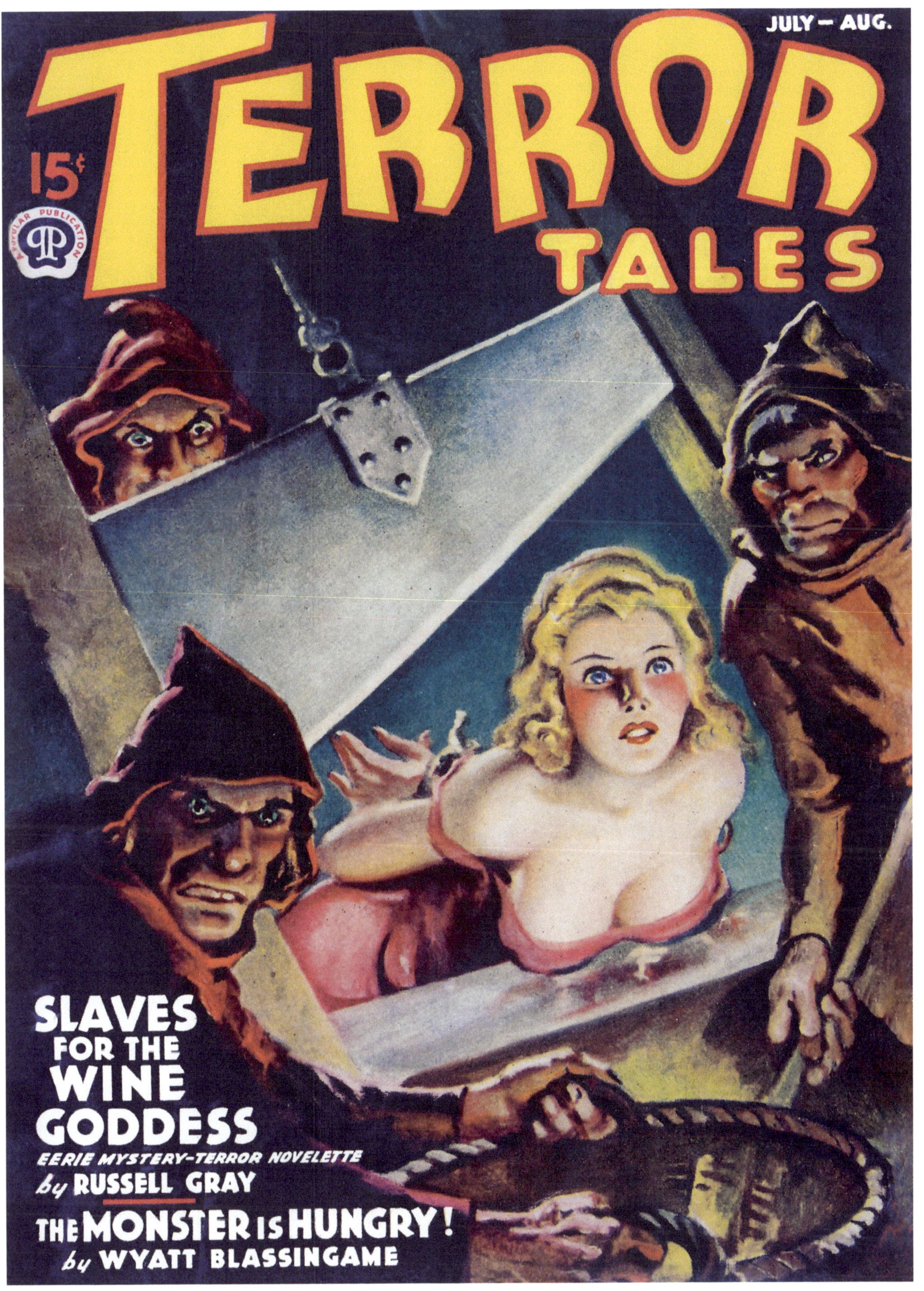

JULY – AUG.
15¢
A POPULAR PUBLICATION
TERROR
TALES
SLAVES
FOR THE
WINE
GODDESS
EERIE MYSTERY-TERROR NOVELETTE
by RUSSELL GRAY
THE MONSTER IS HUNGRY!
by WYATT BLASSINGAME

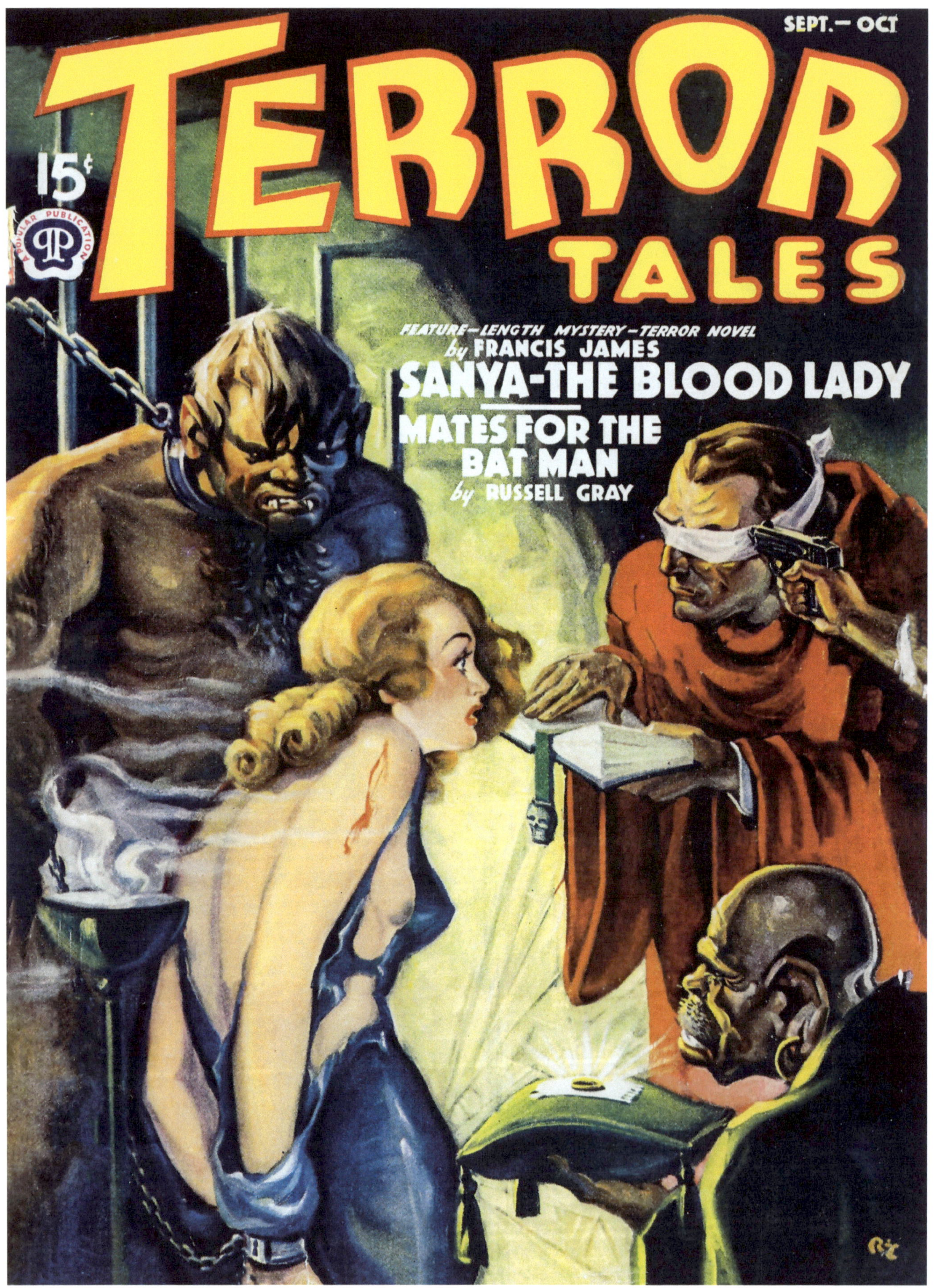

SEPT. — OCT.
15¢
A POPULAR PUBLICATION
TERROR TALES
FEATURE—LENGTH MYSTERY—TERROR NOVEL
by FRANCIS JAMES
SANYA—THE BLOOD LADY
MATES FOR THE BAT MAN
by RUSSELL GRAY

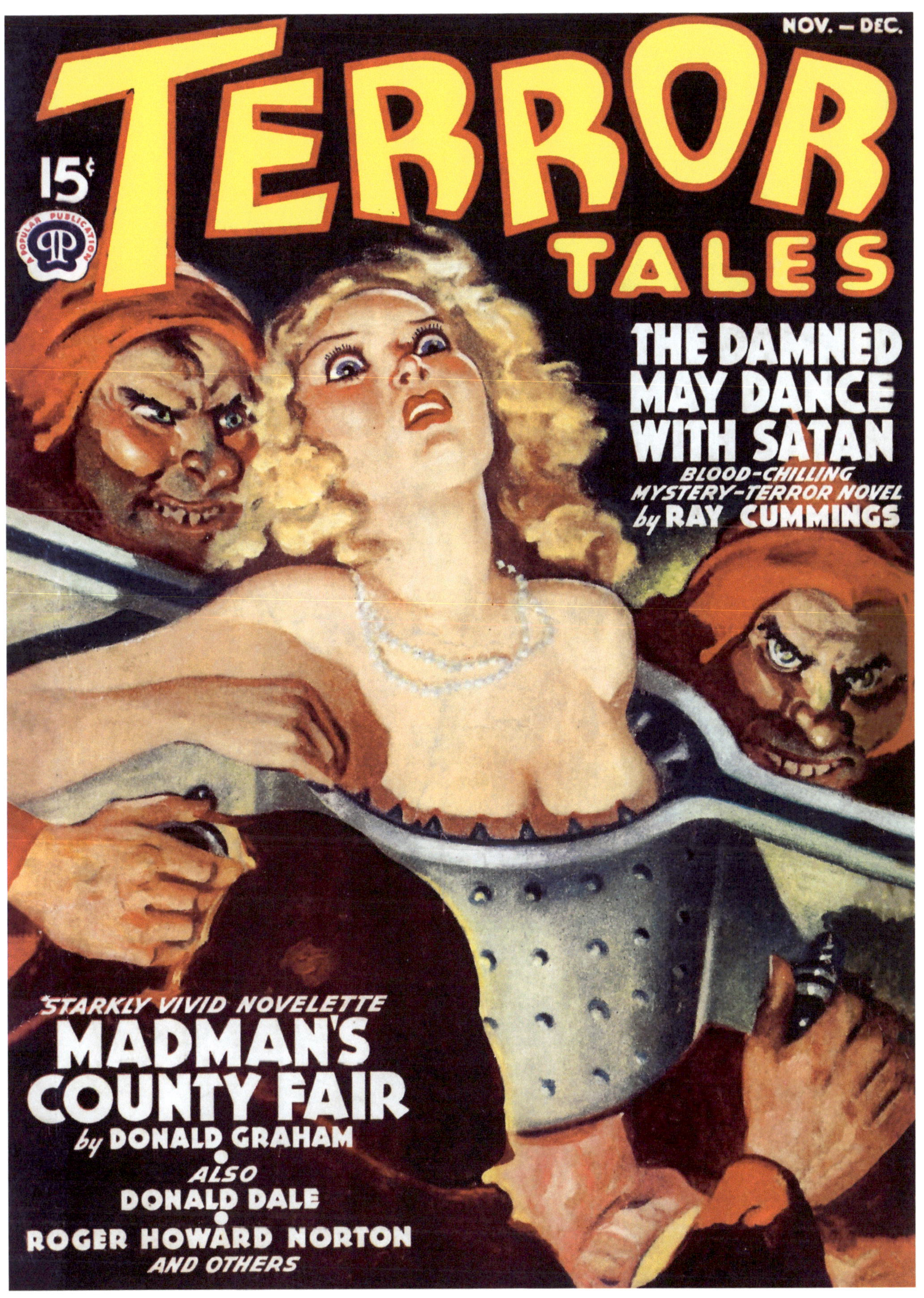

NOV. — DEC.
15¢
A POPULAR PUBLICATION
TERROR TALES
THE DAMNED MAY DANCE WITH SATAN
BLOOD-CHILLING MYSTERY-TERROR NOVEL by RAY CUMMINGS
STARKLY VIVID NOVELETTE
MADMAN'S COUNTY FAIR
by DONALD GRAHAM
ALSO
DONALD DALE
ROGER HOWARD NORTON
AND OTHERS

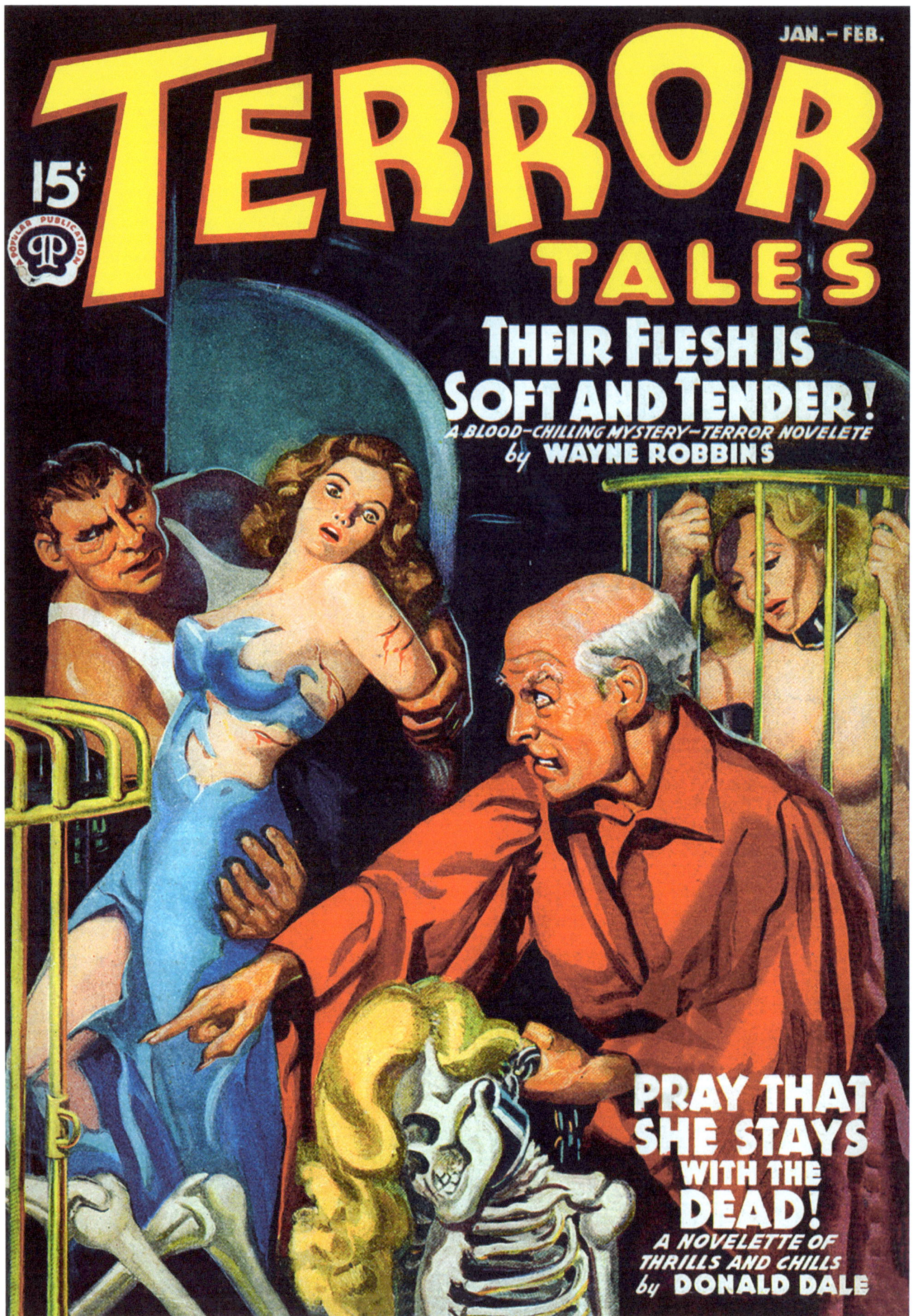

JAN.–FEB.
15¢
A POPULAR PUBLICATION
TERROR TALES
THEIR FLESH IS SOFT AND TENDER!
A BLOOD-CHILLING MYSTERY-TERROR NOVELETE
by WAYNE ROBBINS
PRAY THAT SHE STAYS WITH THE DEAD!
A NOVELETTE OF THRILLS AND CHILLS
by DONALD DALE

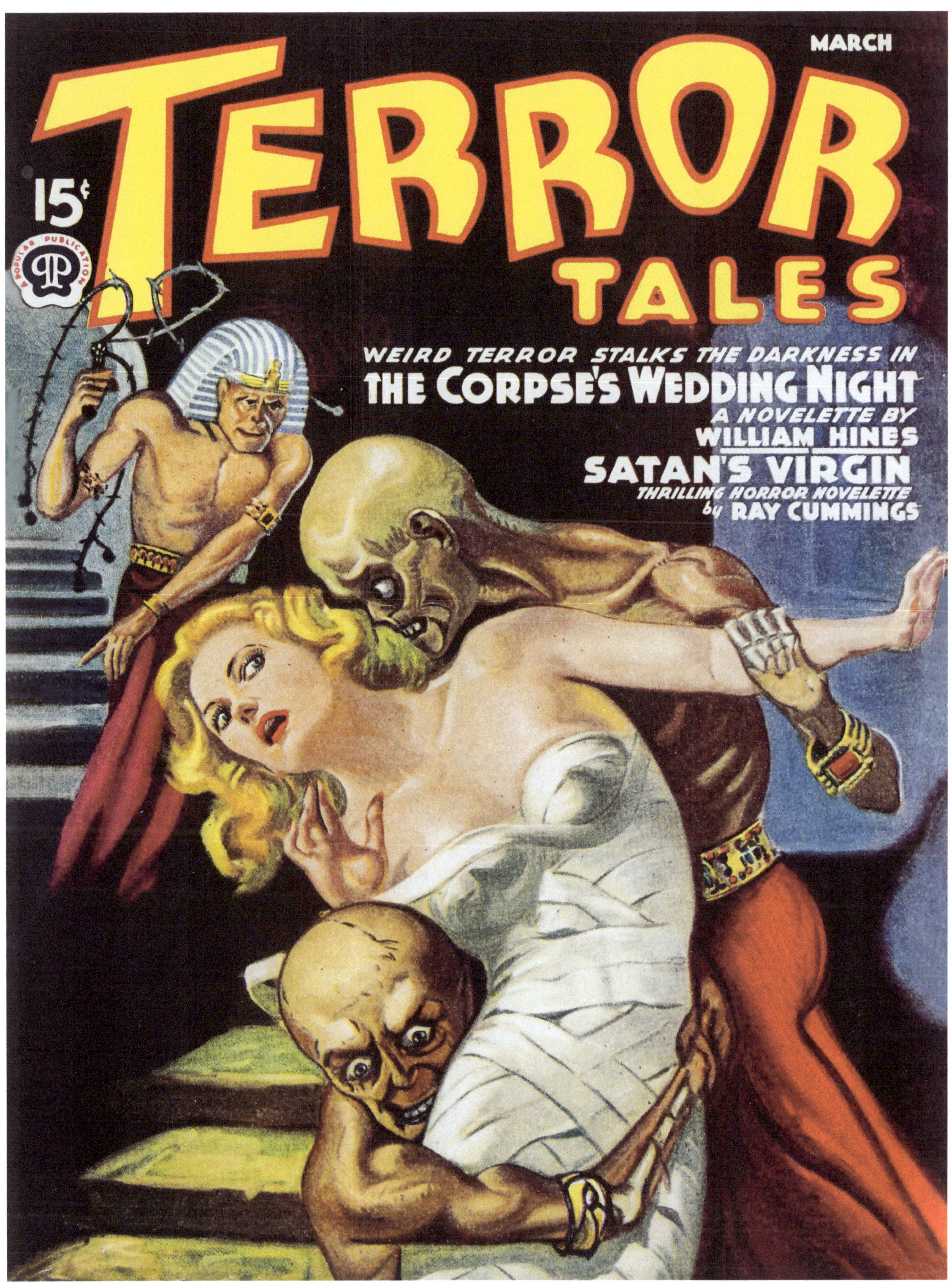# TERROR TALES

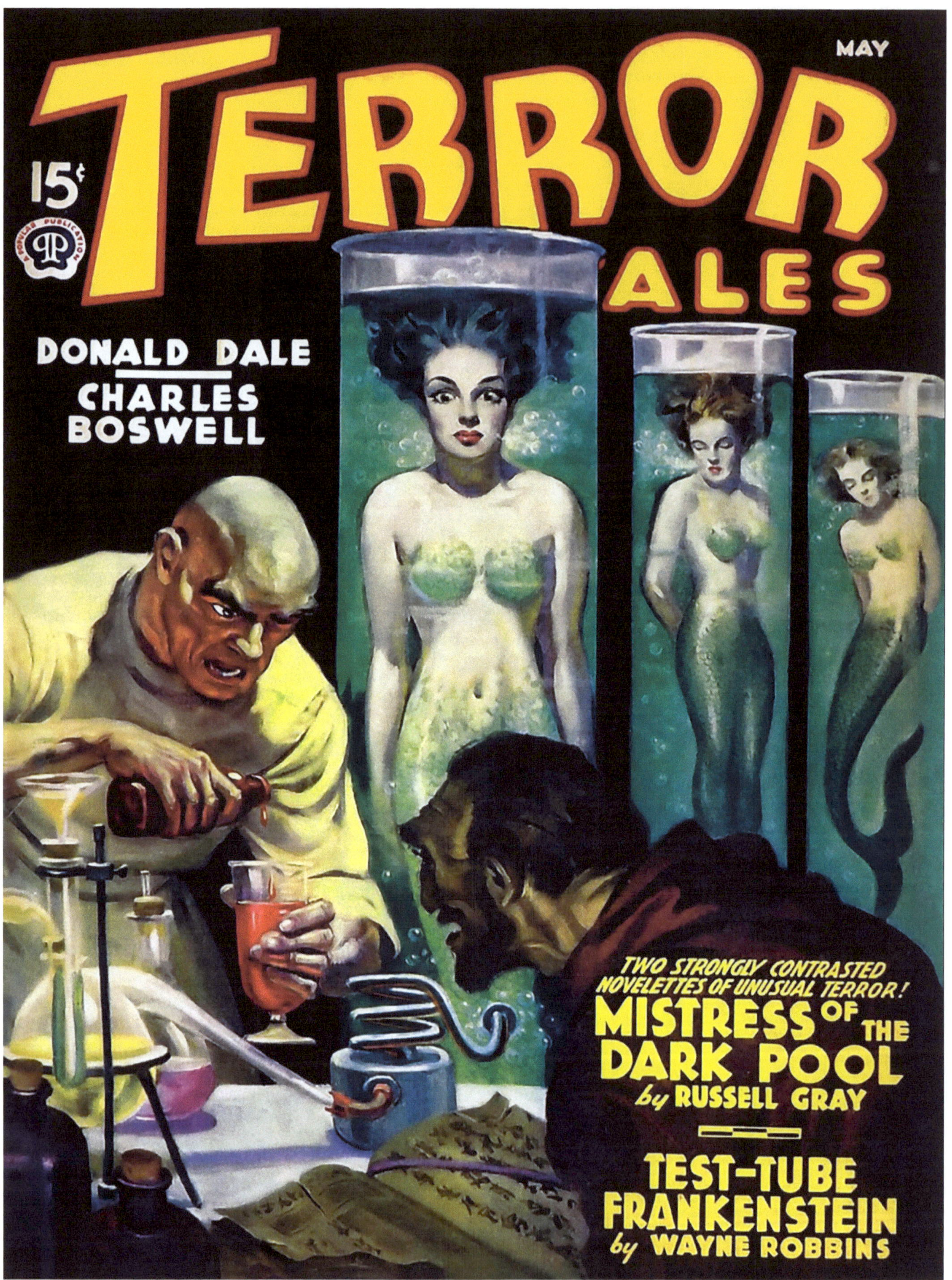

MAY
15¢
TERROR TALES
DONALD DALE
CHARLES BOSWELL
TWO STRONGLY CONTRASTED
NOVELETTES OF UNUSUAL TERROR!
MISTRESS OF THE DARK POOL
by RUSSELL GRAY
TEST-TUBE FRANKENSTEIN
by WAYNE ROBBINS

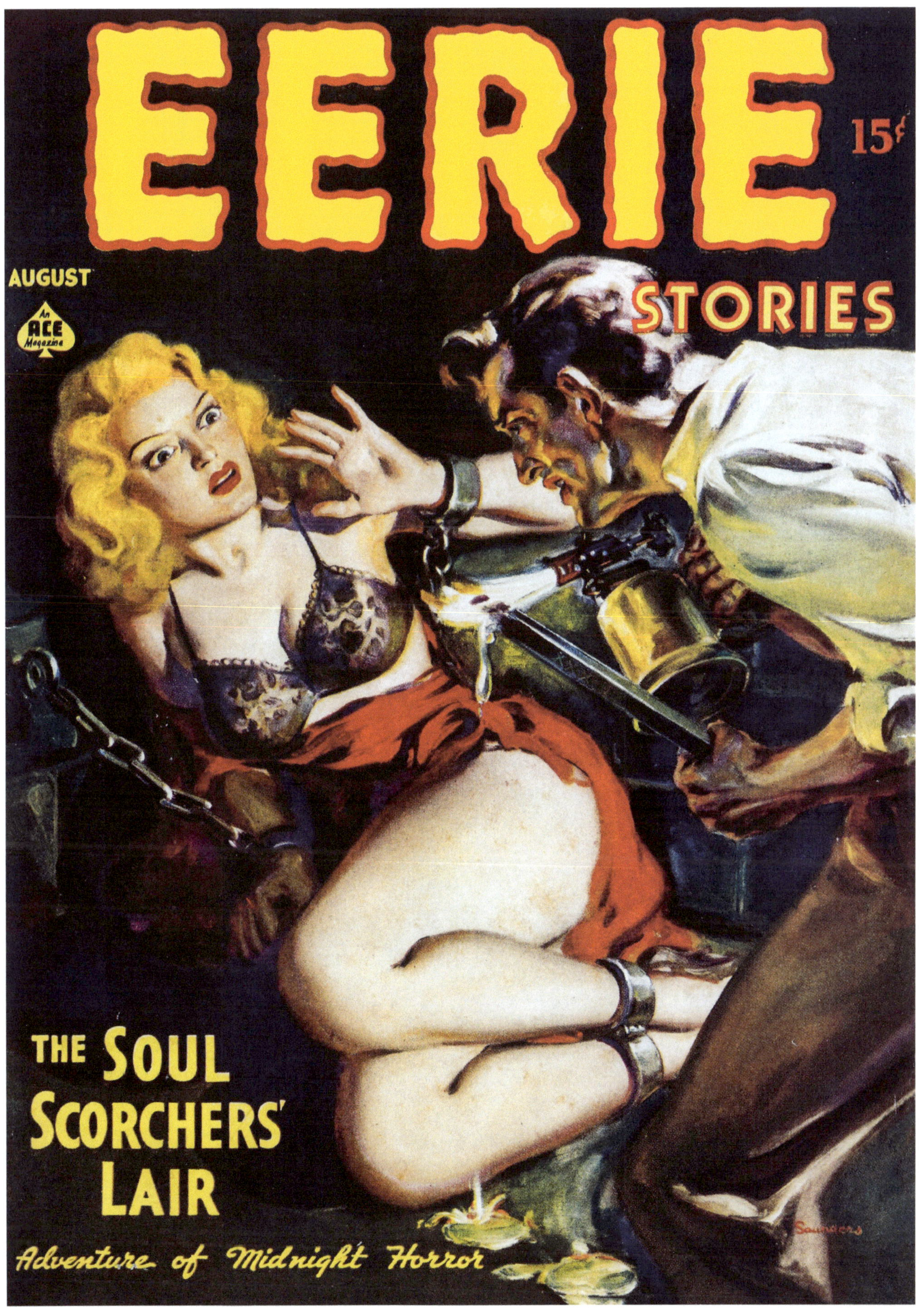

EERIE
STORIES
15¢
AUGUST
An ACE Magazine
THE SOUL
SCORCHERS'
LAIR
Adventure of Midnight Horror

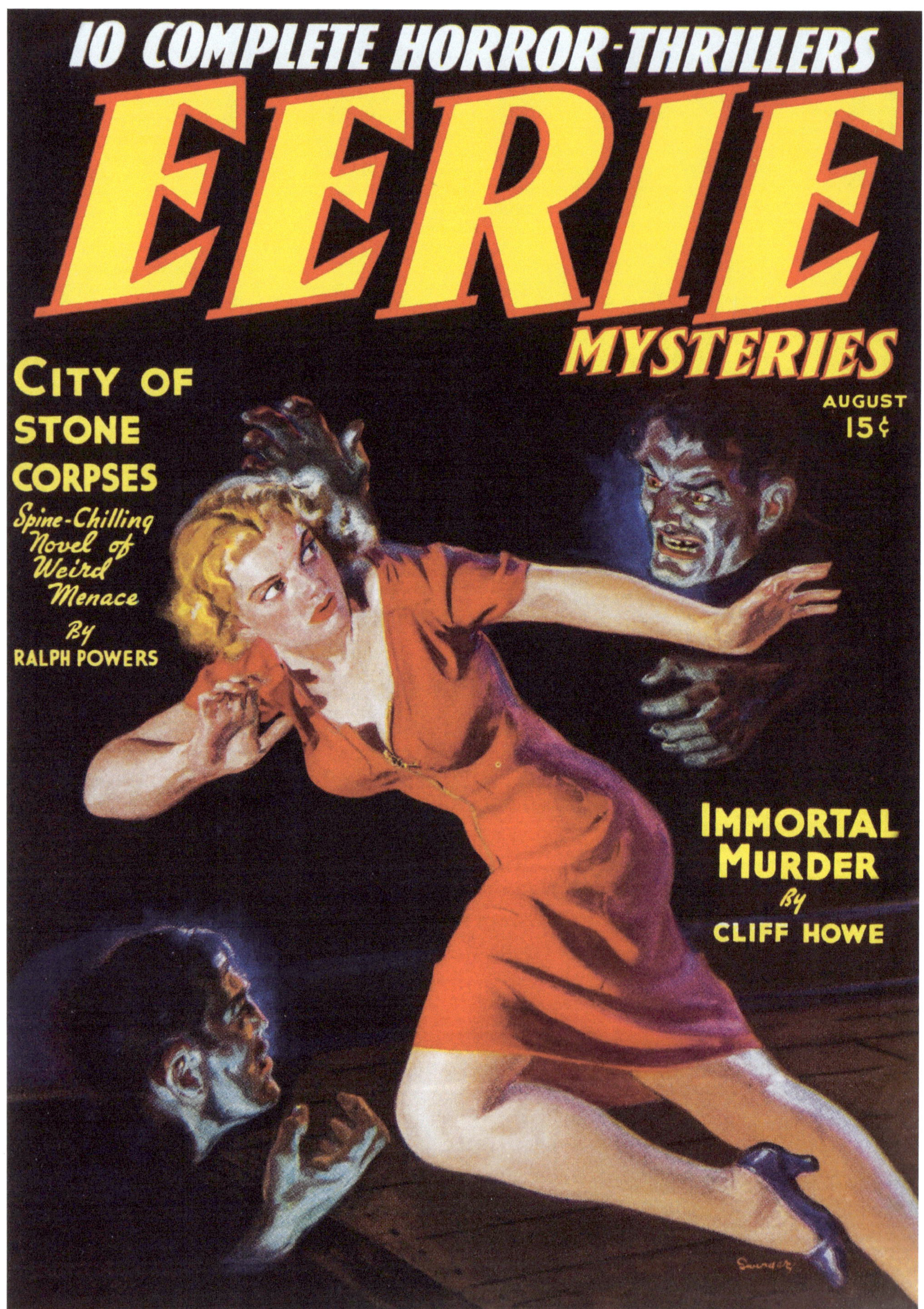

10 COMPLETE HORROR-THRILLERS
EERIE MYSTERIES
AUGUST
15¢
CITY OF STONE CORPSES
Spine-Chilling Novel of Weird Menace
By RALPH POWERS
IMMORTAL MURDER
BY CLIFF HOWE

26

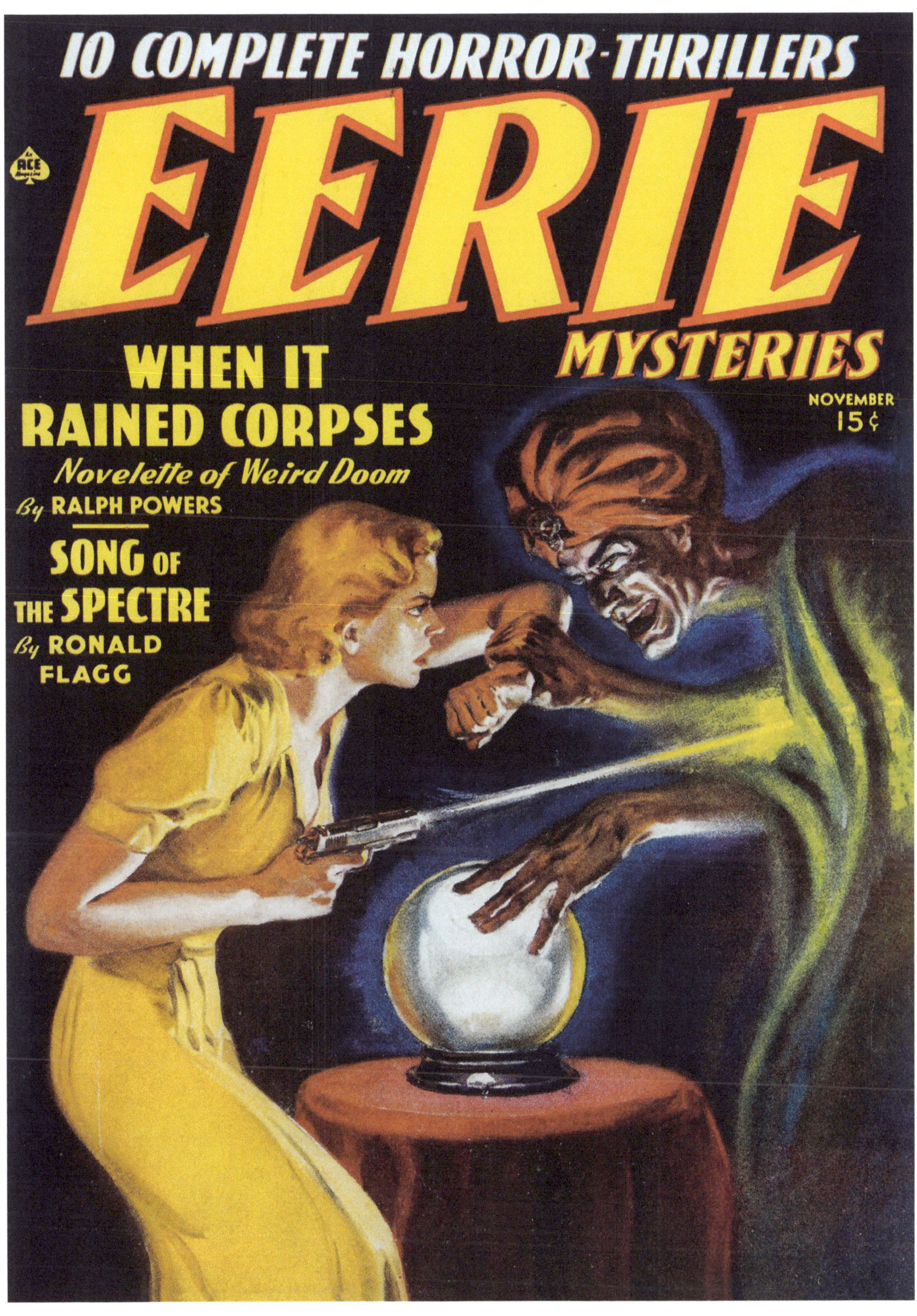

10 COMPLETE HORROR-THRILLERS
EERIE
MYSTERIES
NOVEMBER
15¢
WHEN IT RAINED CORPSES
Novelette of Weird Doom
By RALPH POWERS
SONG of THE SPECTRE
By RONALD FLAGG

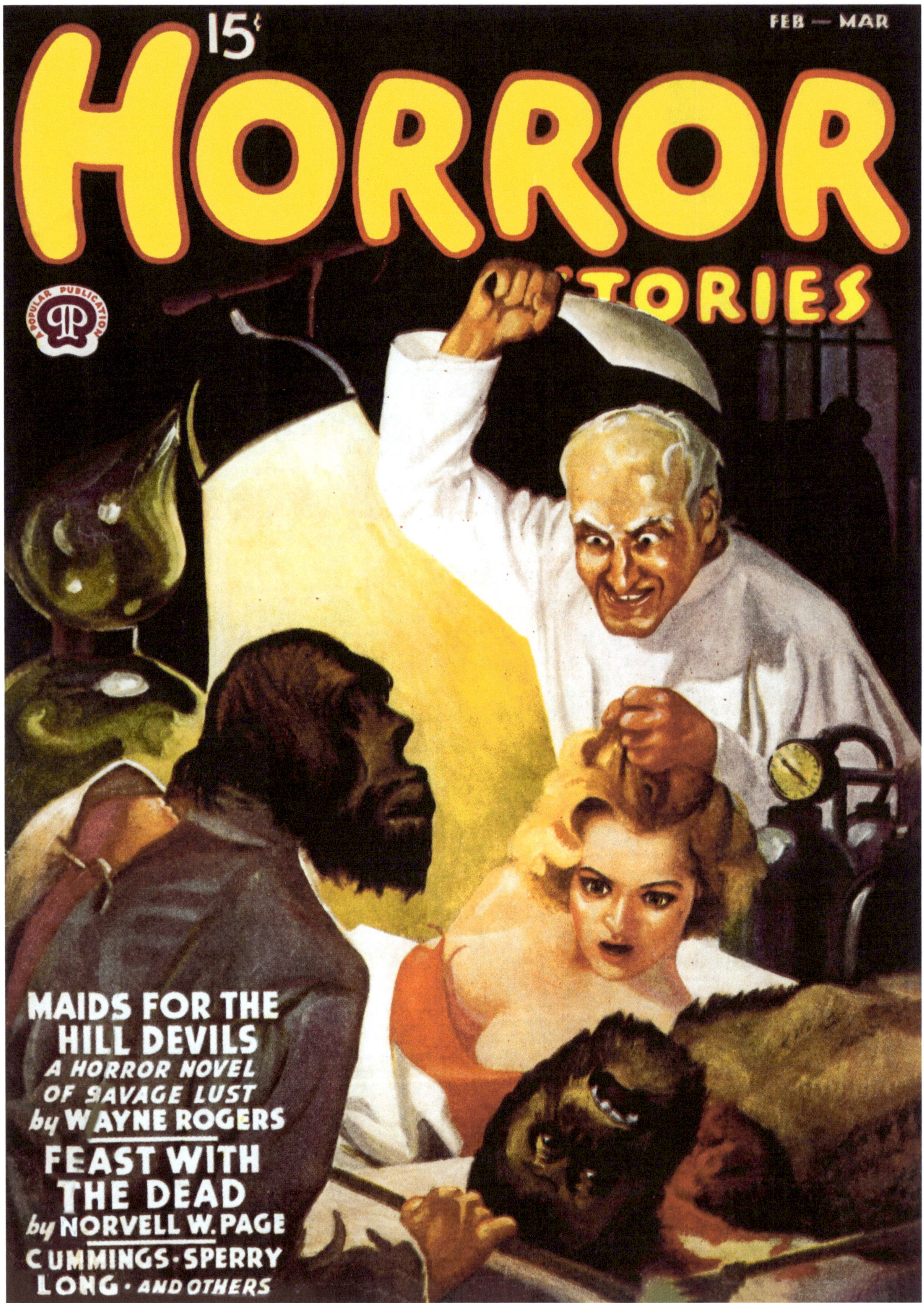

HORROR STORIES

FEBRUARY-MARCH 1938

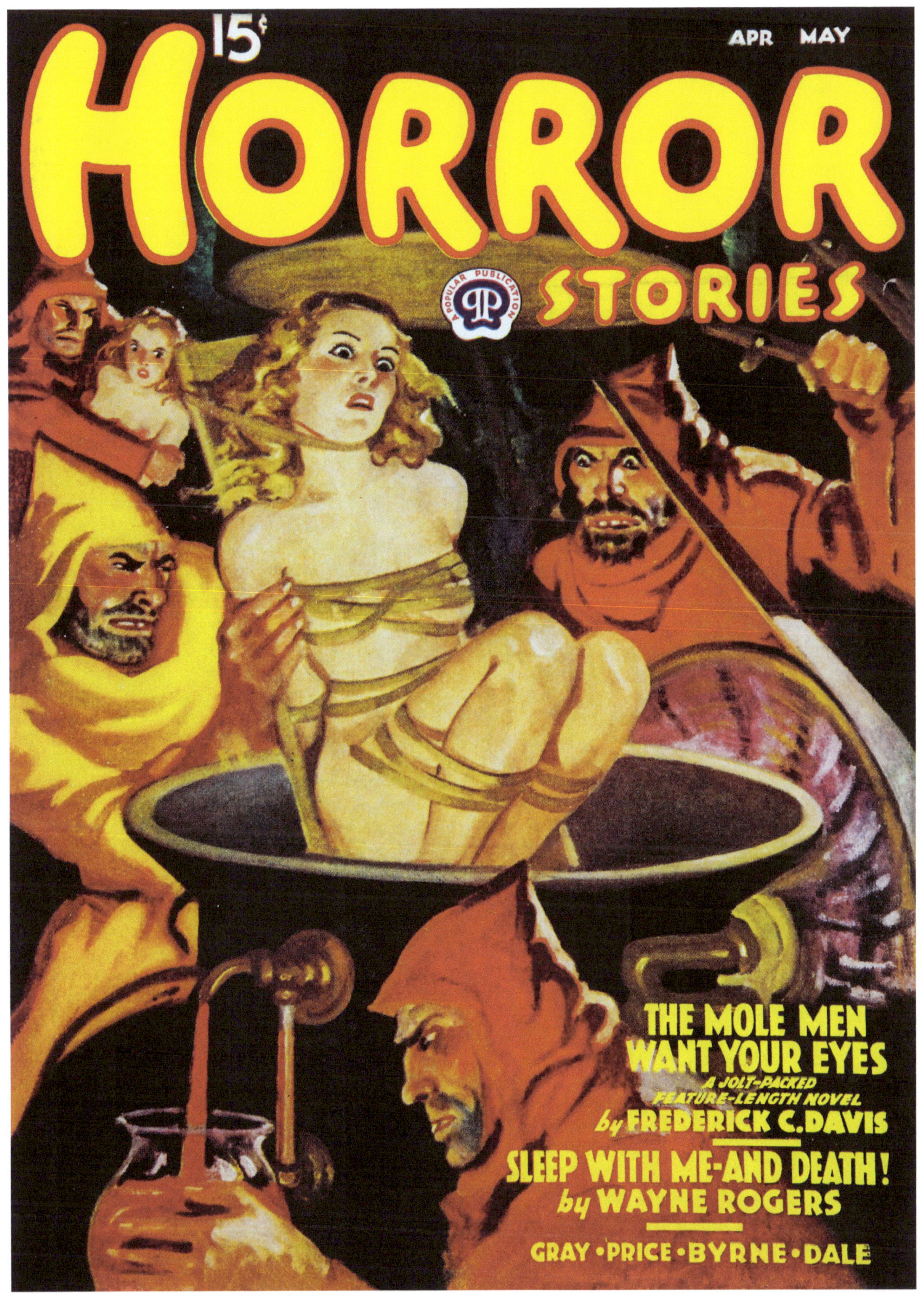
15¢
APR MAY
HORROR STORIES
A POPULAR PUBLICATION
PP
THE MOLE MEN WANT YOUR EYES
A JOLT-PACKED FEATURE-LENGTH NOVEL
by FREDERICK C. DAVIS
SLEEP WITH ME—AND DEATH!
by WAYNE ROGERS
GRAY • PRICE • BYRNE • DALE

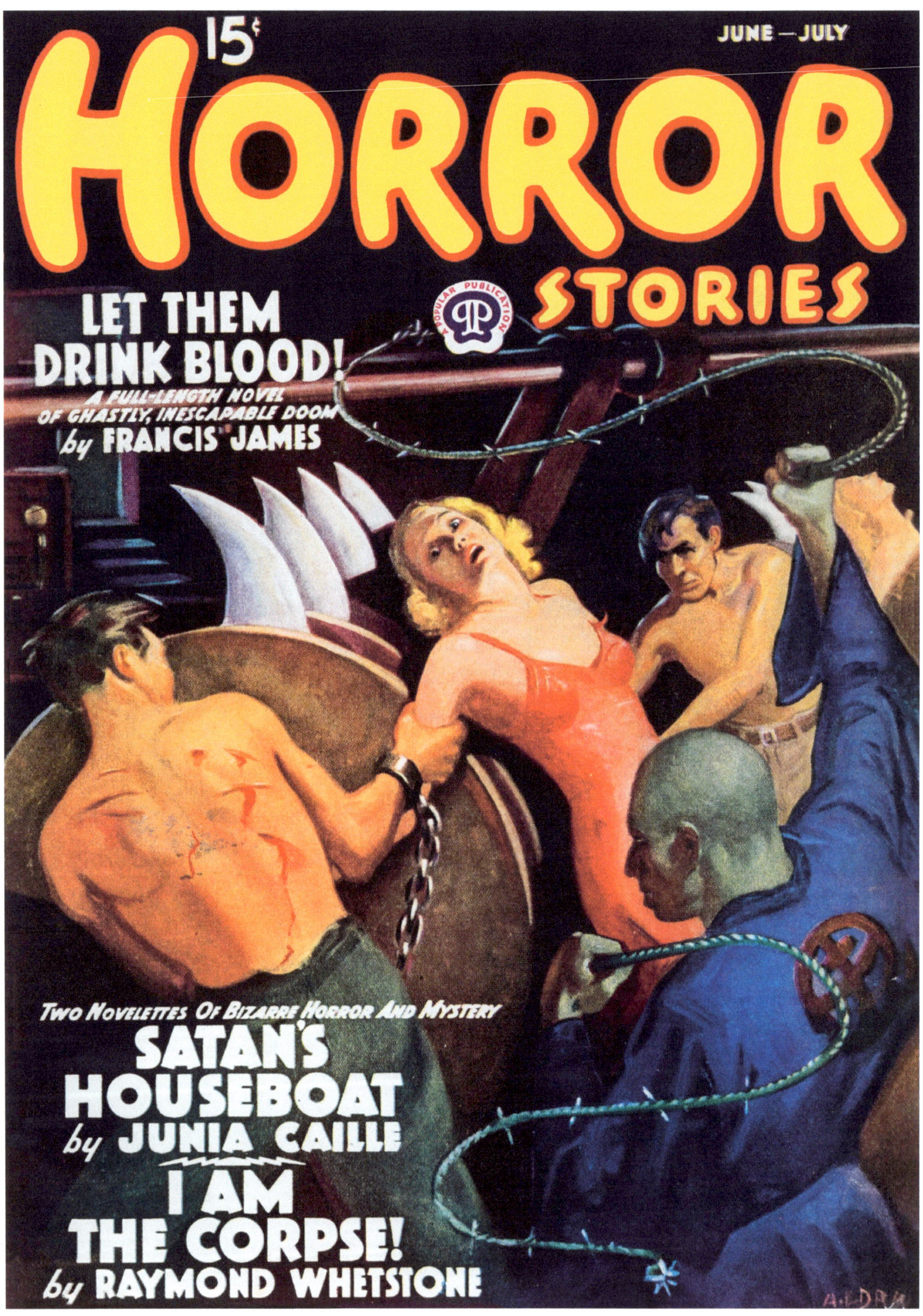

HORROR STORIES

JUNE–JULY 1938

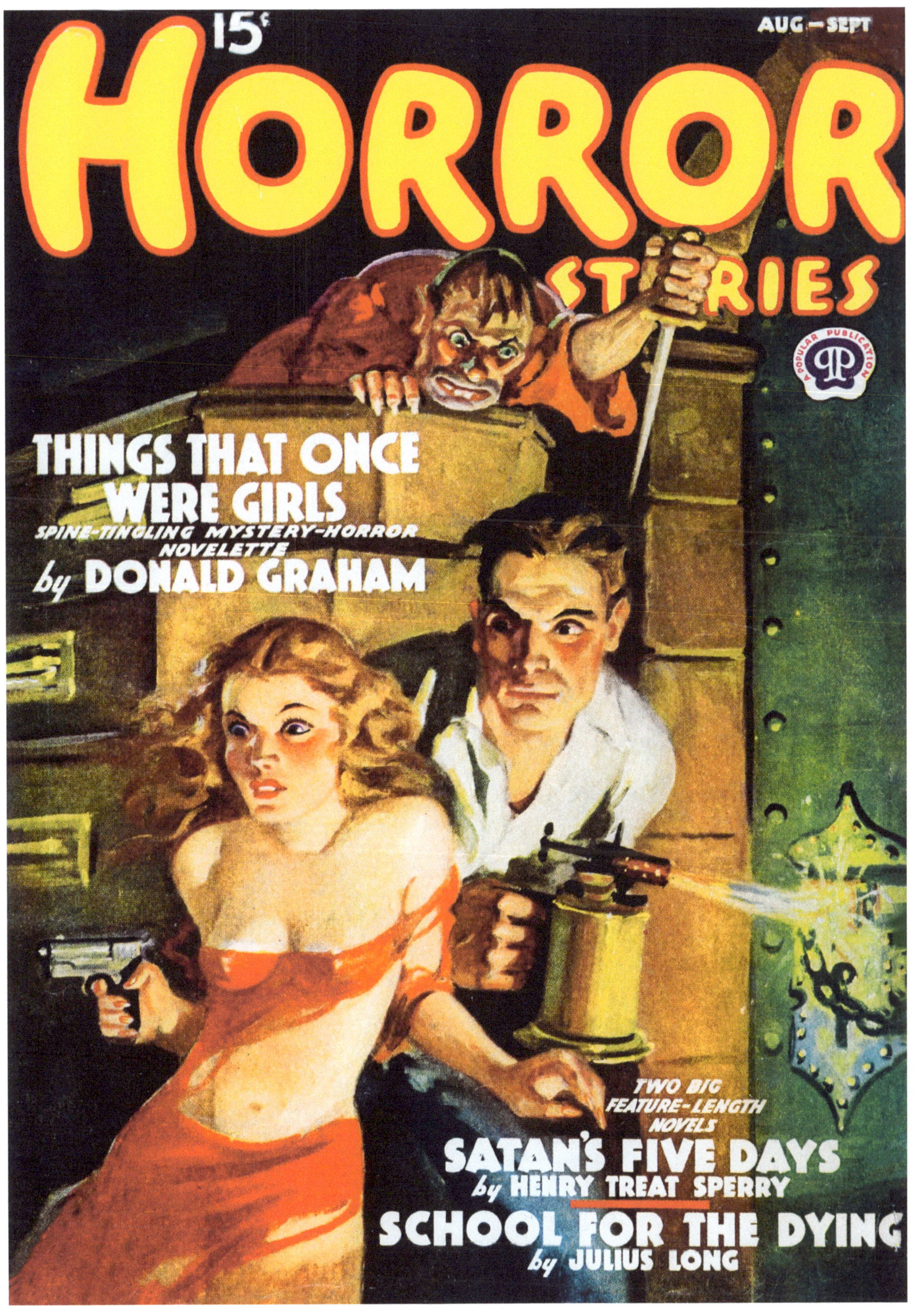

15¢
AUG-SEPT
Horror Stories
A POPULAR PUBLICATION
THINGS THAT ONCE WERE GIRLS
SPINE-TINGLING MYSTERY-HORROR NOVELETTE
by DONALD GRAHAM
TWO BIG FEATURE-LENGTH NOVELS
SATAN'S FIVE DAYS
by HENRY TREAT SPERRY
SCHOOL FOR THE DYING
by JULIUS LONG

31

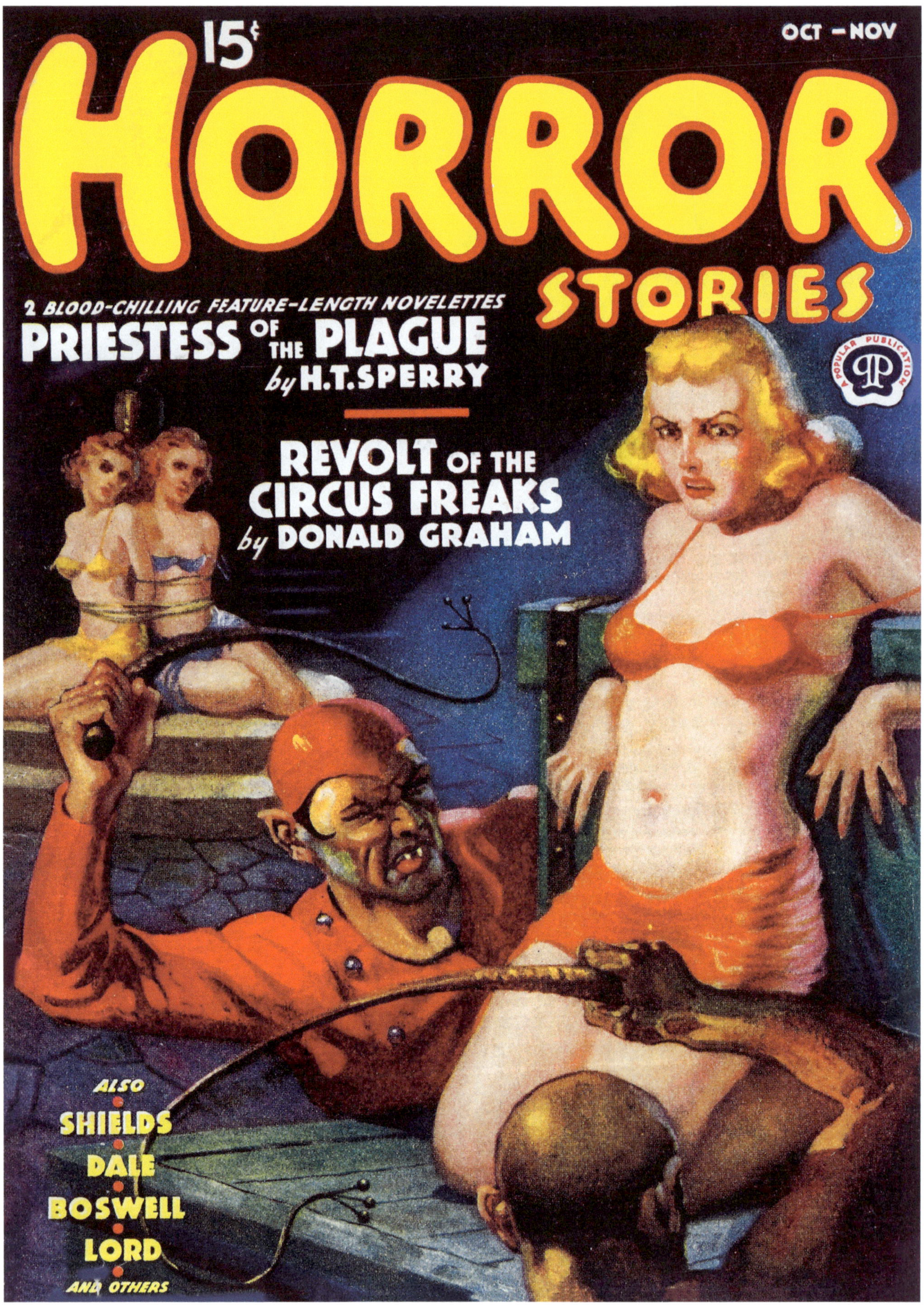

15¢
OCT – NOV
Horror
STORIES
2 BLOOD-CHILLING FEATURE-LENGTH NOVELETTES
PRIESTESS OF THE PLAGUE
by H.T. SPERRY
REVOLT OF THE CIRCUS FREAKS
by DONALD GRAHAM
A POPULAR PUBLICATION
PP
ALSO
SHIELDS
DALE
BOSWELL
LORD
AND OTHERS

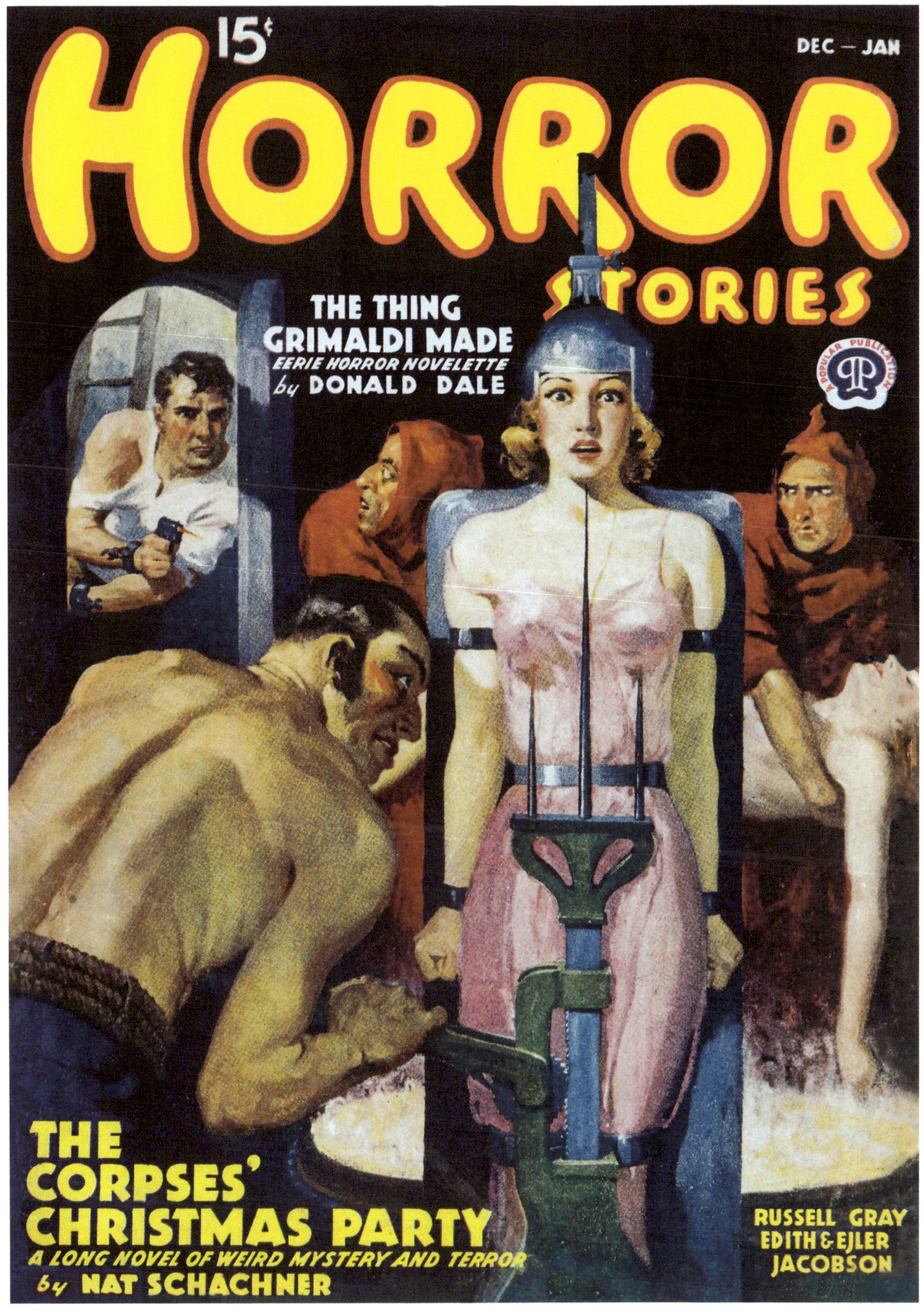

15¢
DEC – JAN
Horror
STORIES
A POPULAR PUBLICATION
THE THING GRIMALDI MADE
EERIE HORROR NOVELETTE
by DONALD DALE
THE CORPSES' CHRISTMAS PARTY
A LONG NOVEL OF WEIRD MYSTERY AND TERROR
by NAT SCHACHNER
RUSSELL GRAY
EDITH & EJLER JACOBSON

33

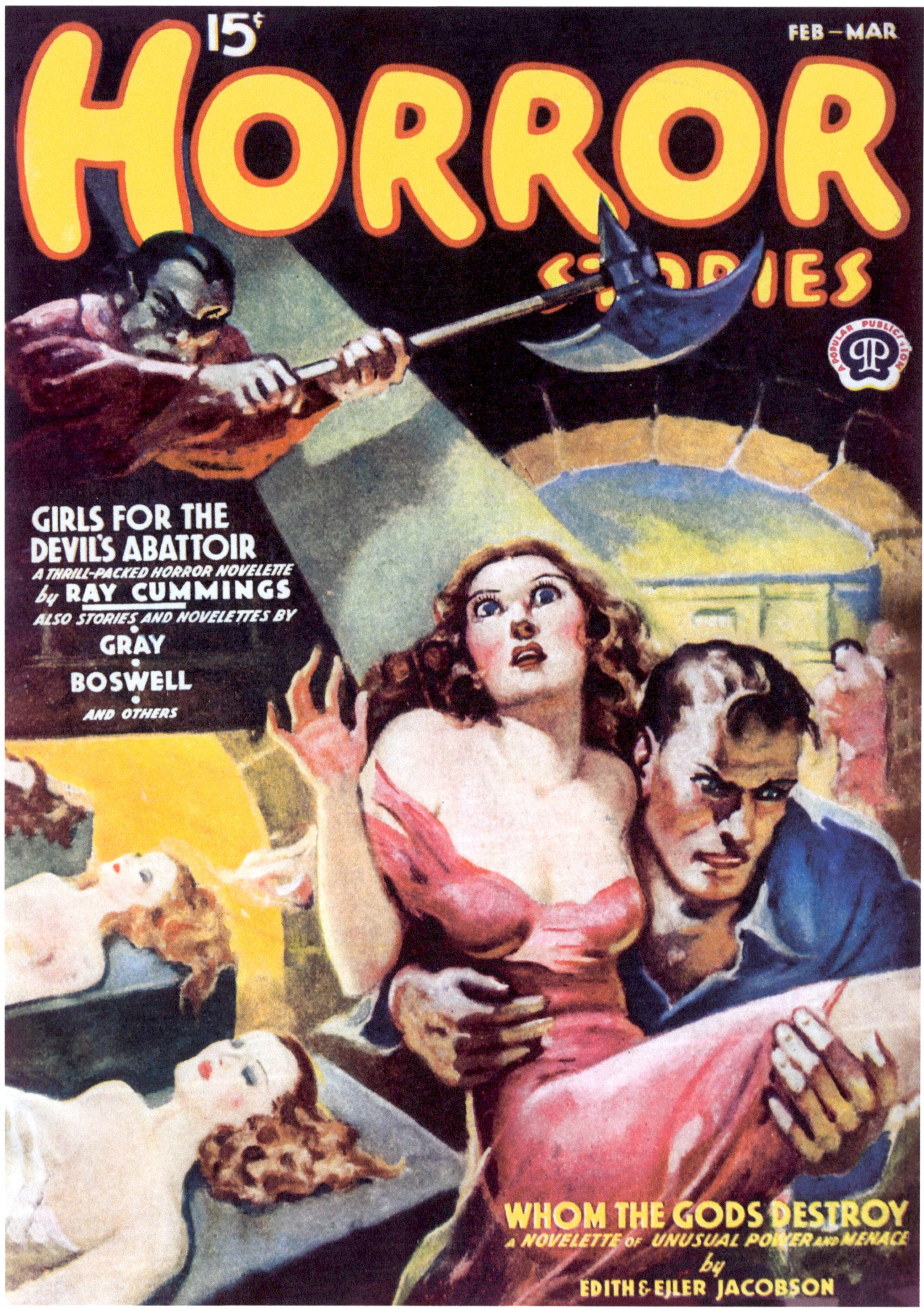
15¢
FEB—MAR
HORROR
STORIES
A POPULAR PUBLICATION
GIRLS FOR THE DEVIL'S ABATTOIR
A THRILL-PACKED HORROR NOVELETTE
by RAY CUMMINGS
ALSO STORIES AND NOVELETTES BY
GRAY
BOSWELL
AND OTHERS
WHOM THE GODS DESTROY
A NOVELETTE of UNUSUAL POWER and MENACE
by
EDITH & EJLER JACOBSON

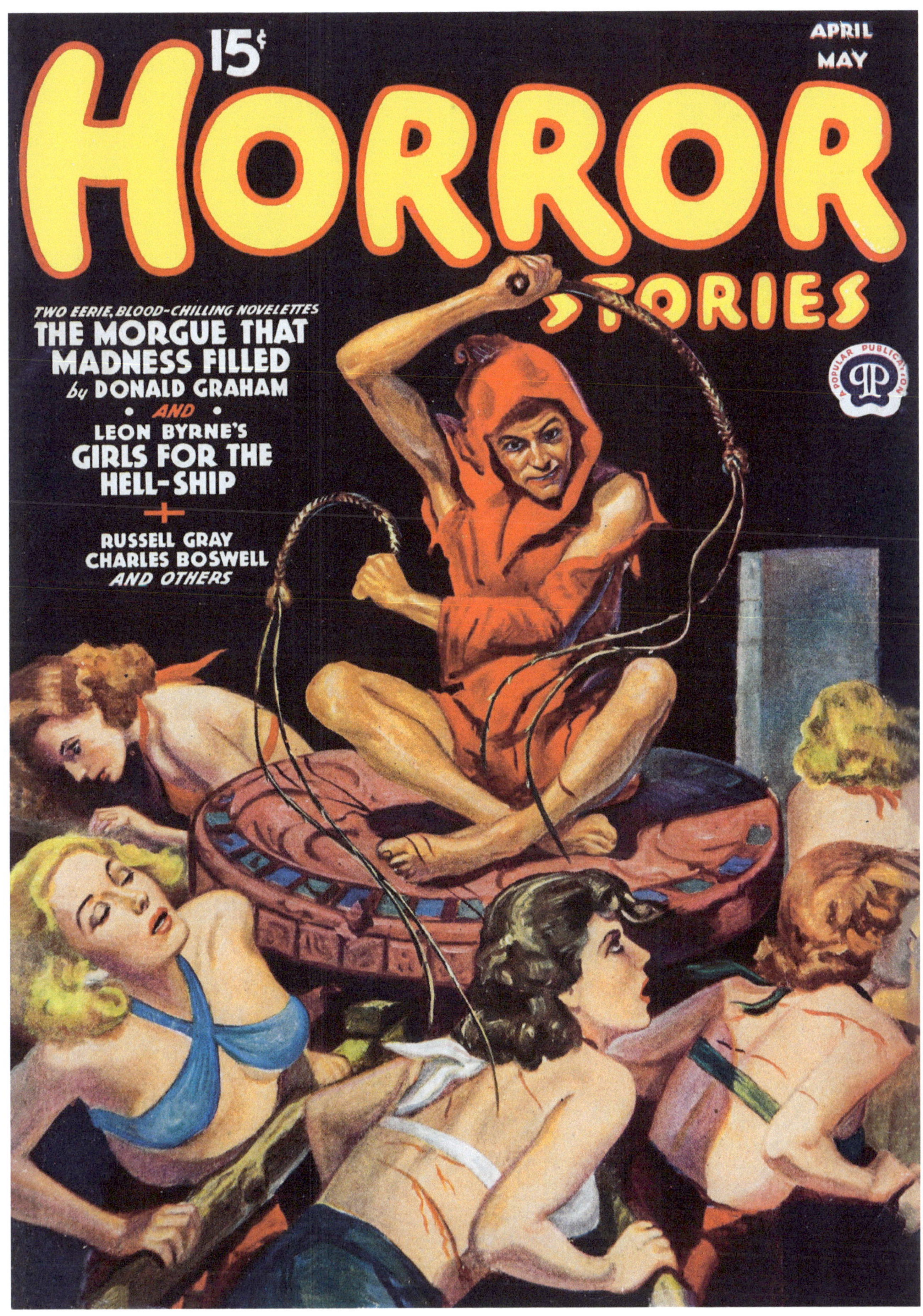
15¢
APRIL
MAY
HORROR STORIES
TWO EERIE, BLOOD-CHILLING NOVELETTES
THE MORGUE THAT MADNESS FILLED
by DONALD GRAHAM
• AND •
LEON BYRNE'S
GIRLS FOR THE HELL-SHIP
RUSSELL GRAY
CHARLES BOSWELL
AND OTHERS
A POPULAR PUBLICATION
PP

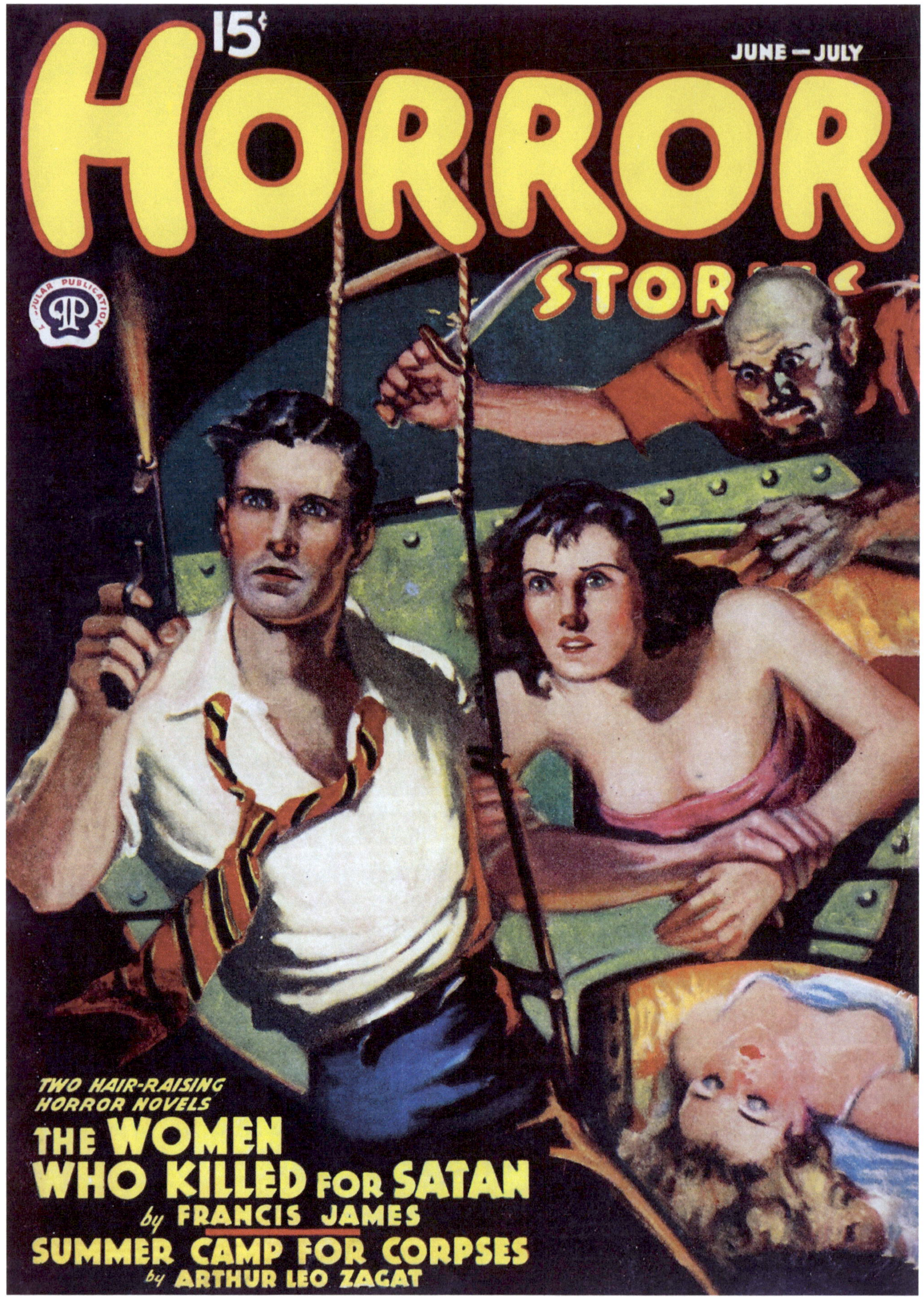

15¢
JUNE — JULY
HORROR STORIES
A POPULAR PUBLICATION
TWO HAIR-RAISING HORROR NOVELS
THE WOMEN WHO KILLED FOR SATAN
by FRANCIS JAMES
SUMMER CAMP FOR CORPSES
by ARTHUR LEO ZAGAT

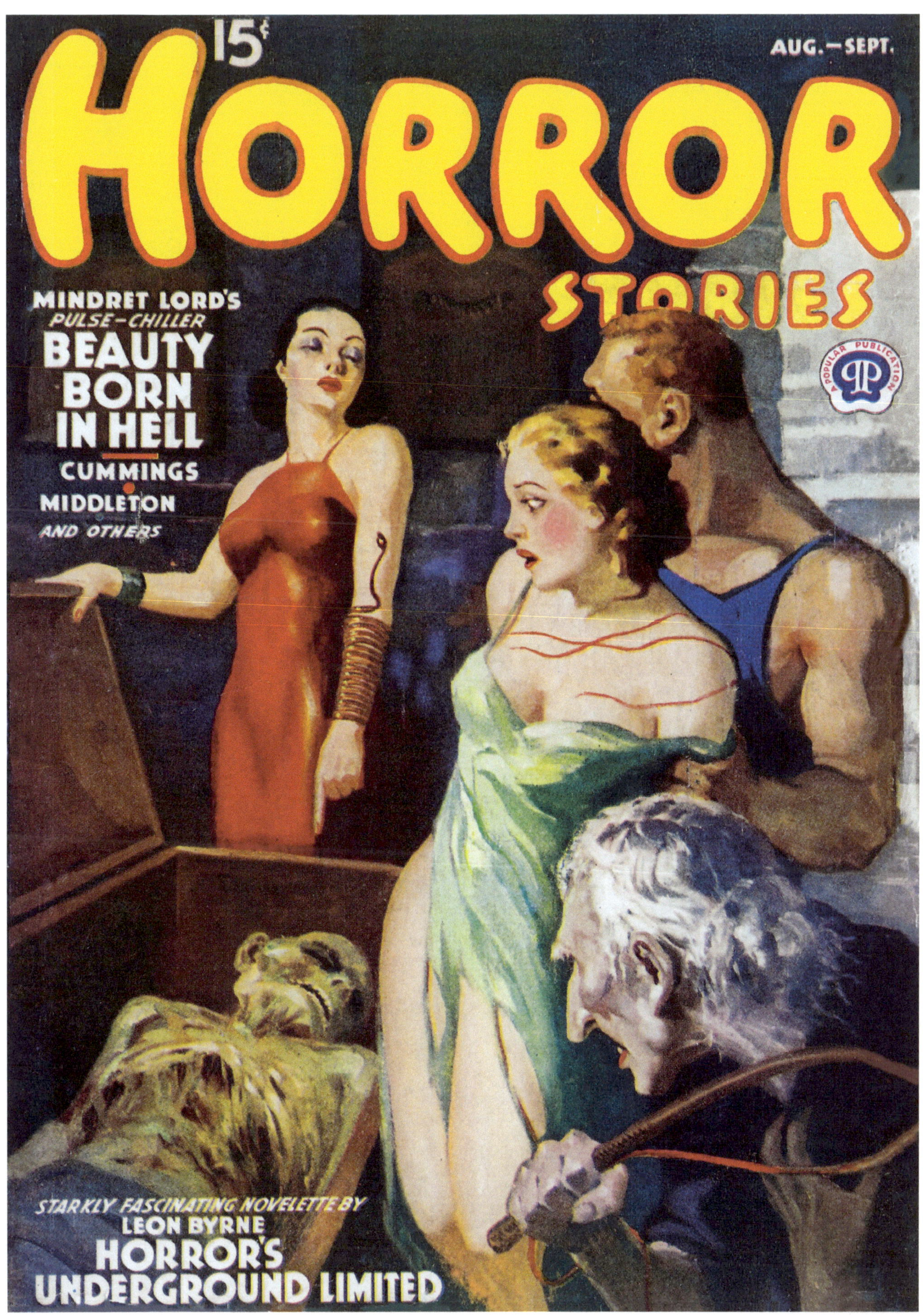

15¢
AUG. - SEPT.
Horror
STORIES
A POPULAR PUBLICATION
PP
MINDRET LORD'S
PULSE-CHILLER
BEAUTY
BORN
IN HELL
CUMMINGS
MIDDLETON
AND OTHERS
STARKLY FASCINATING NOVELETTE BY
LEON BYRNE
HORROR'S
UNDERGROUND LIMITED

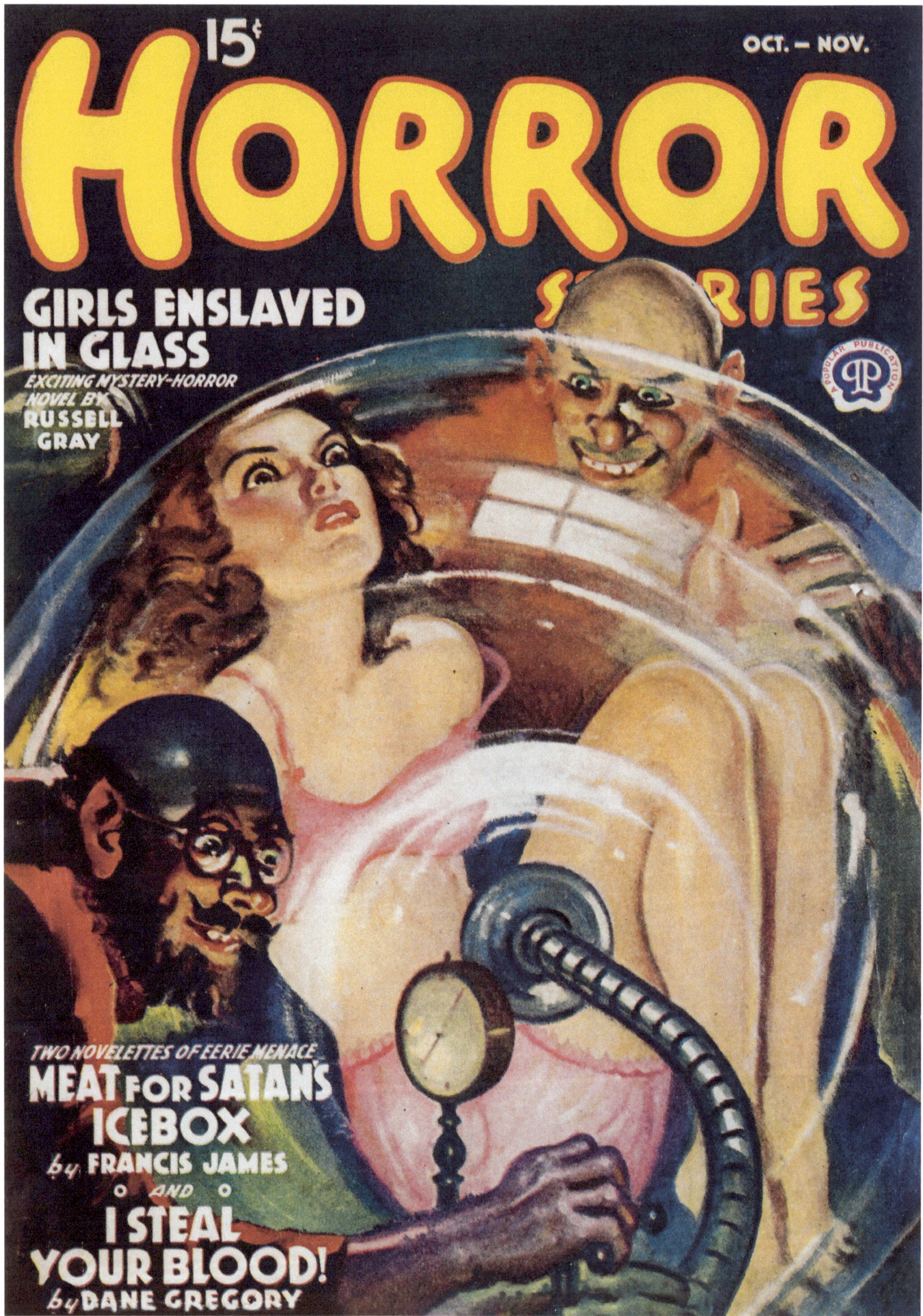

15¢
OCT. – NOV.
Horror Stories
GIRLS ENSLAVED IN GLASS
EXCITING MYSTERY-HORROR NOVEL BY RUSSELL GRAY
A POPULAR PUBLICATION
PP
TWO NOVELETTES OF EERIE MENACE
MEAT FOR SATAN'S ICEBOX
by FRANCIS JAMES
AND
I STEAL YOUR BLOOD!
by DANE GREGORY

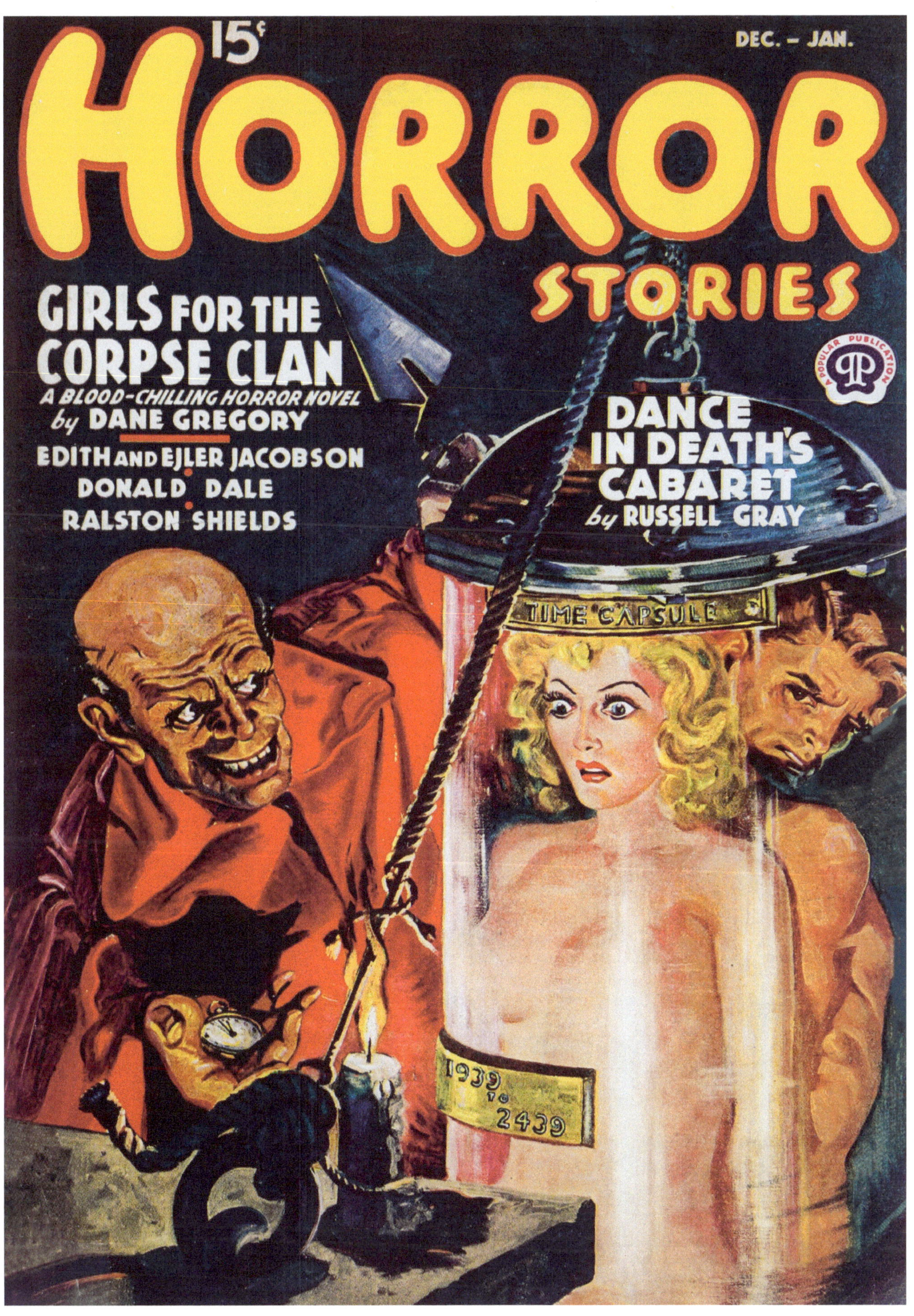

15¢
DEC. - JAN.
HORROR STORIES
GIRLS FOR THE CORPSE CLAN
A BLOOD-CHILLING HORROR NOVEL
by DANE GREGORY
EDITH AND EJLER JACOBSON
DONALD DALE
RALSTON SHIELDS
A POPULAR PUBLICATION
PP
DANCE IN DEATH'S CABARET
by RUSSELL GRAY
TIME CAPSULE
1939 TO 2439

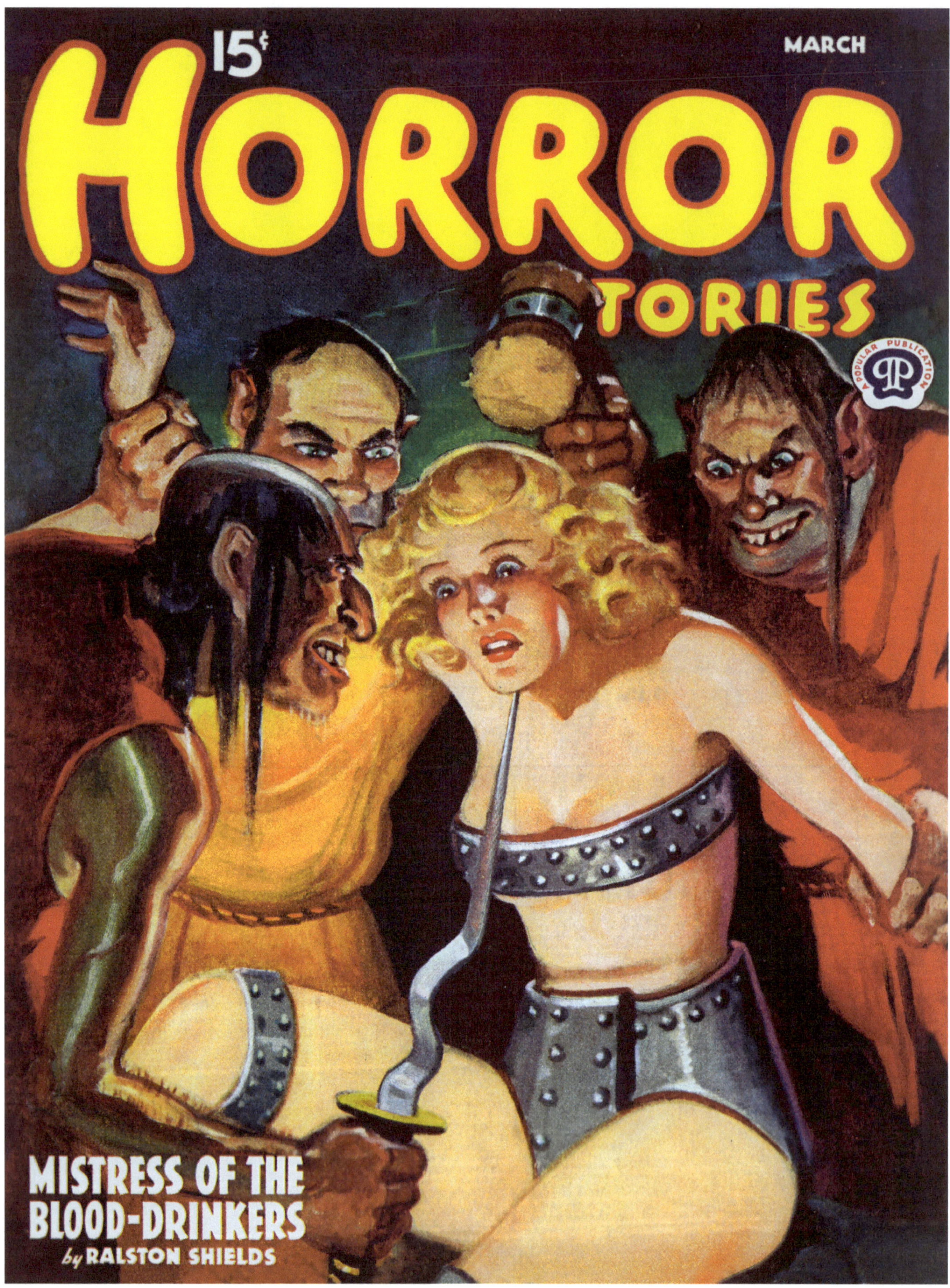

15¢
MARCH
Horror STORIES
A POPULAR PUBLICATION
MISTRESS OF THE
BLOOD-DRINKERS
by RALSTON SHIELDS

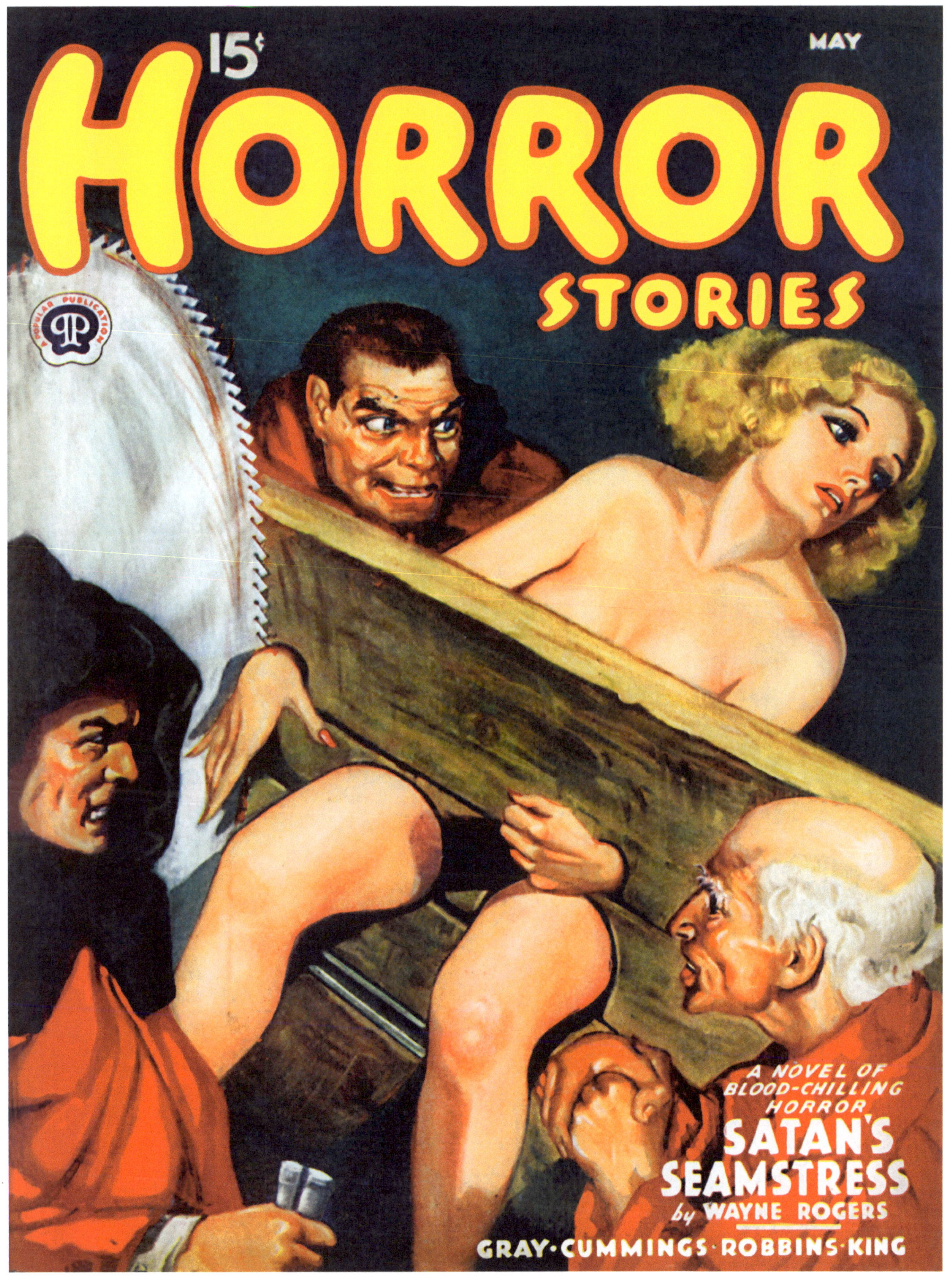
15¢
MAY
Horror
STORIES
A NOVEL OF
BLOOD-CHILLING
HORROR
SATAN'S
SEAMSTRESS
by WAYNE ROGERS
GRAY · CUMMINGS · ROBBINS · KING

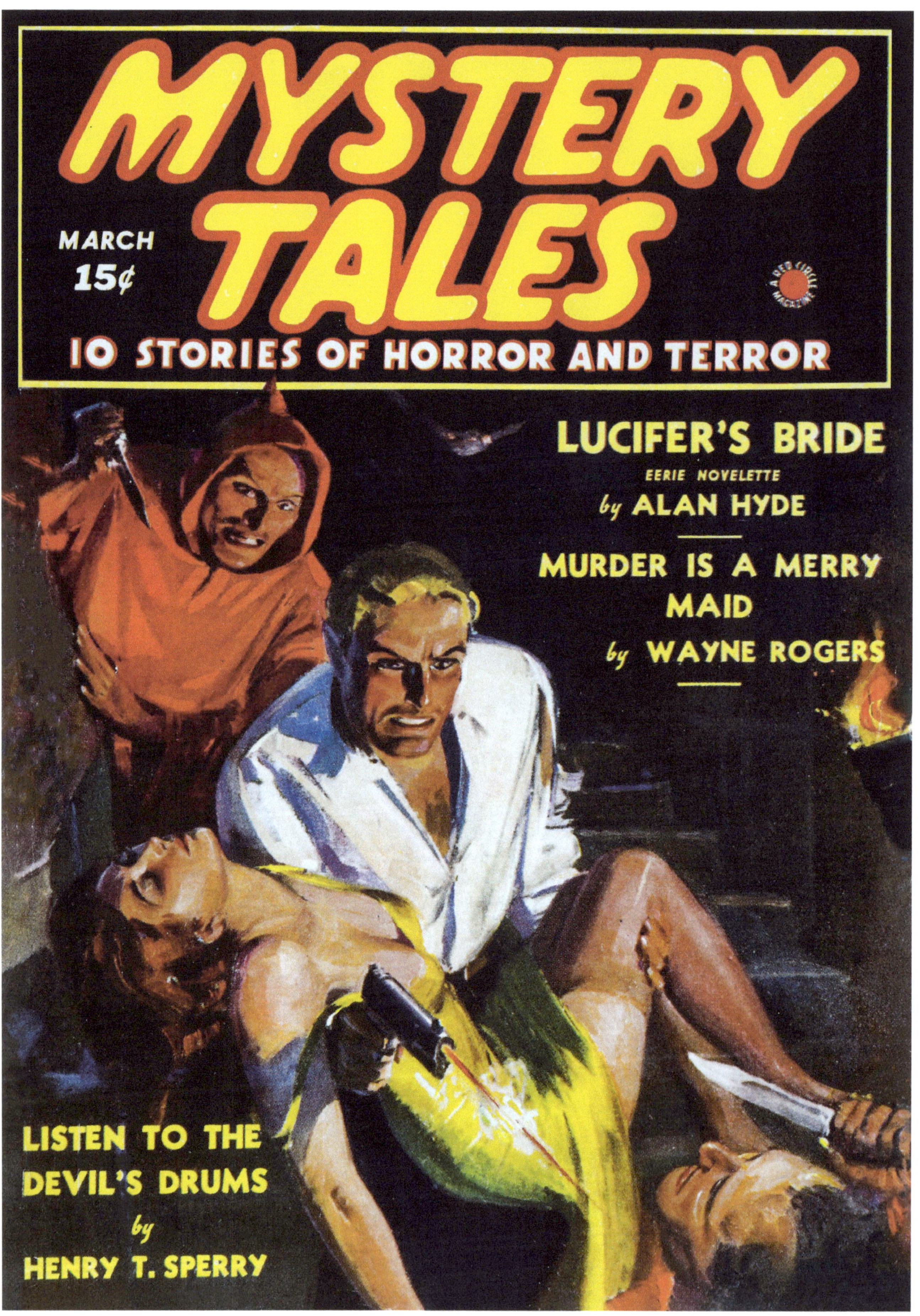

MYSTERY TALES
MARCH
15¢
A RED CIRCLE MAGAZINE
10 STORIES OF HORROR AND TERROR
LUCIFER'S BRIDE
EERIE NOVELETTE
by ALAN HYDE
MURDER IS A MERRY MAID
by WAYNE ROGERS
LISTEN TO THE DEVIL'S DRUMS
by HENRY T. SPERRY

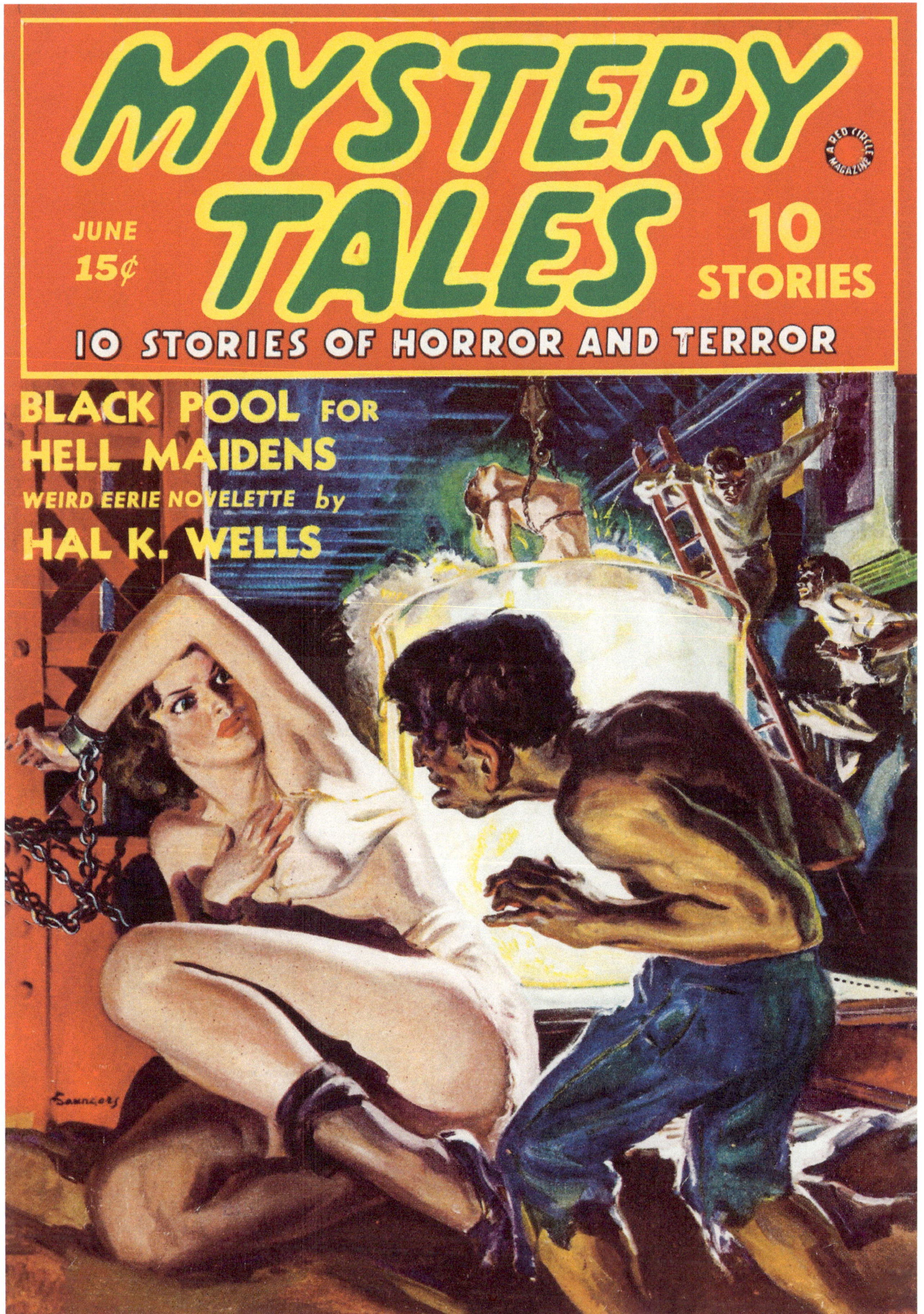

MYSTERY TALES
A RED CIRCLE MAGAZINE
JUNE
15¢
10 STORIES
10 STORIES OF HORROR AND TERROR
BLACK POOL FOR HELL MAIDENS
WEIRD EERIE NOVELETTE by
HAL K. WELLS

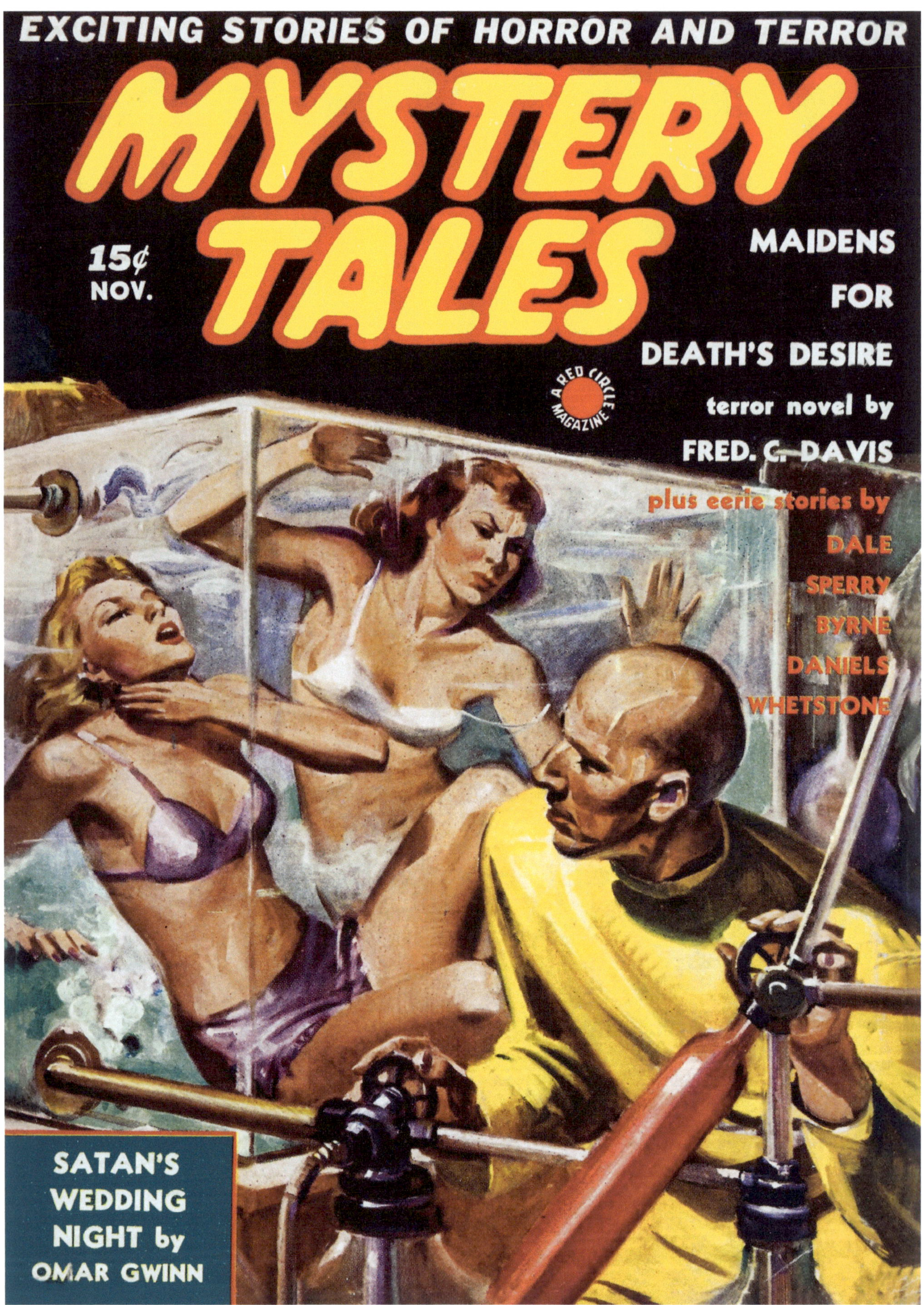

MYSTERY TALES

NOVEMEBER 1938

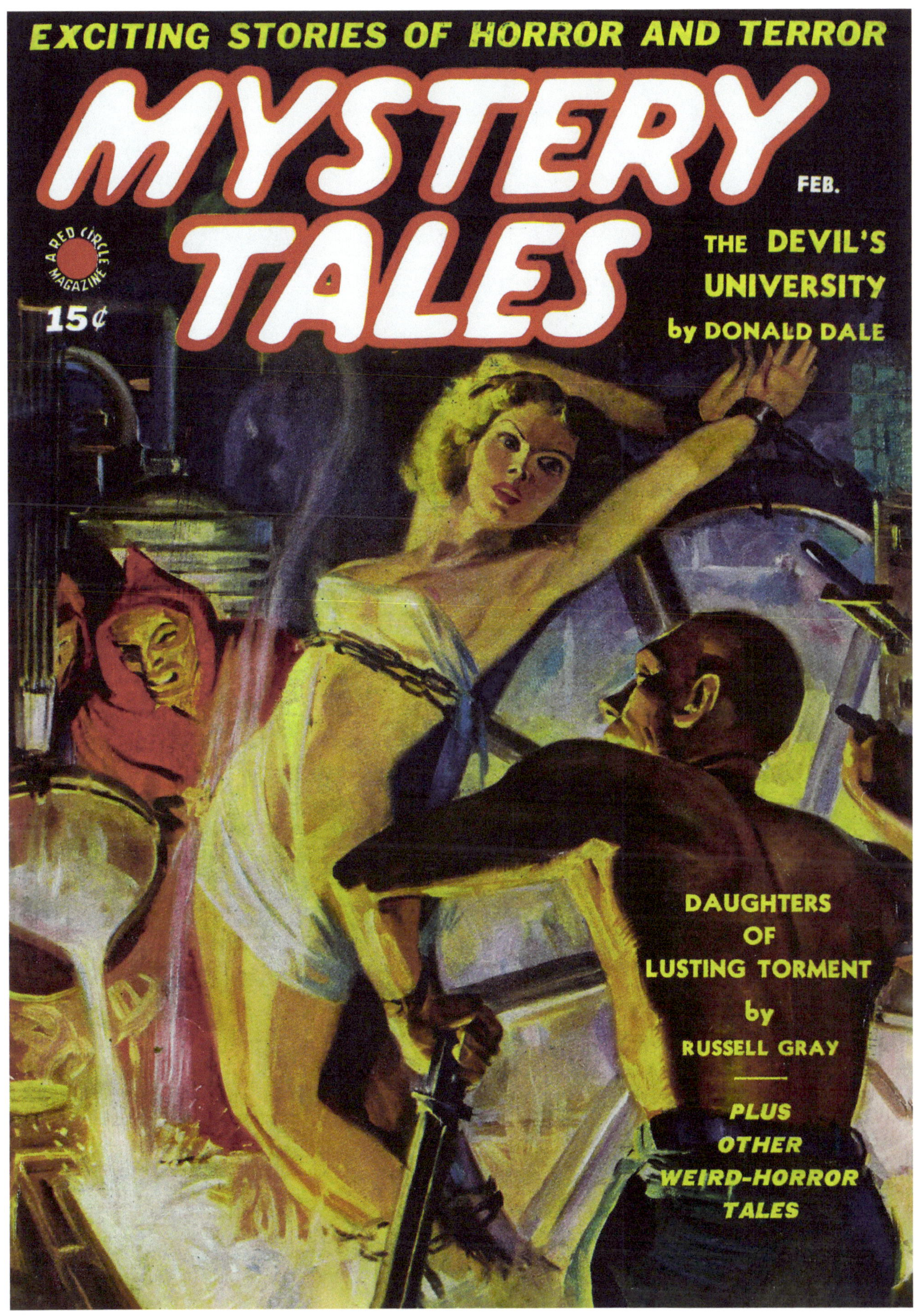

EXCITING STORIES OF HORROR AND TERROR
MYSTERY TALES
FEB.
A RED CIRCLE MAGAZINE
15¢
THE DEVIL'S UNIVERSITY
by DONALD DALE
DAUGHTERS OF LUSTING TORMENT
by RUSSELL GRAY
PLUS OTHER WEIRD-HORROR TALES

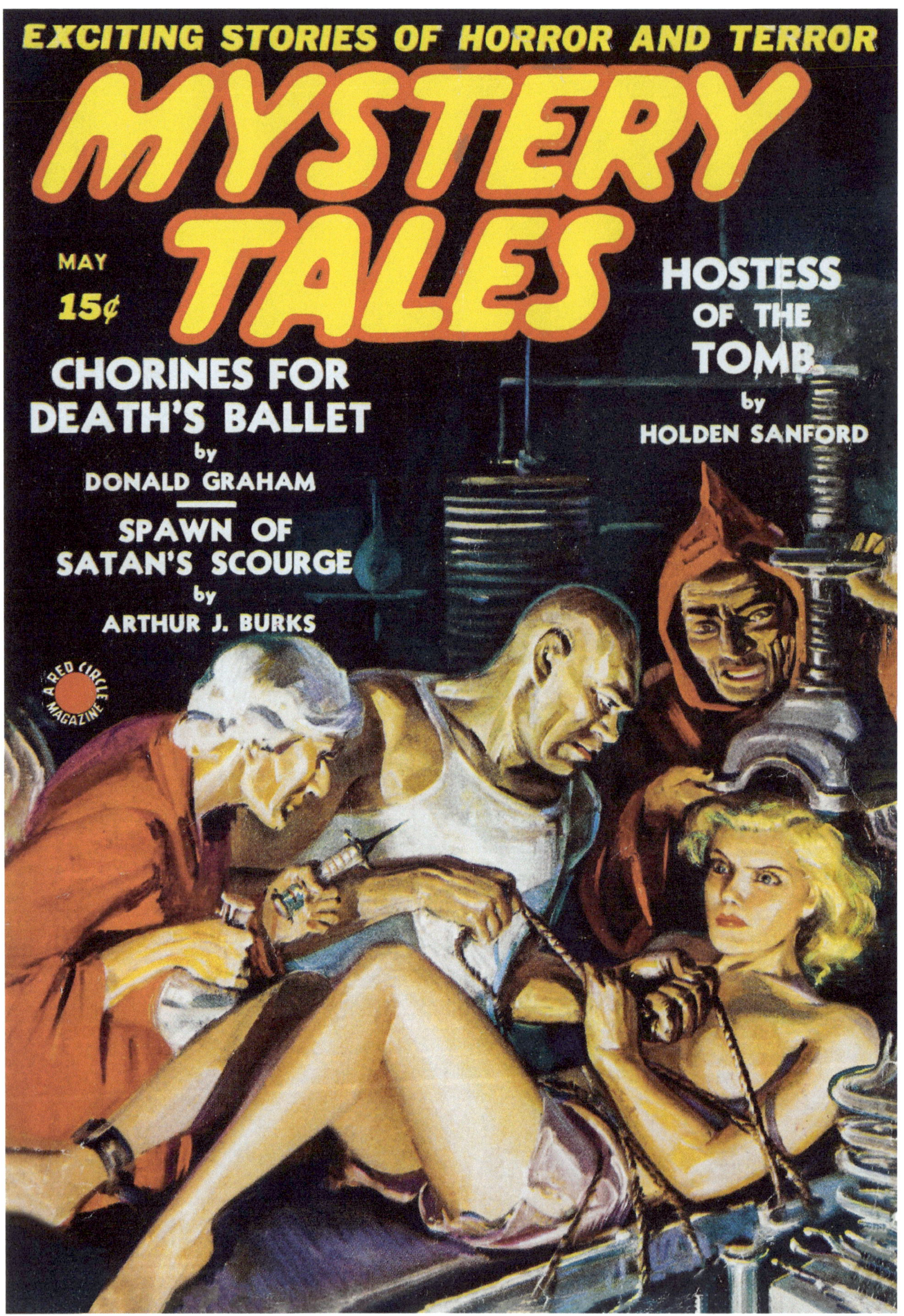

EXCITING STORIES OF HORROR AND TERROR
MYSTERY TALES
MAY
15¢
CHORINES FOR DEATH'S BALLET
by
DONALD GRAHAM
SPAWN OF SATAN'S SCOURGE
by
ARTHUR J. BURKS
HOSTESS OF THE TOMB
by
HOLDEN SANFORD
A RED CIRCLE MAGAZINE

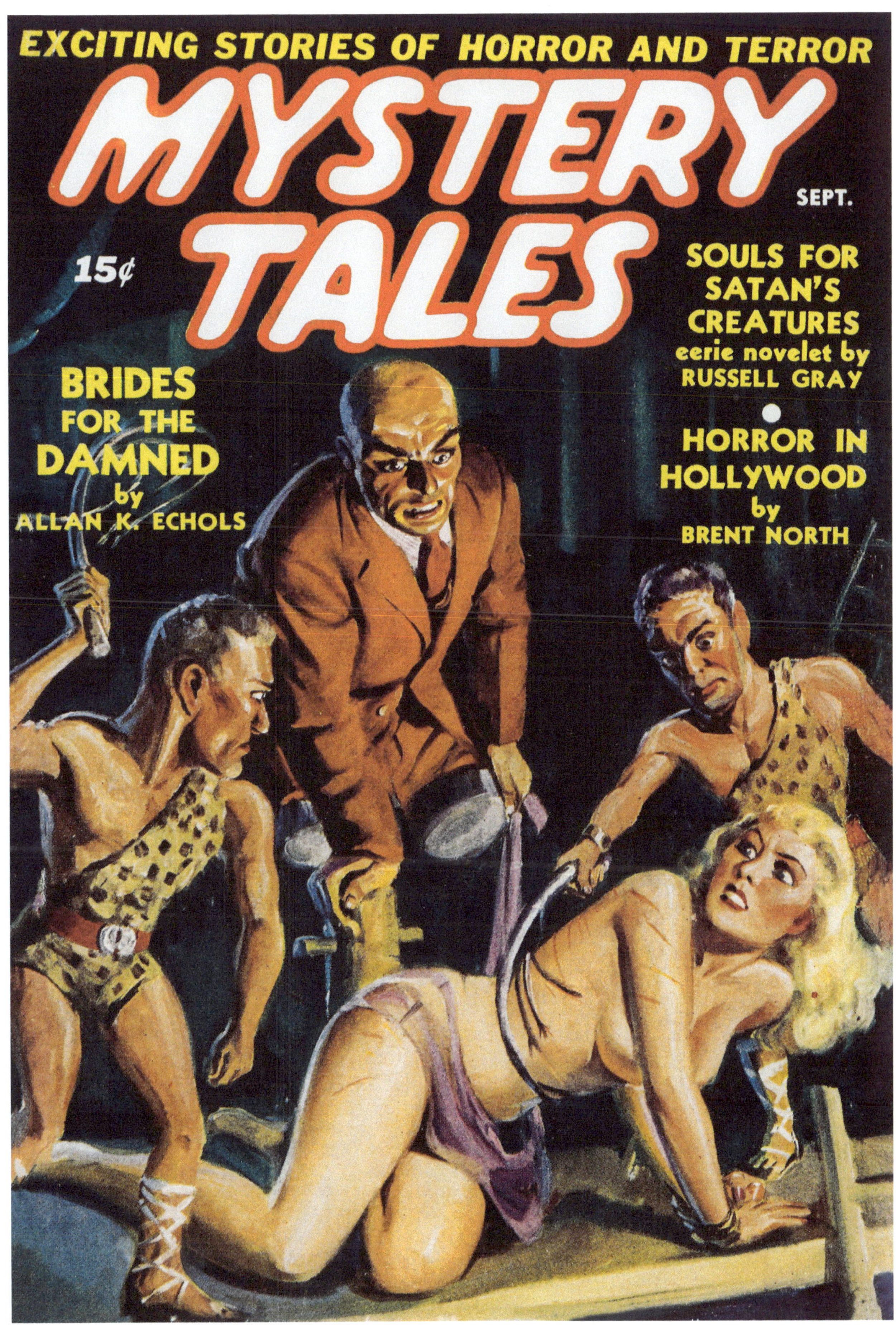

EXCITING STORIES OF HORROR AND TERROR
MYSTERY TALES
SEPT.
15¢
SOULS FOR SATAN'S CREATURES
eerie novelet by RUSSELL GRAY
BRIDES FOR THE DAMNED
by ALLAN K. ECHOLS
HORROR IN HOLLYWOOD
by BRENT NORTH

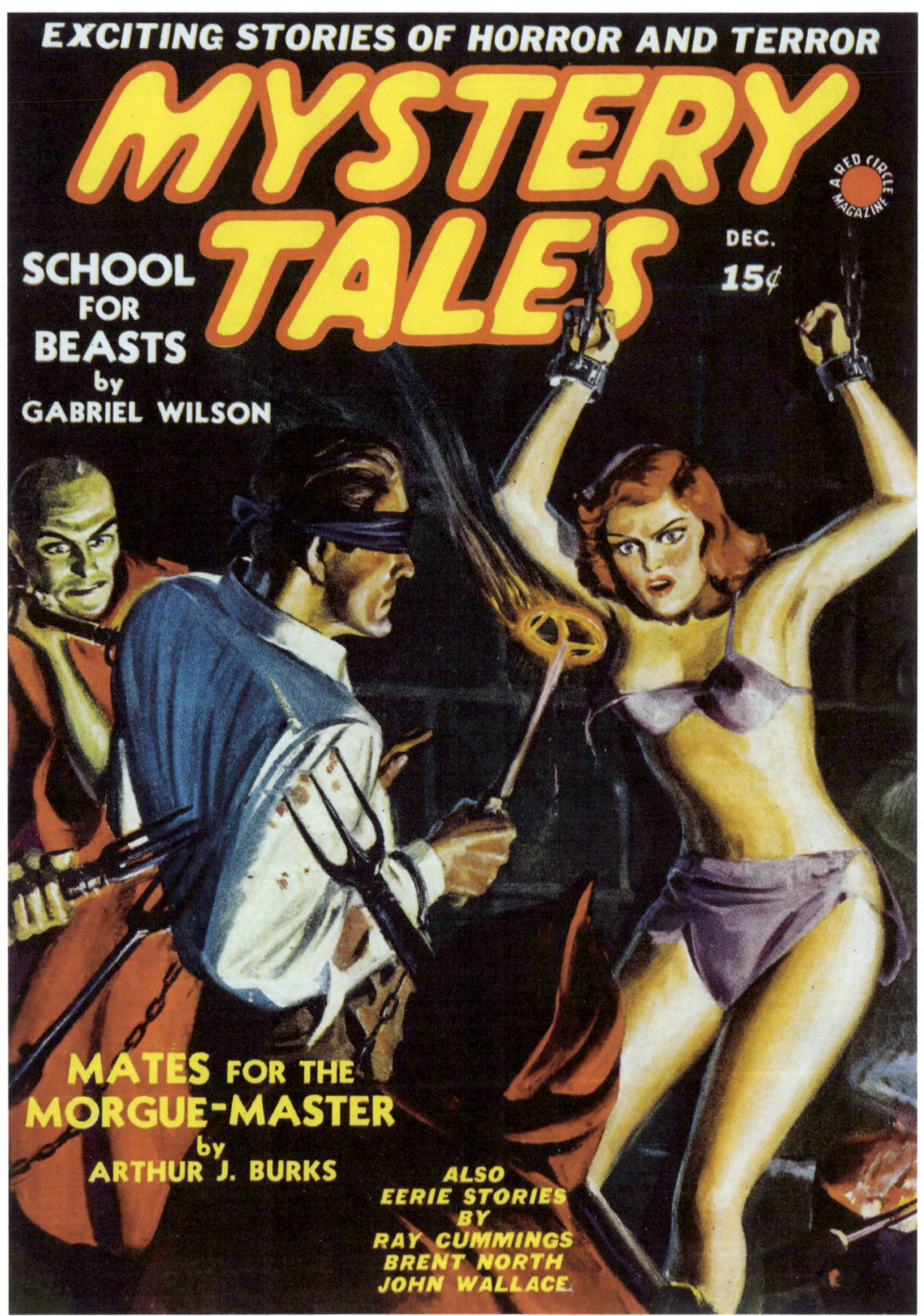

MYSTERY TALES

DECEMBER 1939

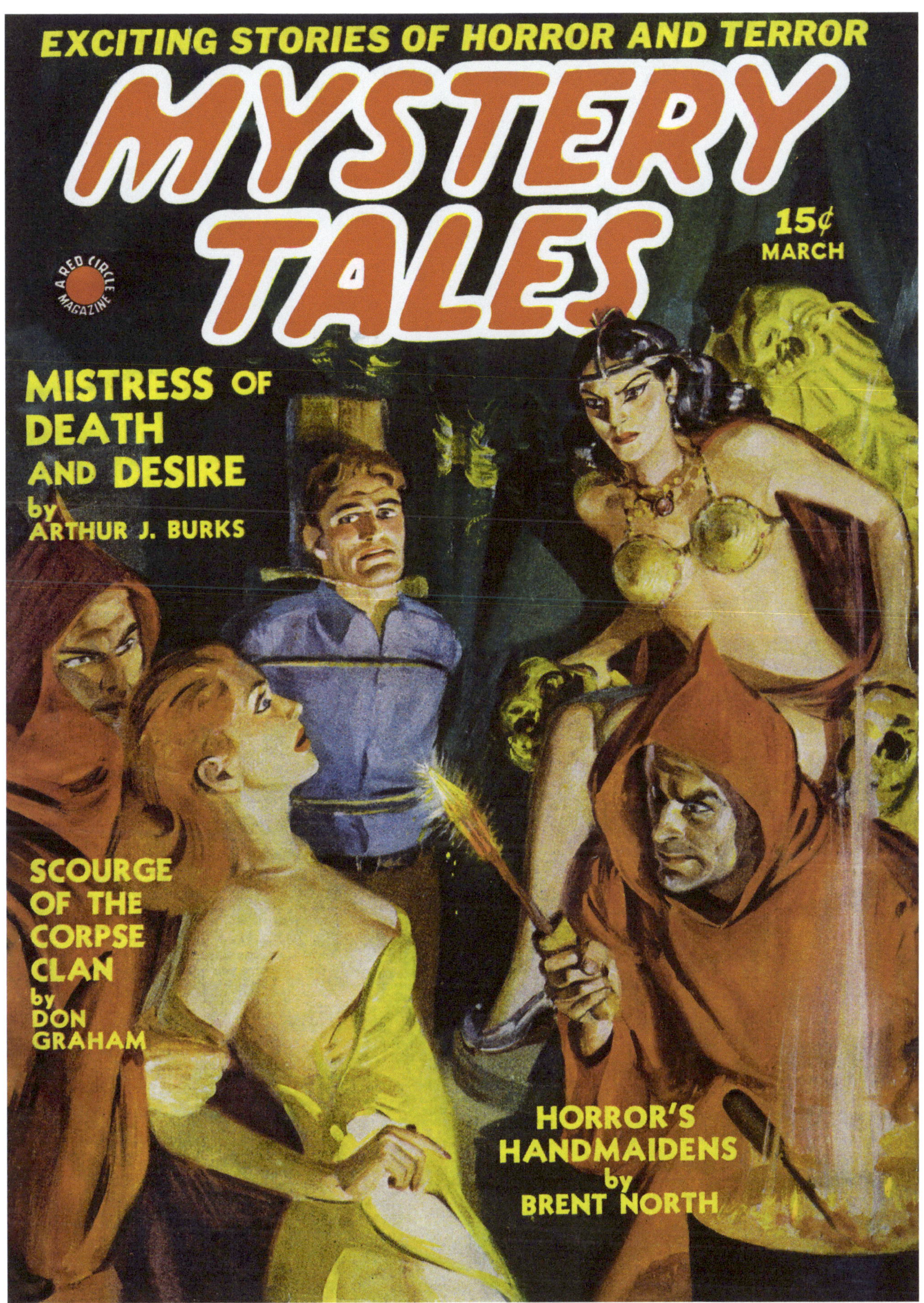

EXCITING STORIES OF HORROR AND TERROR
MYSTERY TALES
15¢
MARCH
A RED CIRCLE MAGAZINE
MISTRESS OF DEATH AND DESIRE
by ARTHUR J. BURKS
SCOURGE OF THE CORPSE CLAN
by DON GRAHAM
HORROR'S HANDMAIDENS
by BRENT NORTH

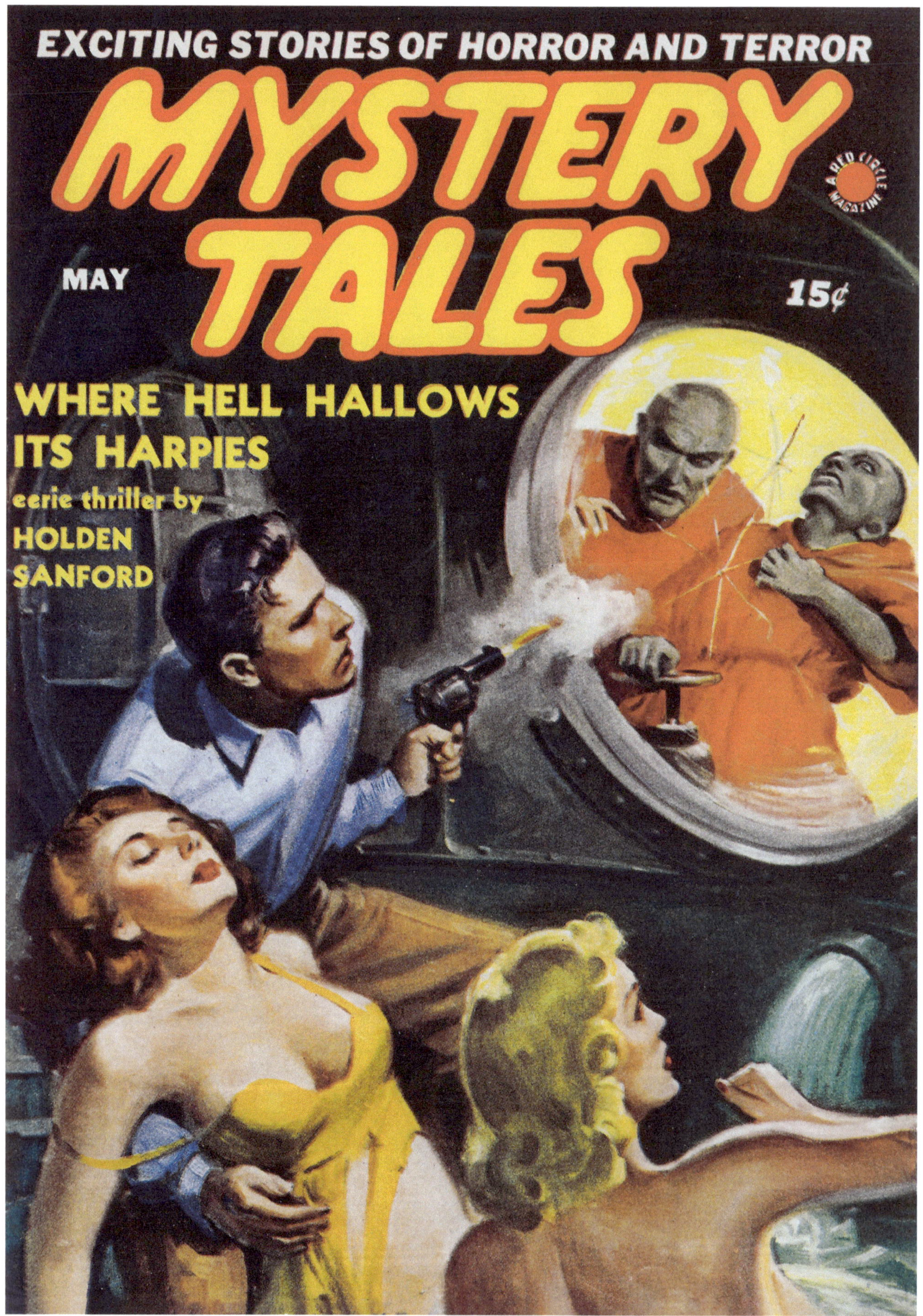
EXCITING STORIES OF HORROR AND TERROR
MYSTERY TALES
A RED CIRCLE MAGAZINE
MAY
15¢
WHERE HELL HALLOWS ITS HARPIES
eerie thriller by
HOLDEN SANFORD

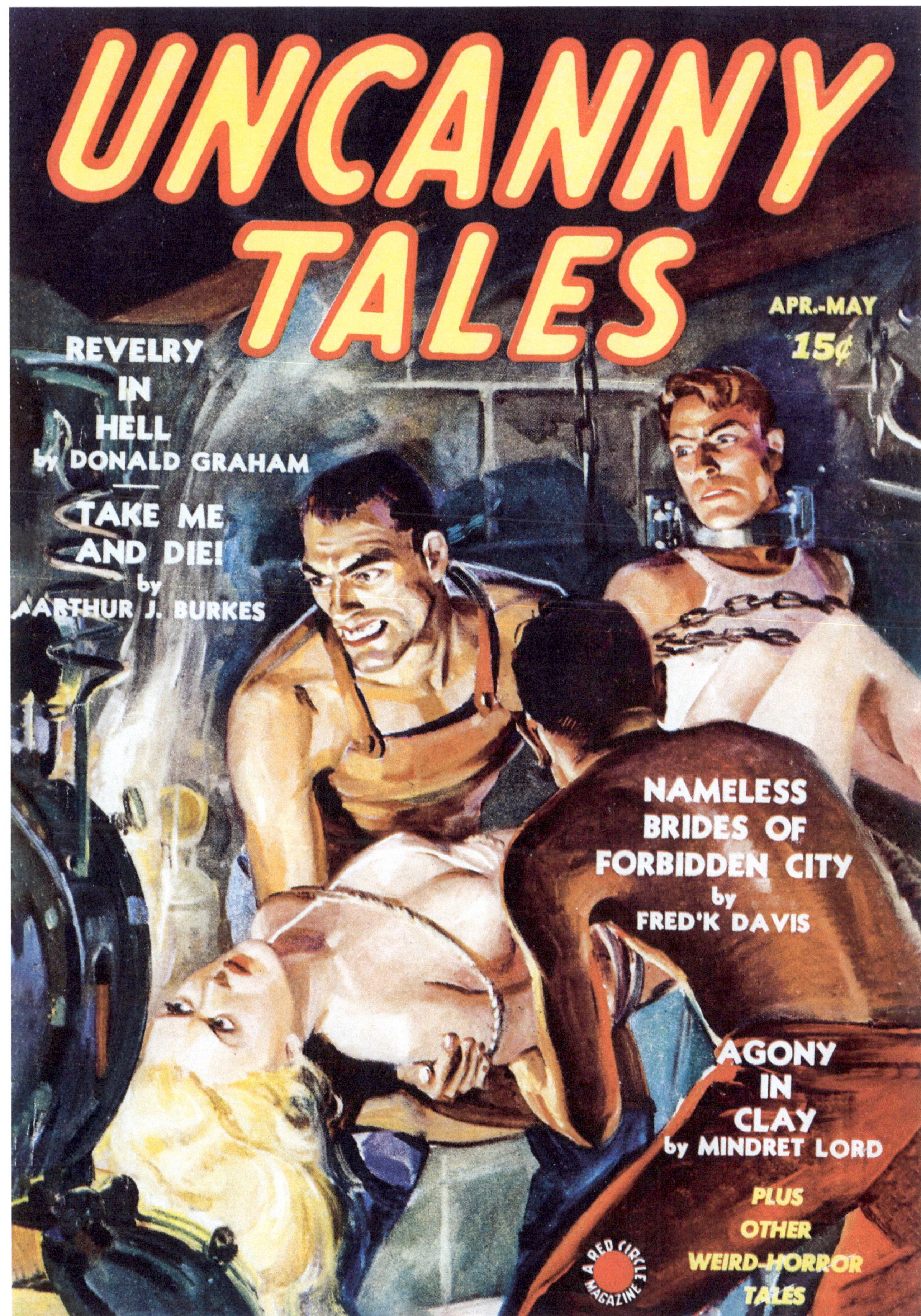

UNCANNY TALES
APR.-MAY
15¢
REVELRY IN HELL
by DONALD GRAHAM
TAKE ME AND DIE!
by ARTHUR J. BURKES
NAMELESS BRIDES OF FORBIDDEN CITY
by FRED'K DAVIS
AGONY IN CLAY
by MINDRET LORD
PLUS OTHER WEIRD-HORROR TALES
A RED CIRCLE MAGAZINE

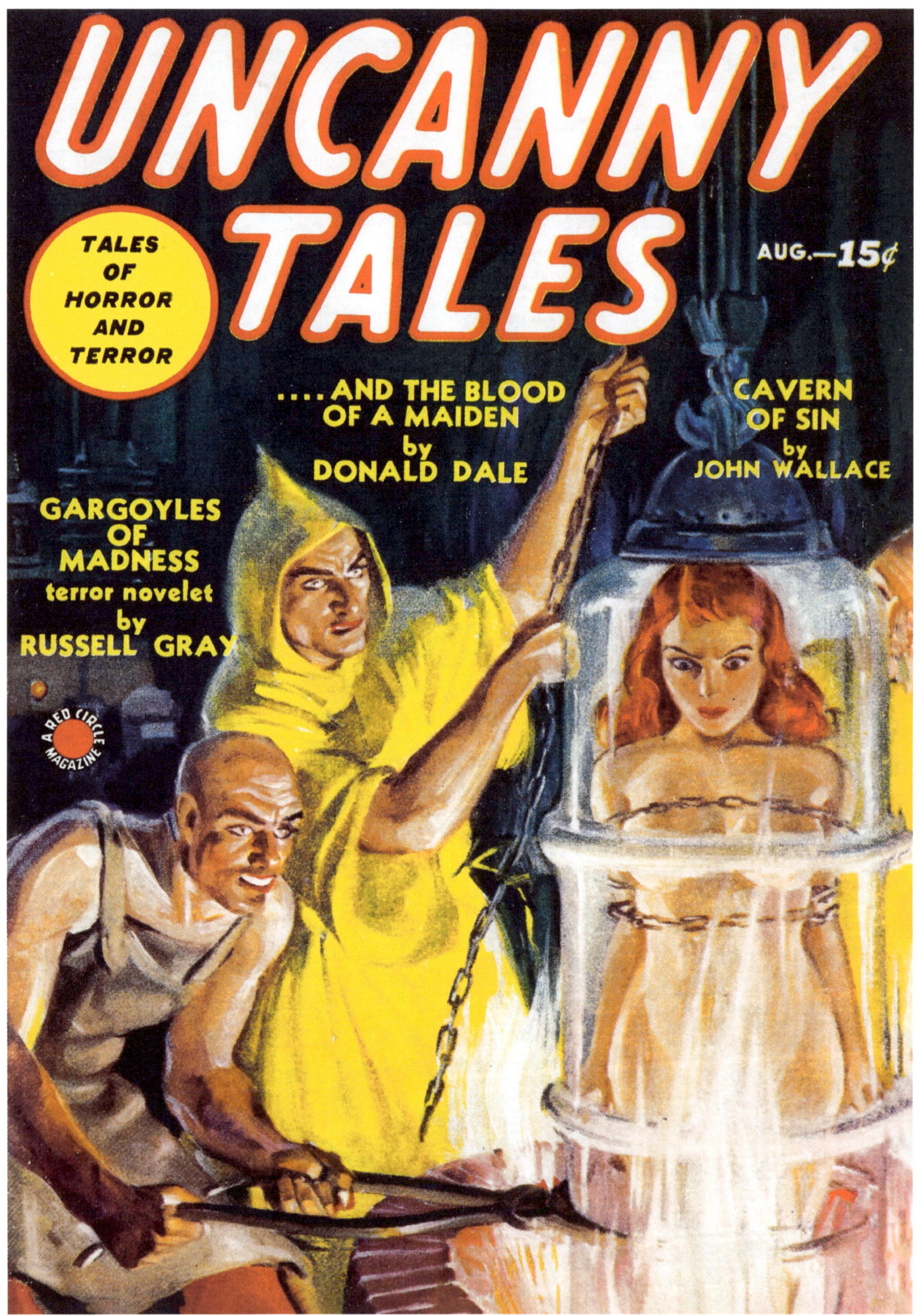

UNCANNY TALES
TALES OF HORROR AND TERROR
AUG.—15¢
....AND THE BLOOD OF A MAIDEN
by DONALD DALE
CAVERN OF SIN
by JOHN WALLACE
GARGOYLES OF MADNESS
terror novelet
by RUSSELL GRAY
A RED CIRCLE MAGAZINE

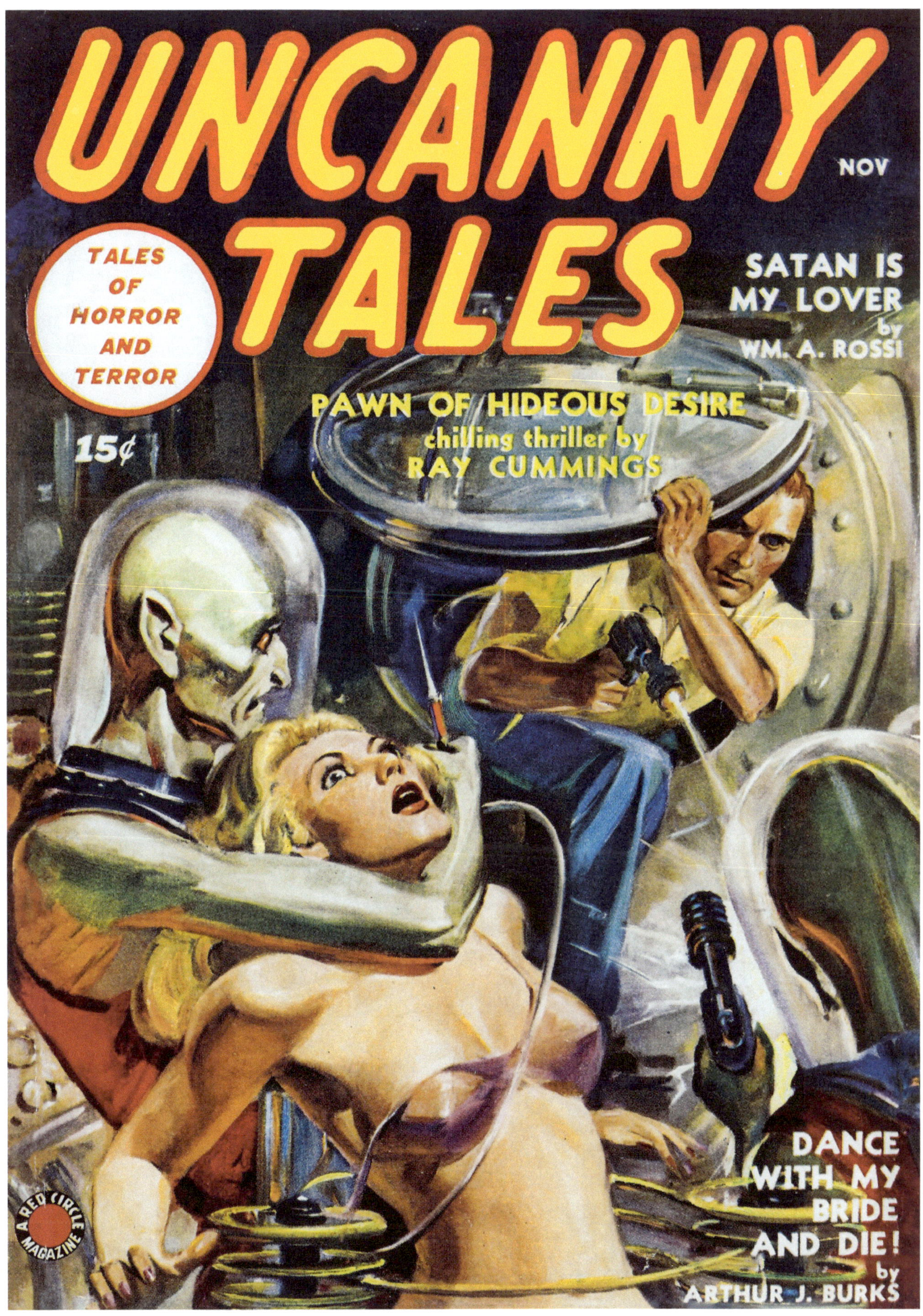

UNCANNY
TALES
NOV
TALES OF HORROR AND TERROR
15¢
SATAN IS MY LOVER
by
WM. A. ROSSI
PAWN OF HIDEOUS DESIRE
chilling thriller by
RAY CUMMINGS
DANCE WITH MY BRIDE AND DIE!
by
ARTHUR J. BURKS
A RED CIRCLE MAGAZINE

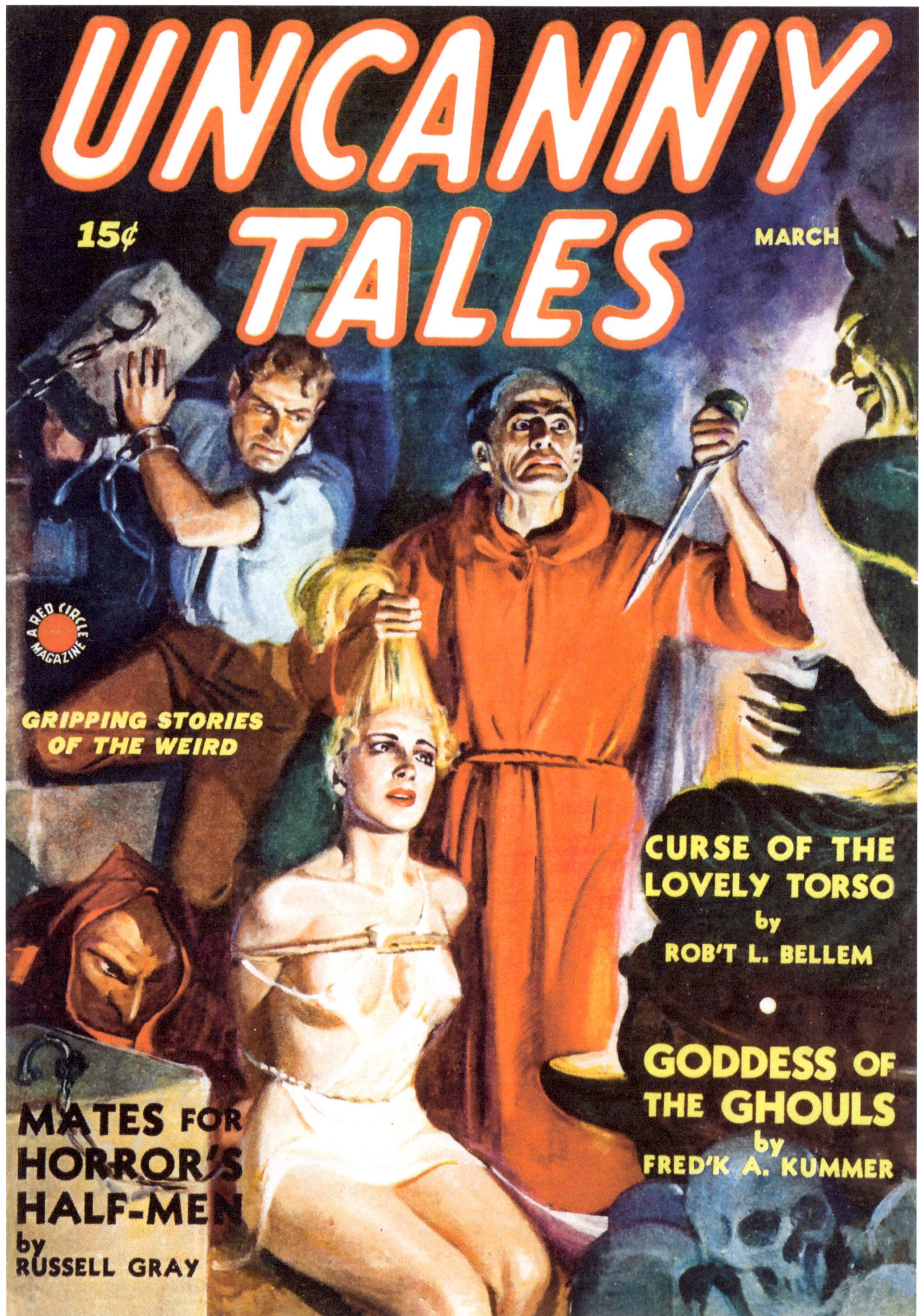

UNCANNY TALES

MARCH 1940

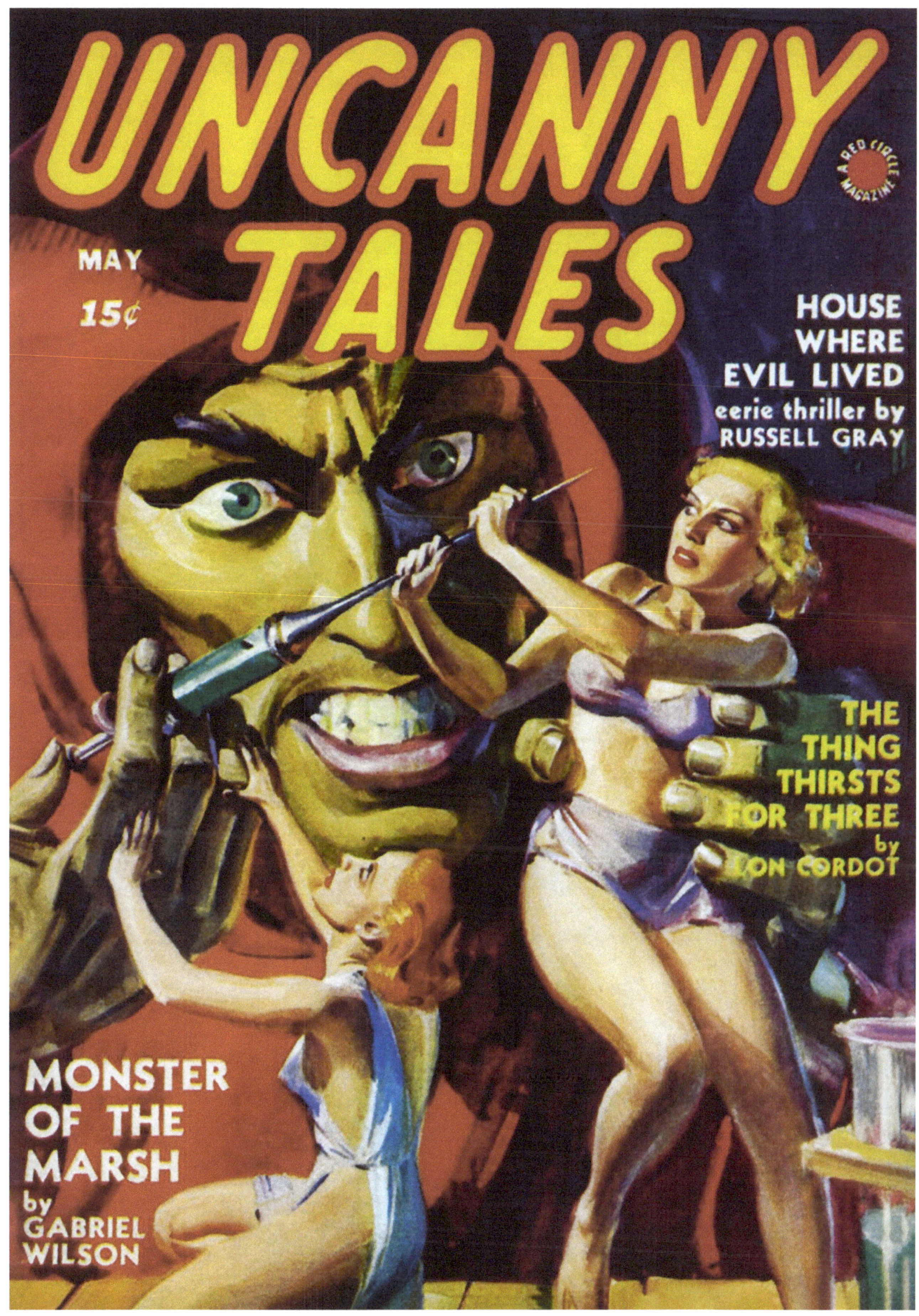

UNCANNY TALES
A RED CIRCLE MAGAZINE
MAY
15¢
HOUSE WHERE EVIL LIVED
eerie thriller by
RUSSELL GRAY
THE THING THIRSTS FOR THREE
by LON CORDOT
MONSTER OF THE MARSH
by GABRIEL WILSON

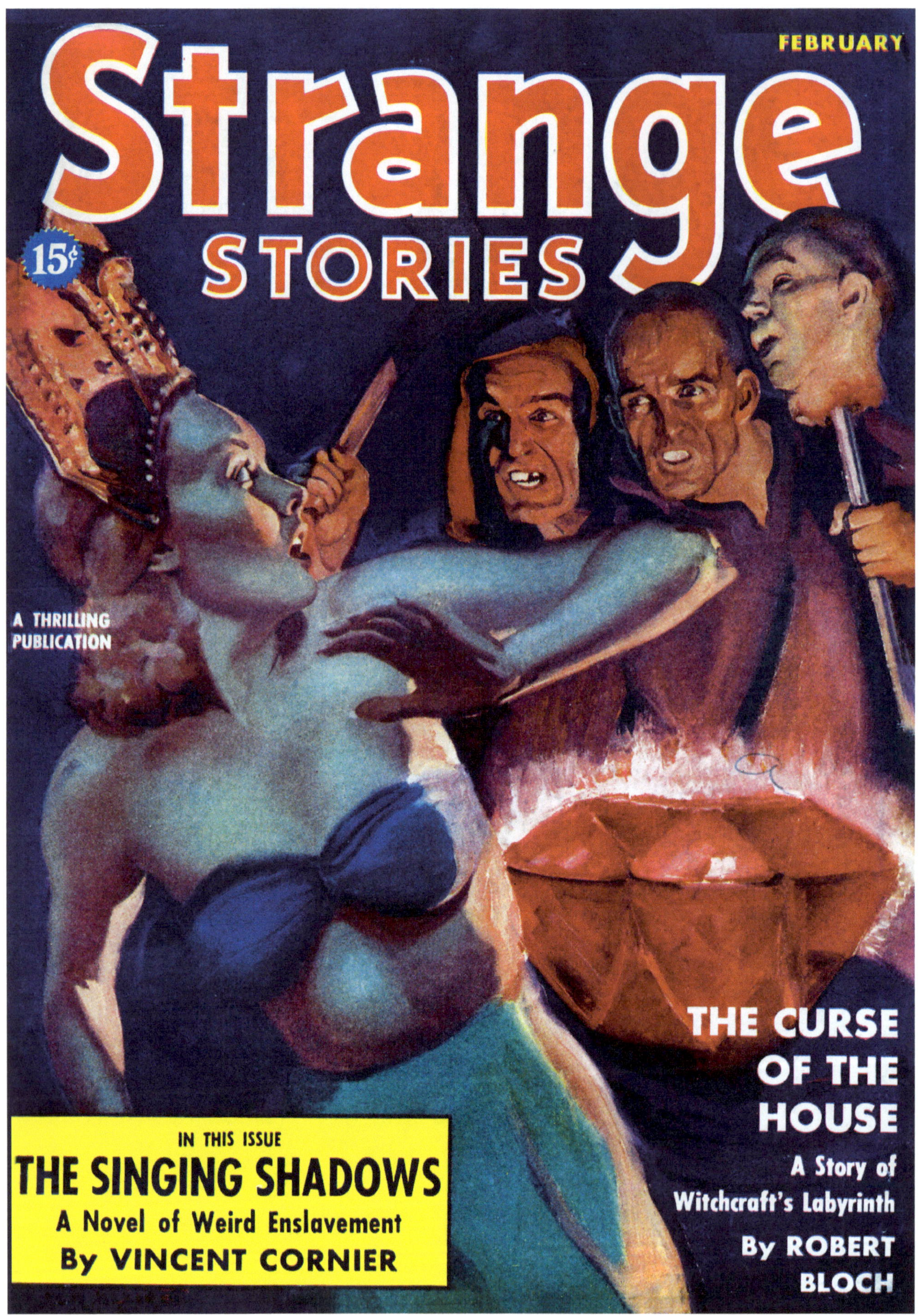

FEBRUARY
Strange
STORIES
15¢
A THRILLING
PUBLICATION
THE CURSE
OF THE
HOUSE
A Story of
Witchcraft's Labyrinth
By ROBERT
BLOCH
IN THIS ISSUE
THE SINGING SHADOWS
A Novel of Weird Enslavement
By VINCENT CORNIER

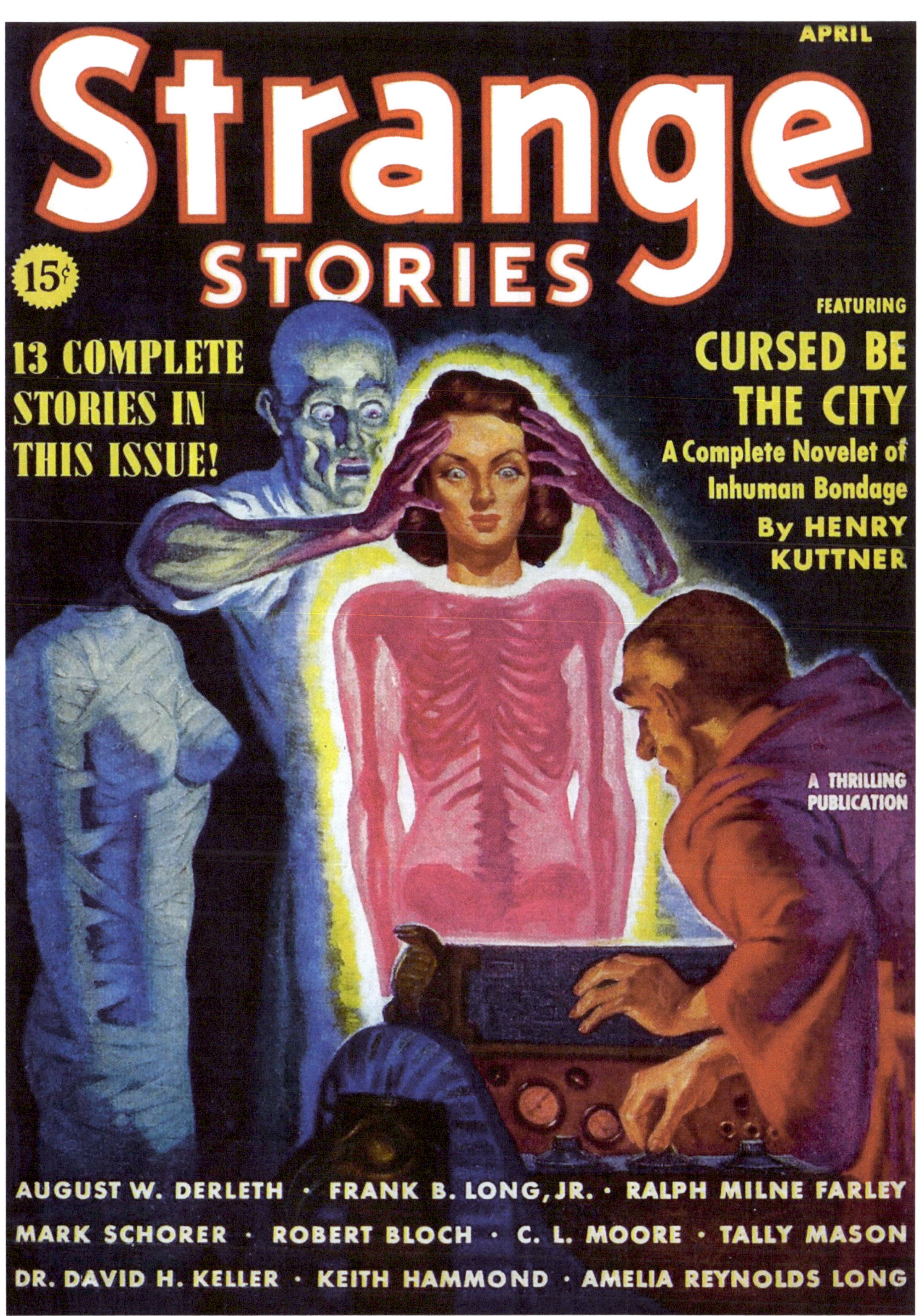

APRIL
15¢
Strange
STORIES
13 COMPLETE STORIES IN THIS ISSUE!
FEATURING
CURSED BE THE CITY
A Complete Novelet of Inhuman Bondage
By HENRY KUTTNER
A THRILLING PUBLICATION
AUGUST W. DERLETH · FRANK B. LONG, JR. · RALPH MILNE FARLEY
MARK SCHORER · ROBERT BLOCH · C. L. MOORE · TALLY MASON
DR. DAVID H. KELLER · KEITH HAMMOND · AMELIA REYNOLDS LONG

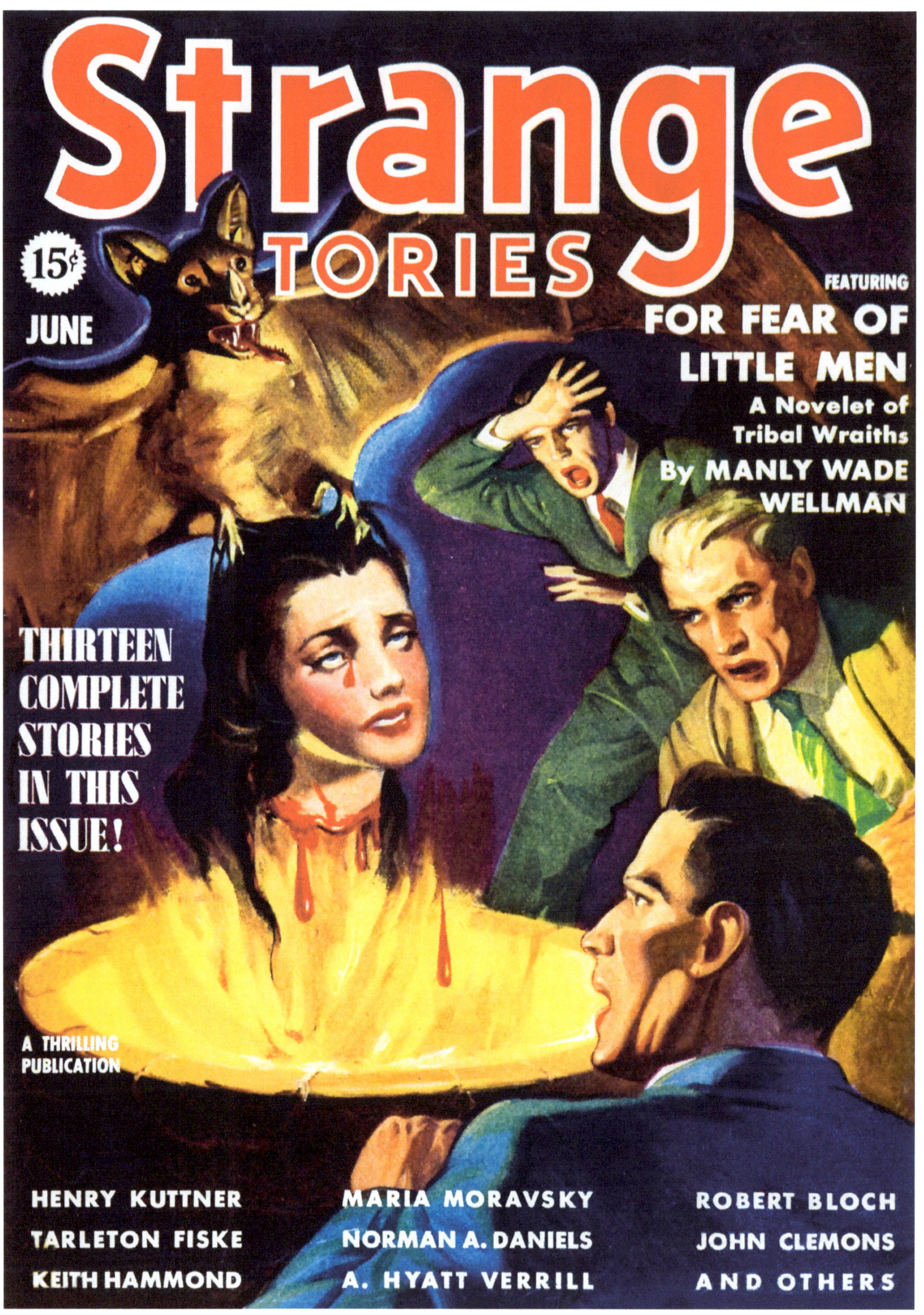

STRANGE STORIES

JUNE 1939

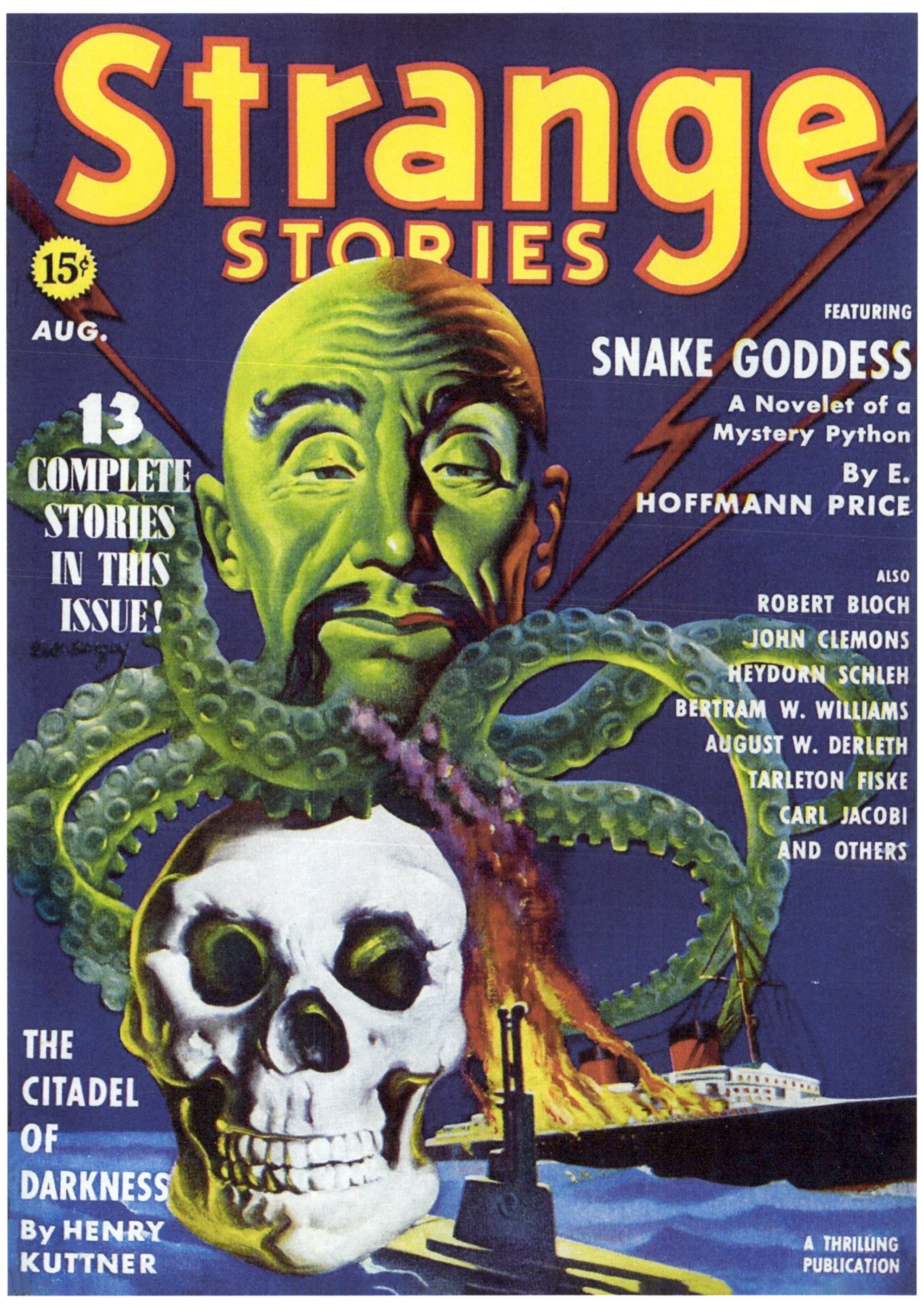

Strange STORIES
15¢
AUG.
13 COMPLETE STORIES IN THIS ISSUE!
FEATURING
SNAKE GODDESS
A Novelet of a Mystery Python
By E. HOFFMANN PRICE
ALSO
ROBERT BLOCH
JOHN CLEMONS
HEYDORN SCHLEH
BERTRAM W. WILLIAMS
AUGUST W. DERLETH
TARLETON FISKE
CARL JACOBI
AND OTHERS
THE CITADEL OF DARKNESS
By HENRY KUTTNER
A THRILLING PUBLICATION

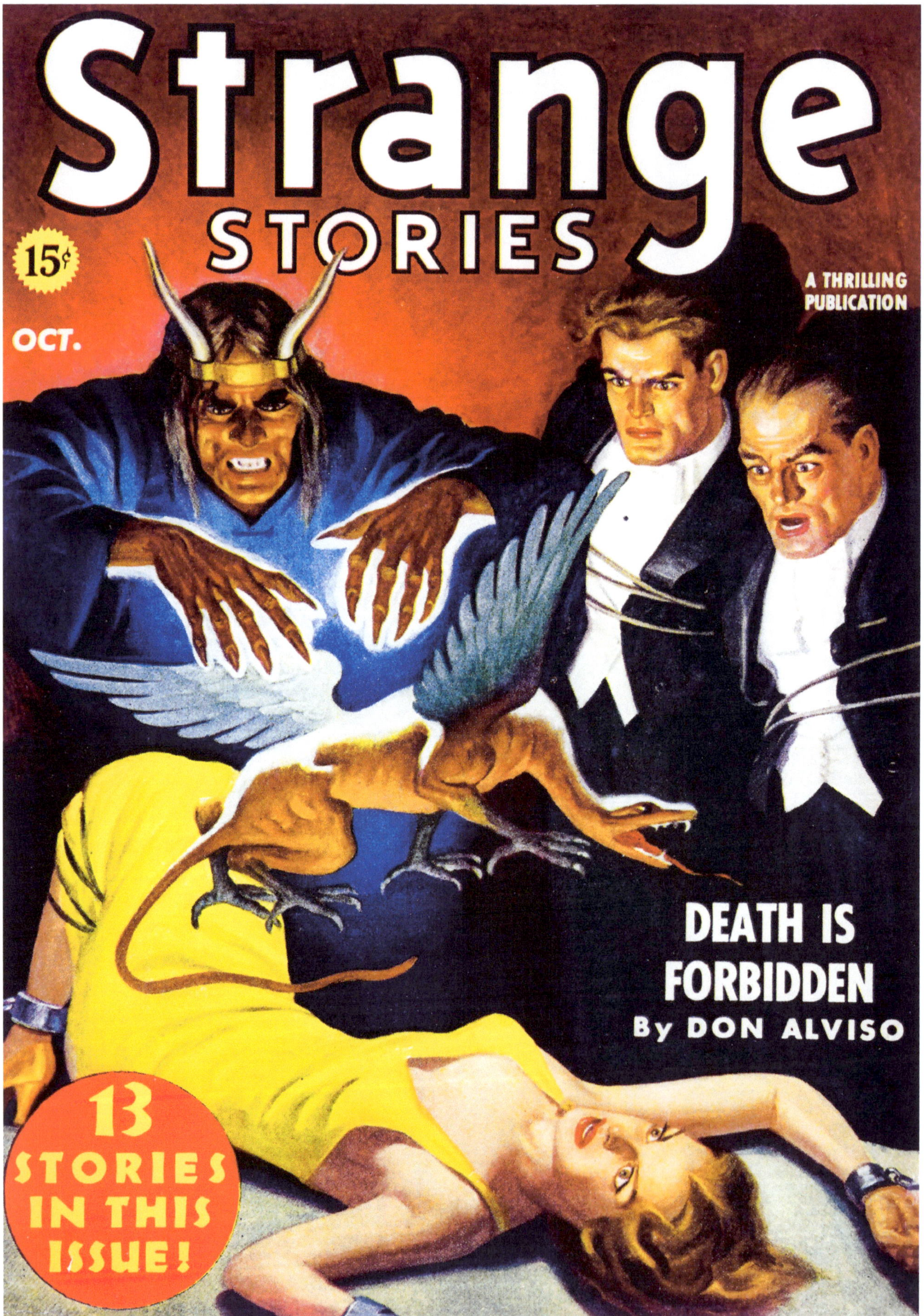

Strange
STORIES
A THRILLING PUBLICATION
15¢
OCT.
DEATH IS FORBIDDEN
By DON ALVISO
13 STORIES IN THIS ISSUE!

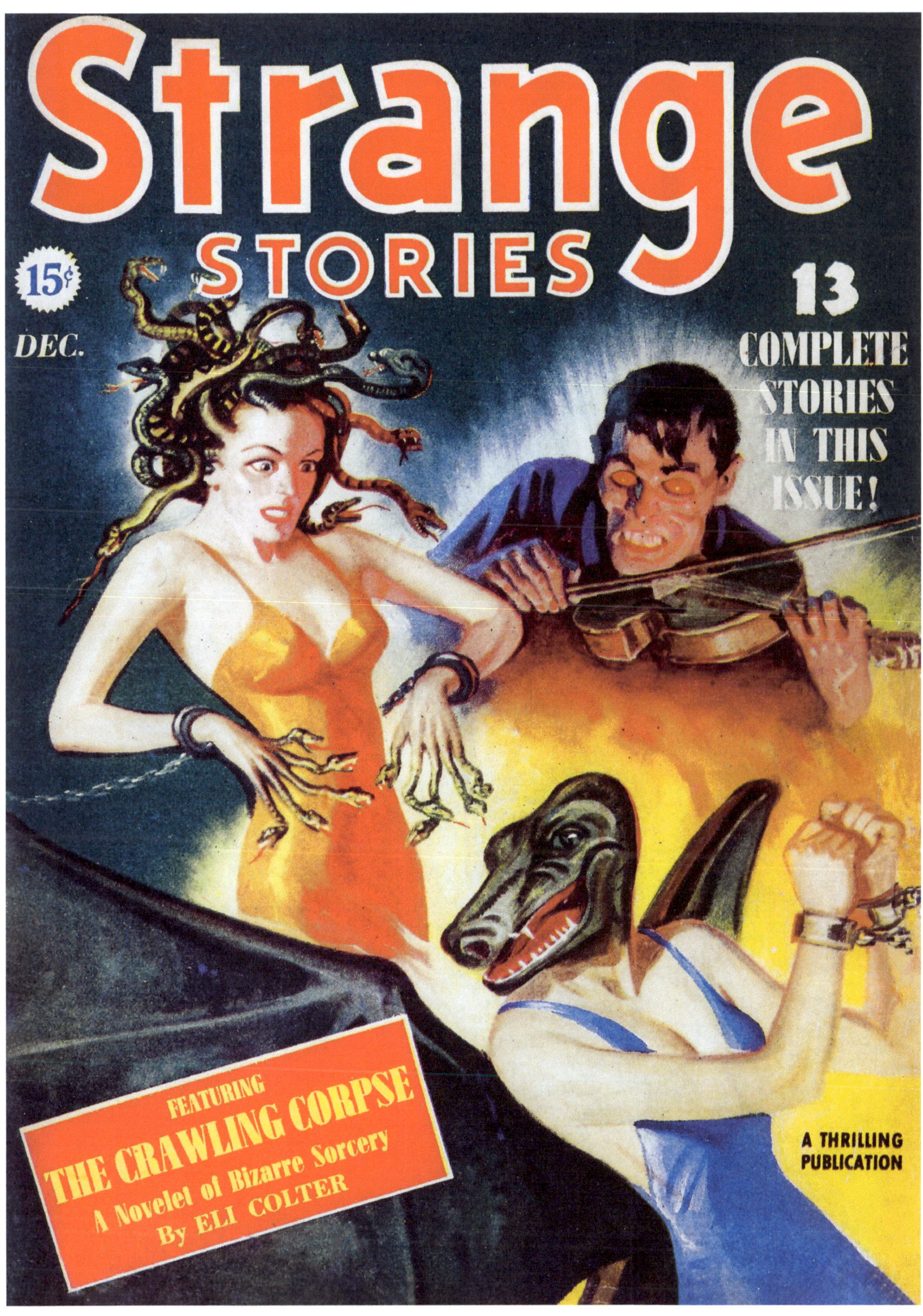

Strange
STORIES
15¢
DEC.
13 COMPLETE STORIES IN THIS ISSUE!
FEATURING
THE CRAWLING CORPSE
A Novelet of Bizarre Sorcery
By ELI COLTER
A THRILLING PUBLICATION

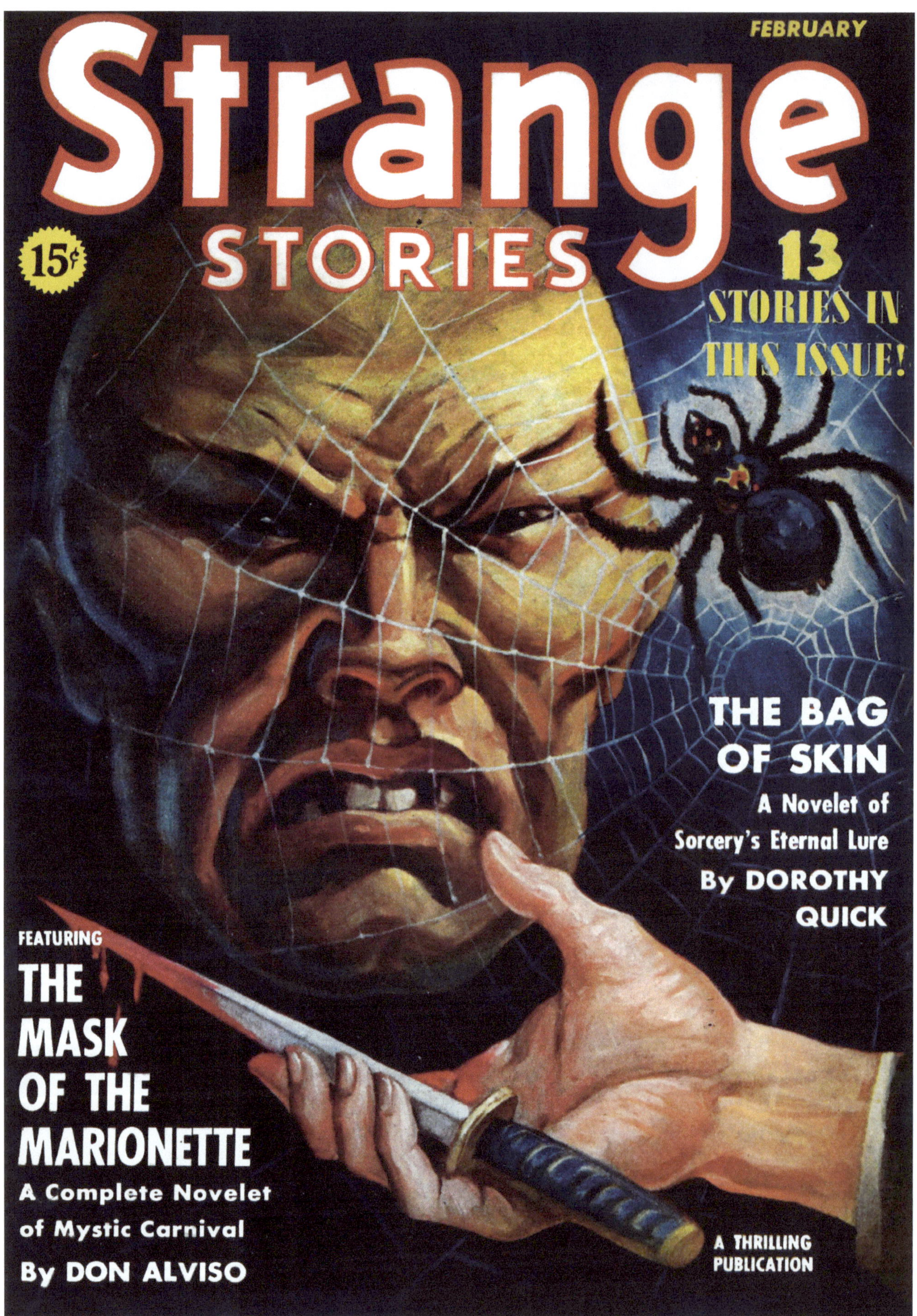

FEBRUARY
Strange
STORIES
15¢
13
STORIES IN
THIS ISSUE!
THE BAG
OF SKIN
A Novelet of
Sorcery's Eternal Lure
By DOROTHY
QUICK
FEATURING
THE
MASK
OF THE
MARIONETTE
A Complete Novelet
of Mystic Carnival
By DON ALVISO
A THRILLING
PUBLICATION

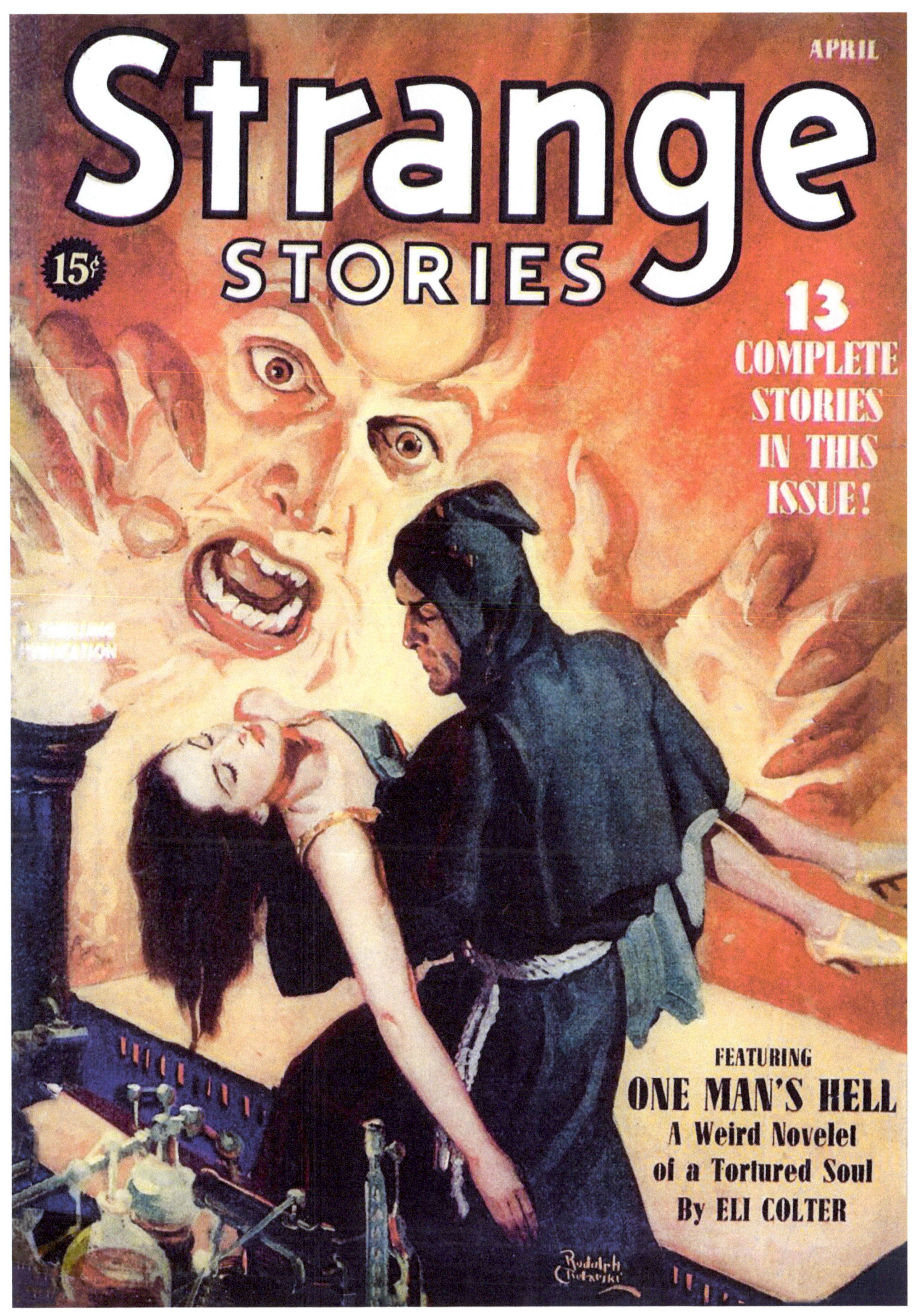

APRIL
Strange
STORIES
15¢
13 COMPLETE STORIES IN THIS ISSUE!
A THRILLING PUBLICATION
FEATURING
ONE MAN'S HELL
A Weird Novelet
of a Tortured Soul
By ELI COLTER

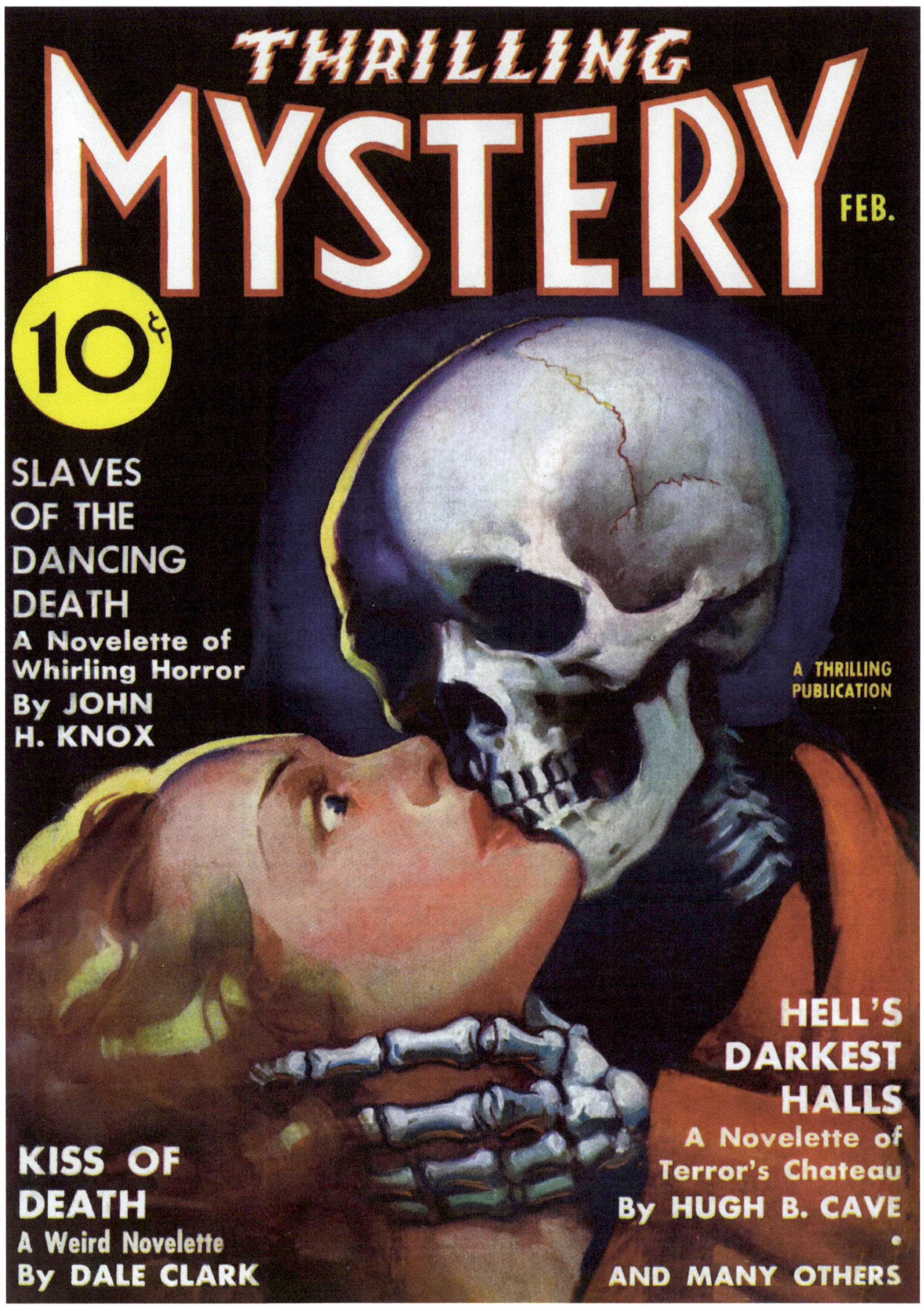

THRILLING MYSTERY

FEBRUARY 1937

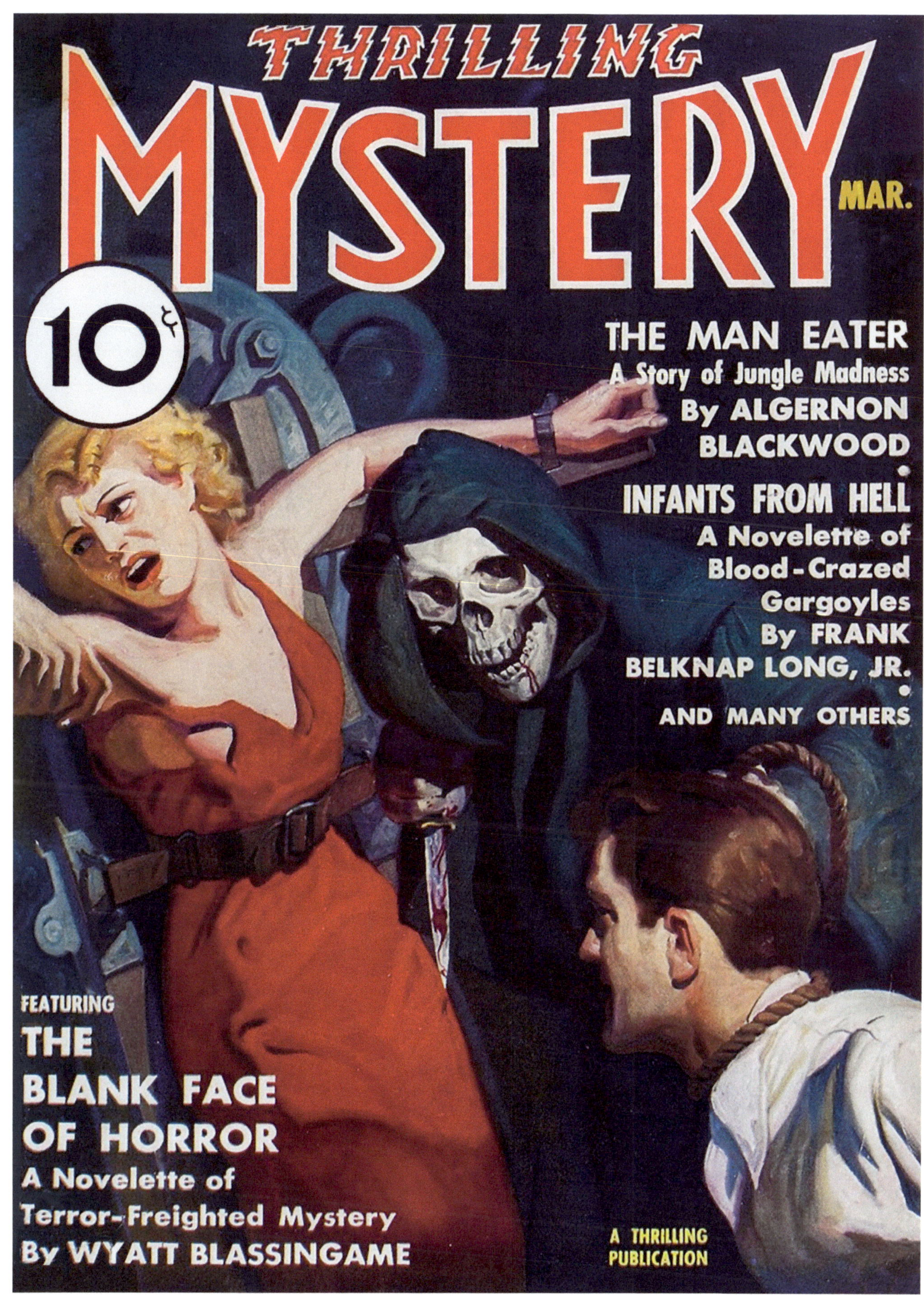

THRILLING
MYSTERY
MAR.
10¢
THE MAN EATER
A Story of Jungle Madness
By ALGERNON BLACKWOOD
INFANTS FROM HELL
A Novelette of Blood-Crazed Gargoyles
By FRANK BELKNAP LONG, JR.
AND MANY OTHERS
FEATURING
THE BLANK FACE OF HORROR
A Novelette of Terror-Freighted Mystery
By WYATT BLASSINGAME
A THRILLING PUBLICATION

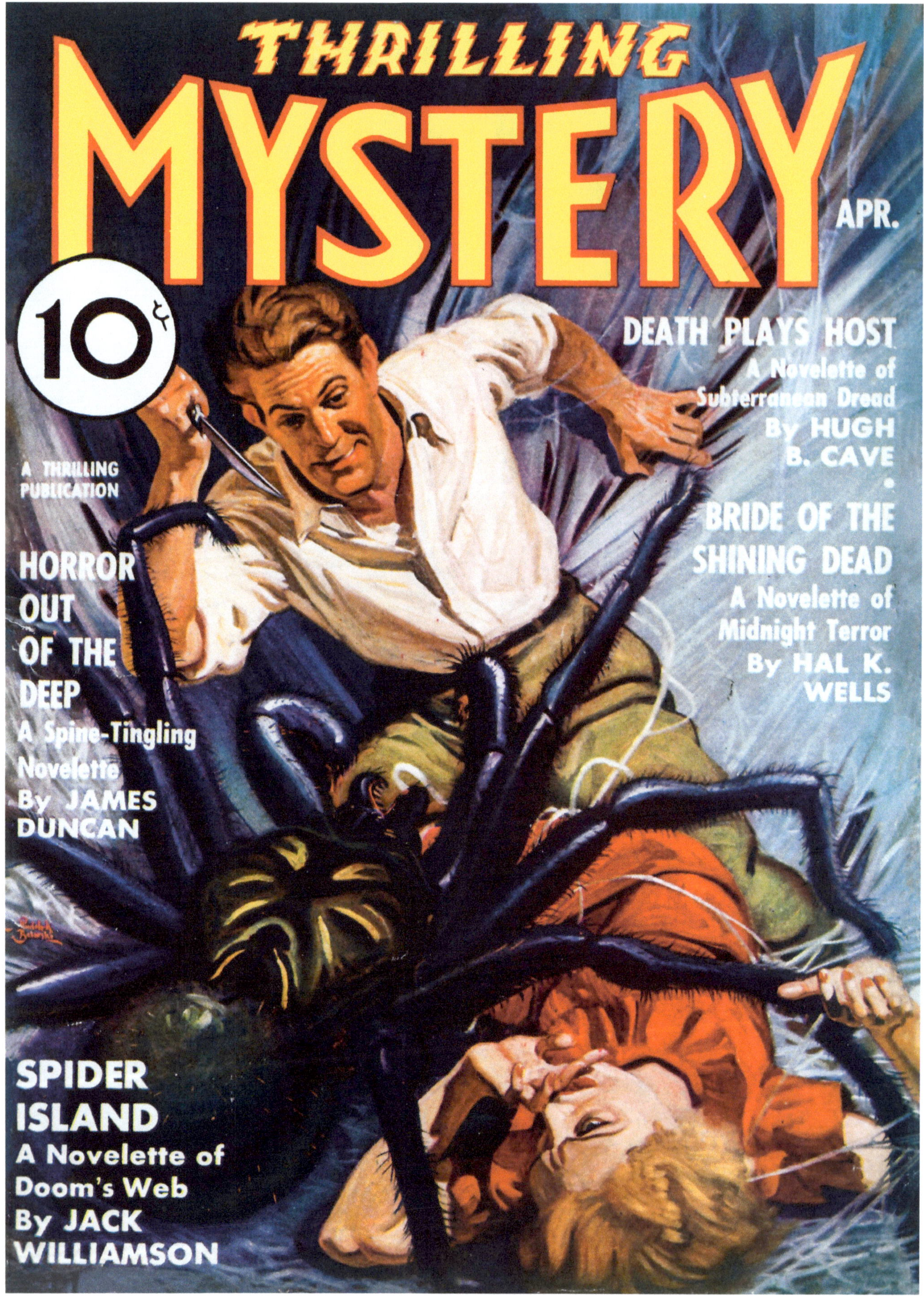

THRILLING MYSTERY

APRIL 1937

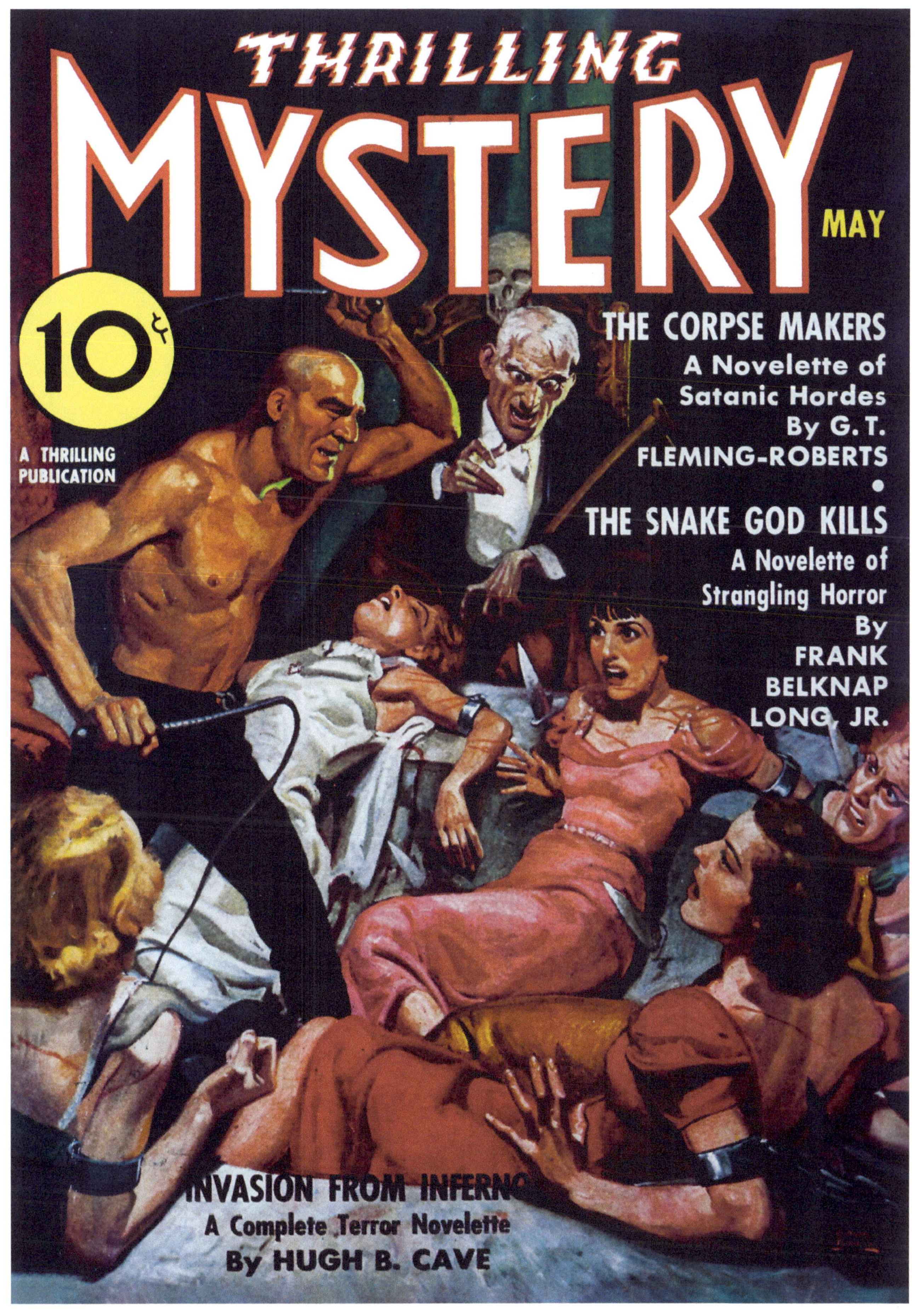

THRILLING MYSTERY

MAY 1937

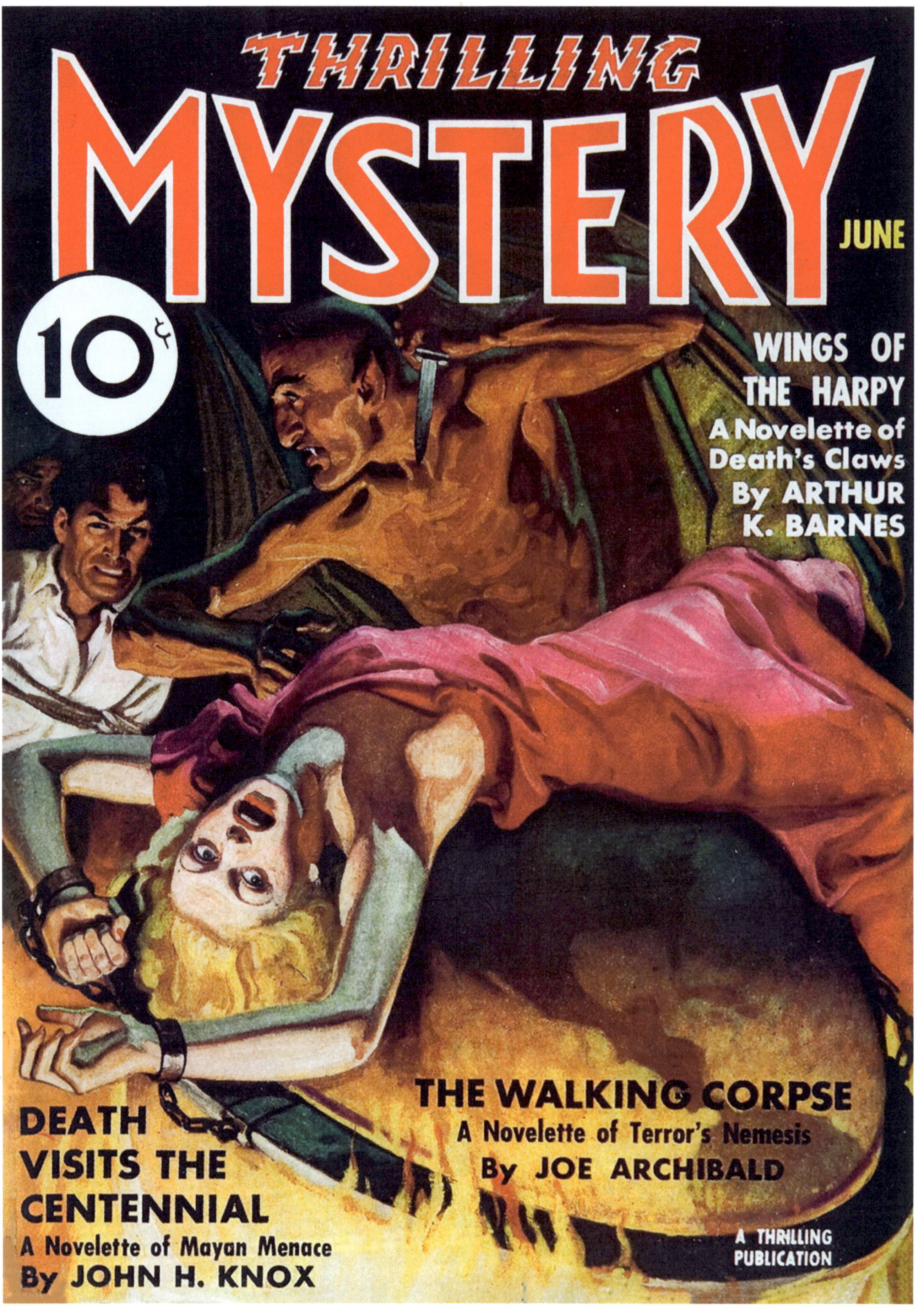

THRILLING MYSTERY

JUNE 1937

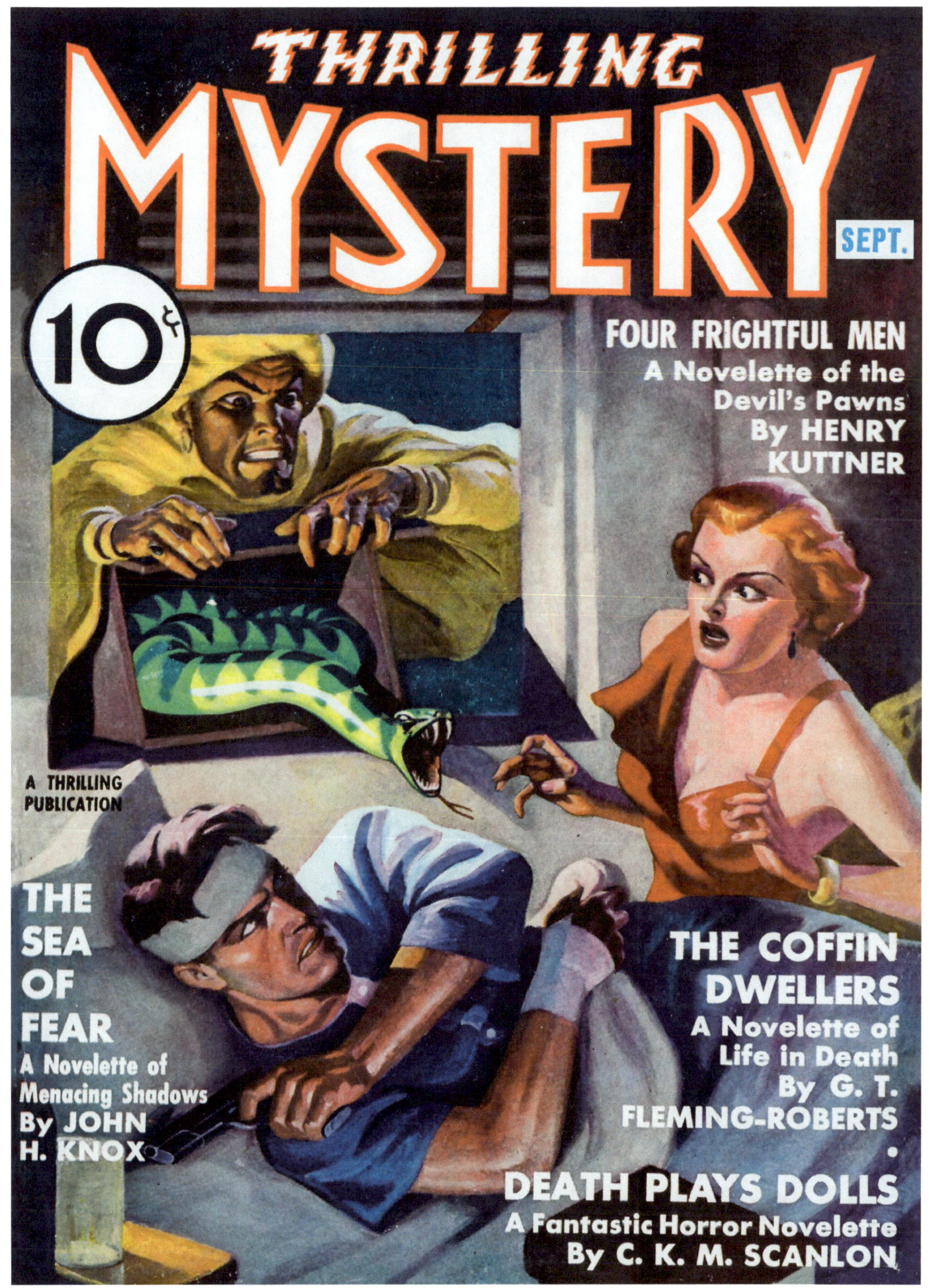

THRILLING
MYSTERY
SEPT.
10¢
A THRILLING PUBLICATION
FOUR FRIGHTFUL MEN
A Novelette of the Devil's Pawns
By HENRY KUTTNER
THE SEA OF FEAR
A Novelette of Menacing Shadows
By JOHN H. KNOX
THE COFFIN DWELLERS
A Novelette of Life in Death
By G. T. FLEMING-ROBERTS
DEATH PLAYS DOLLS
A Fantastic Horror Novelette
By C. K. M. SCANLON

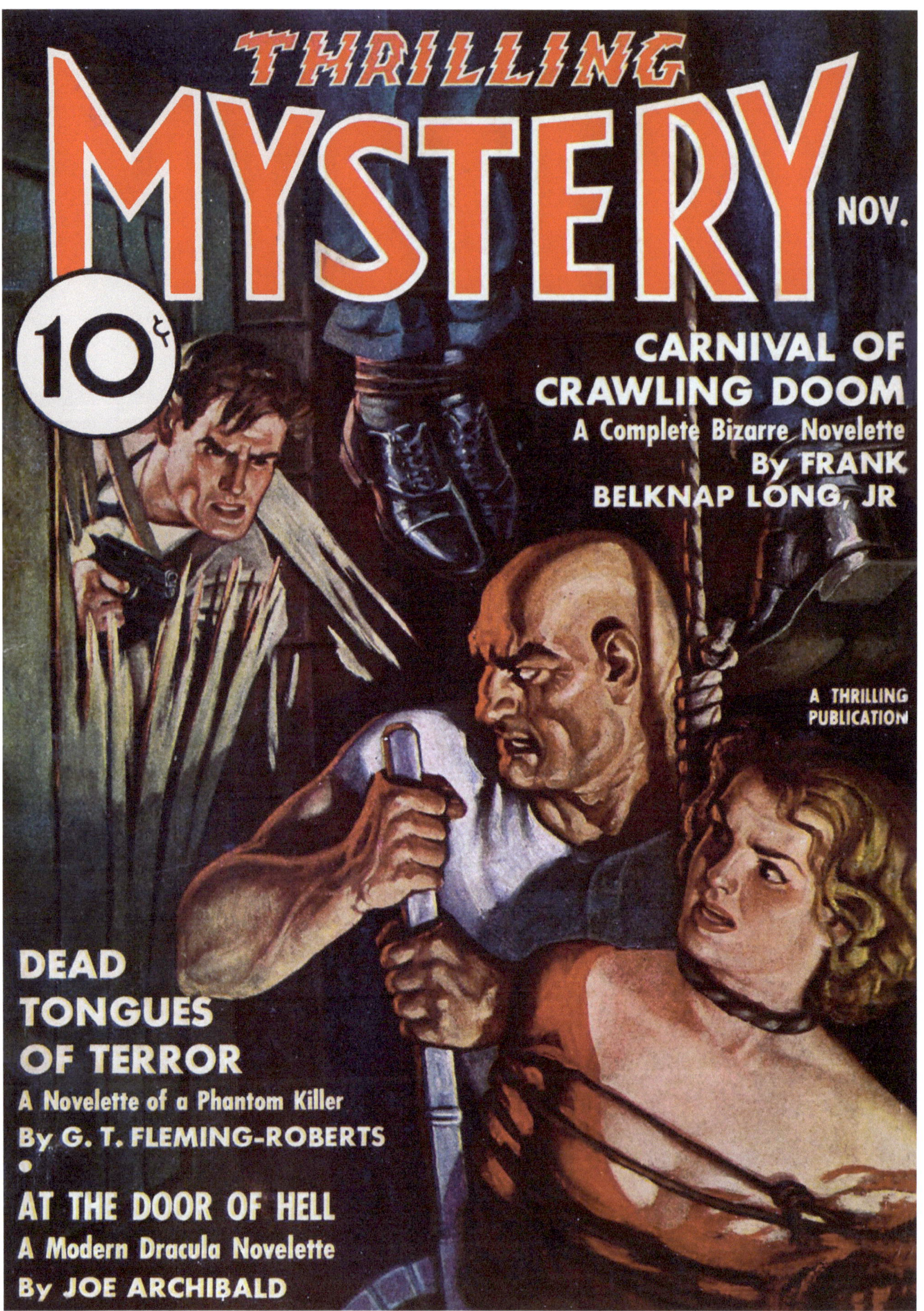
THRILLING
MYSTERY
NOV.
10¢
CARNIVAL OF
CRAWLING DOOM
A Complete Bizarre Novelette
BY FRANK
BELKNAP LONG, JR
A THRILLING
PUBLICATION
DEAD
TONGUES
OF TERROR
A Novelette of a Phantom Killer
By G. T. FLEMING-ROBERTS
AT THE DOOR OF HELL
A Modern Dracula Novelette
By JOE ARCHIBALD

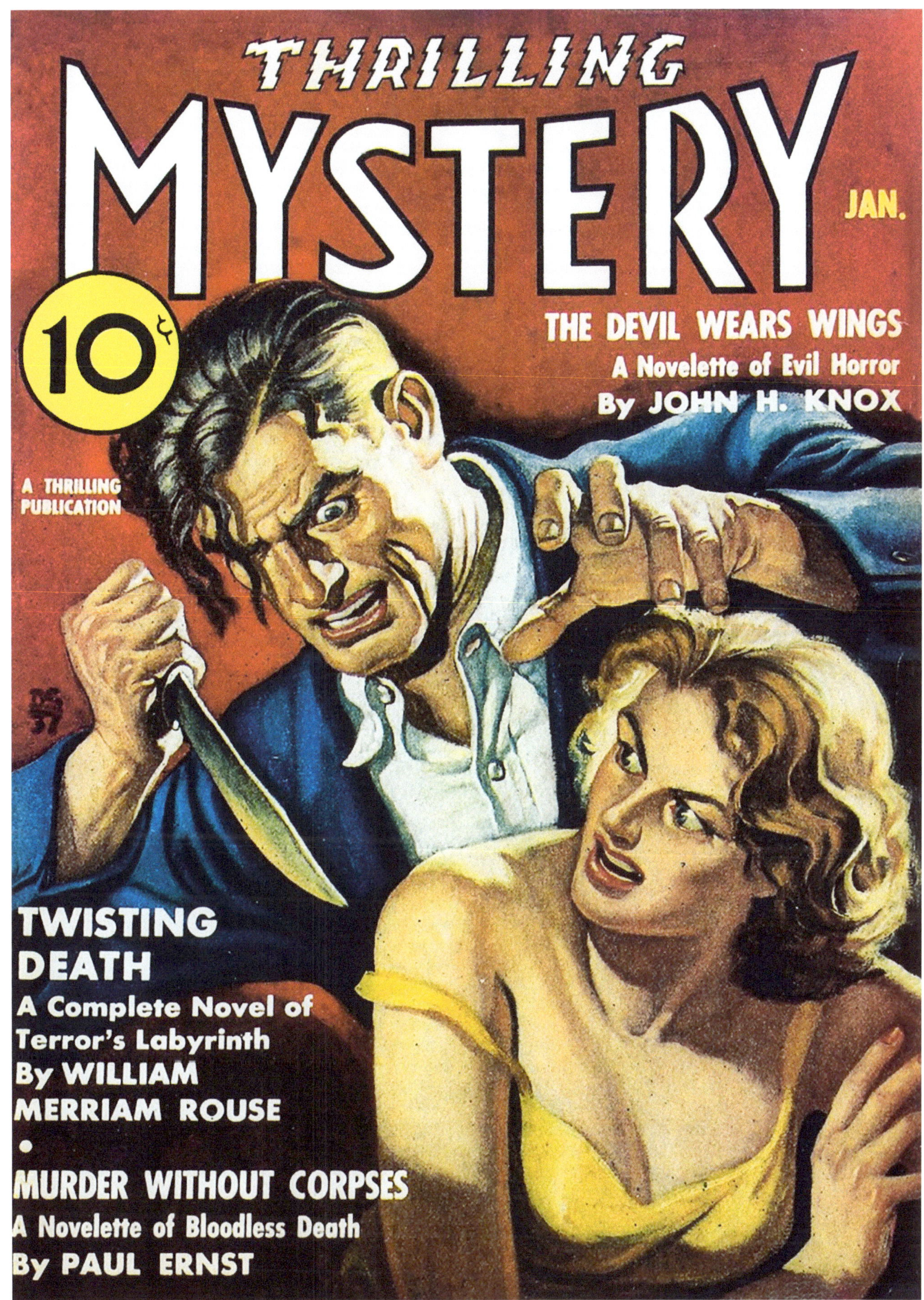
THRILLING
MYSTERY
JAN.
10¢
A THRILLING
PUBLICATION
THE DEVIL WEARS WINGS
A Novelette of Evil Horror
By JOHN H. KNOX
TWISTING DEATH
A Complete Novel of
Terror's Labyrinth
By WILLIAM
MERRIAM ROUSE
•
MURDER WITHOUT CORPSES
A Novelette of Bloodless Death
By PAUL ERNST

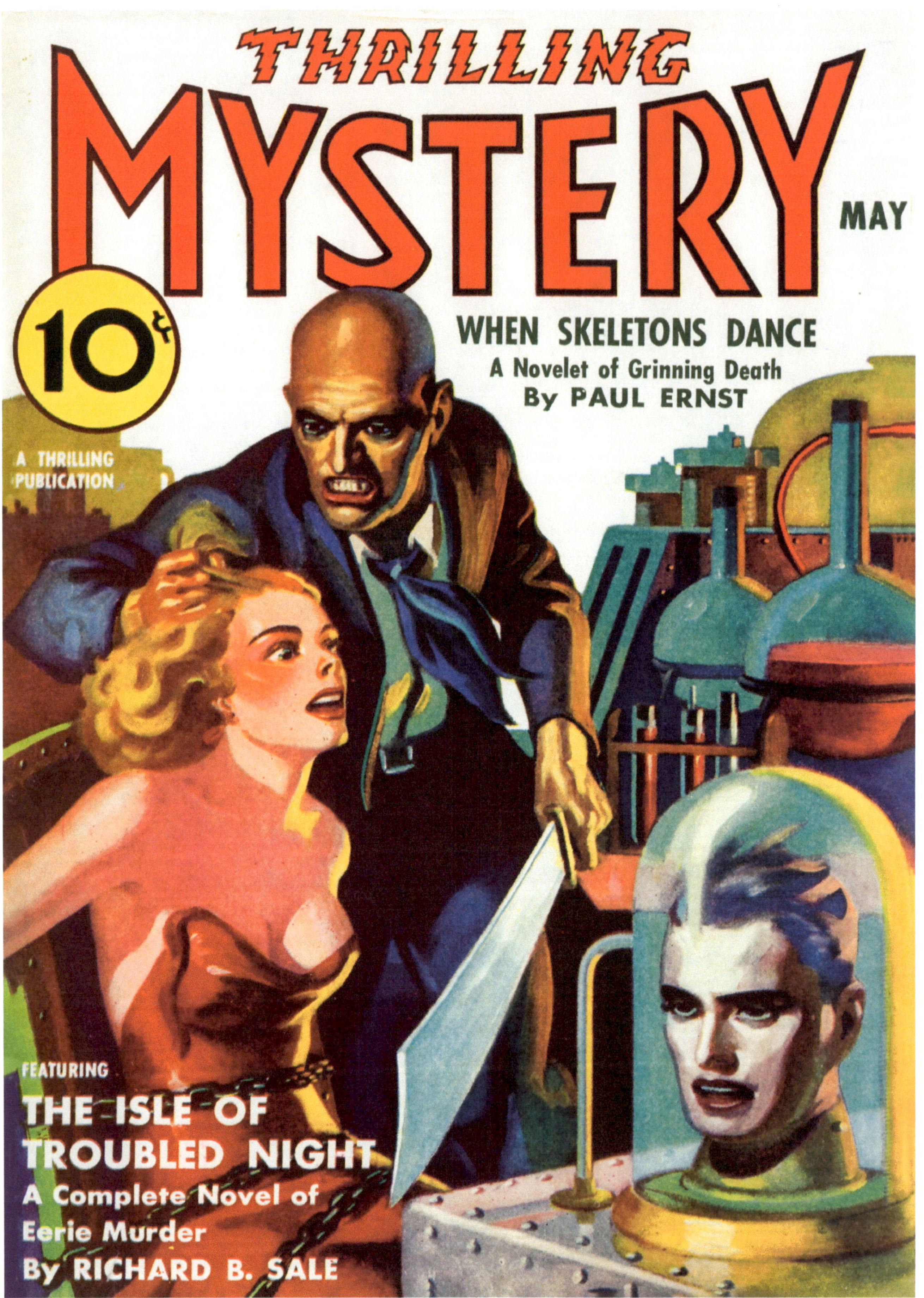

THRILLING MYSTERY

MAY 1938

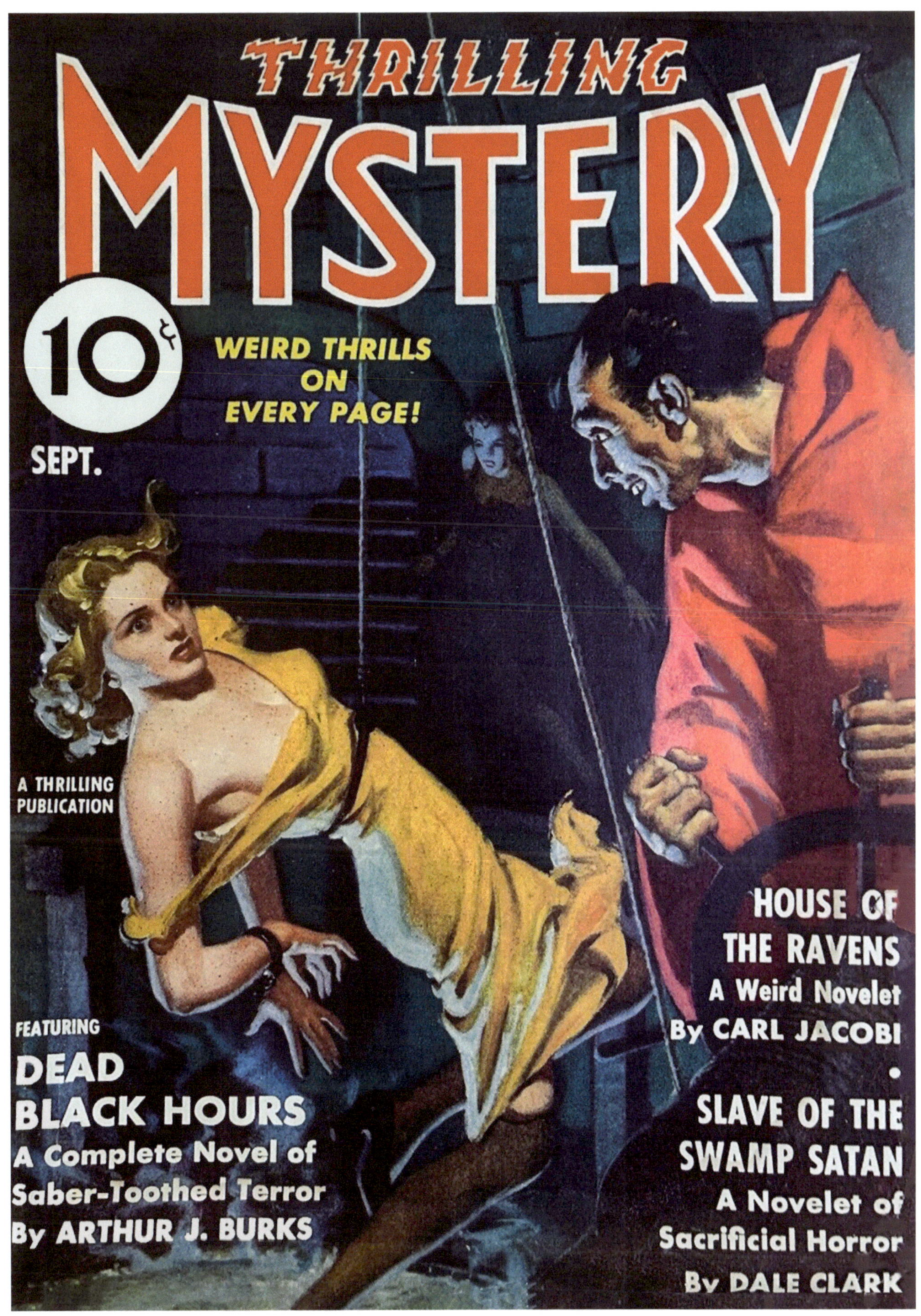

THRILLING
MYSTERY
10¢
WEIRD THRILLS ON EVERY PAGE!
SEPT.
A THRILLING PUBLICATION
FEATURING
DEAD BLACK HOURS
A Complete Novel of Saber-Toothed Terror
By ARTHUR J. BURKS
HOUSE OF THE RAVENS
A Weird Novelet
By CARL JACOBI
SLAVE OF THE SWAMP SATAN
A Novelet of Sacrificial Horror
By DALE CLARK

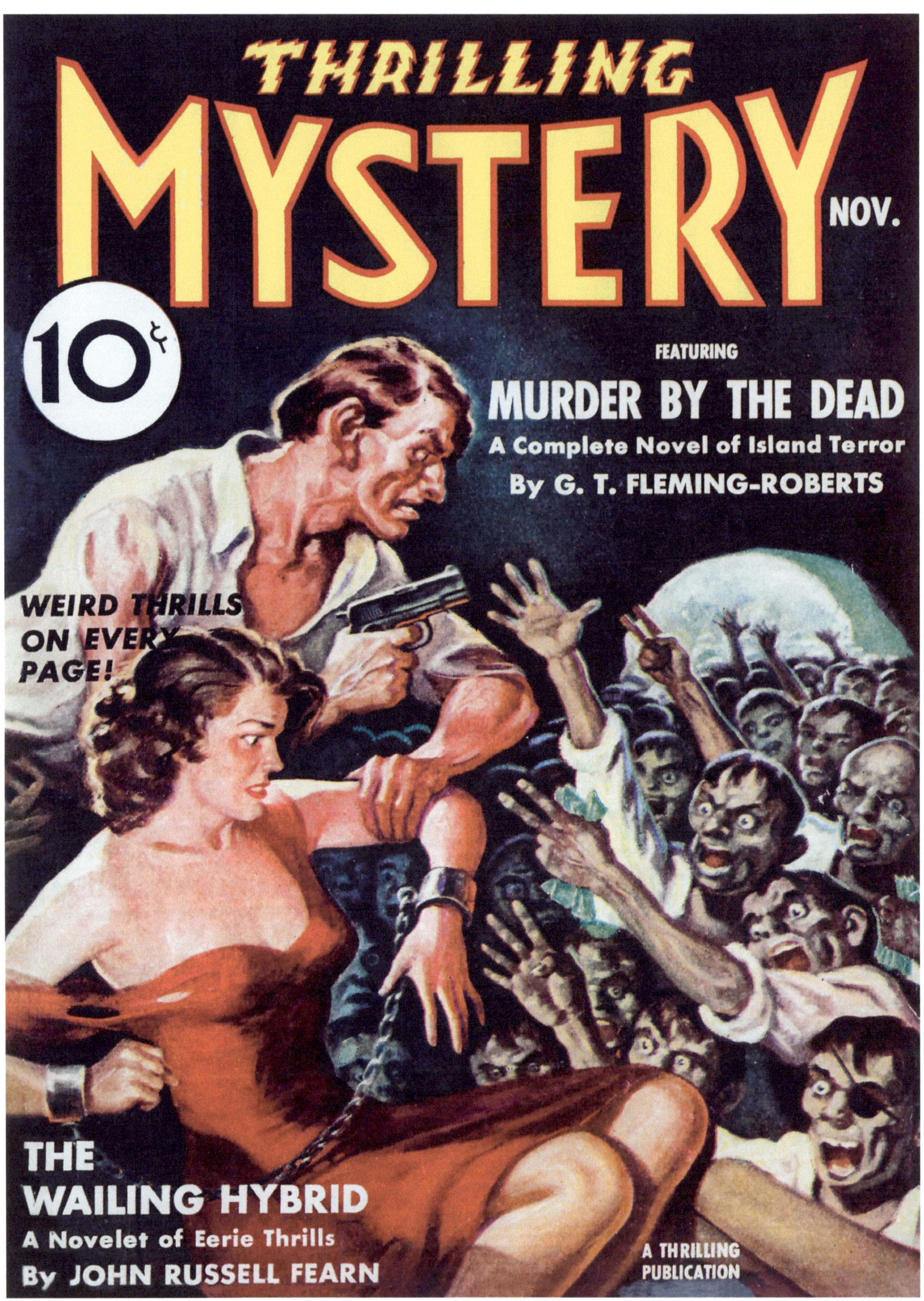

THRILLING
MYSTERY
NOV.
10¢
FEATURING
MURDER BY THE DEAD
A Complete Novel of Island Terror
By G. T. FLEMING-ROBERTS
WEIRD THRILLS ON EVERY PAGE!
THE WAILING HYBRID
A Novelet of Eerie Thrills
By JOHN RUSSELL FEARN
A THRILLING PUBLICATION

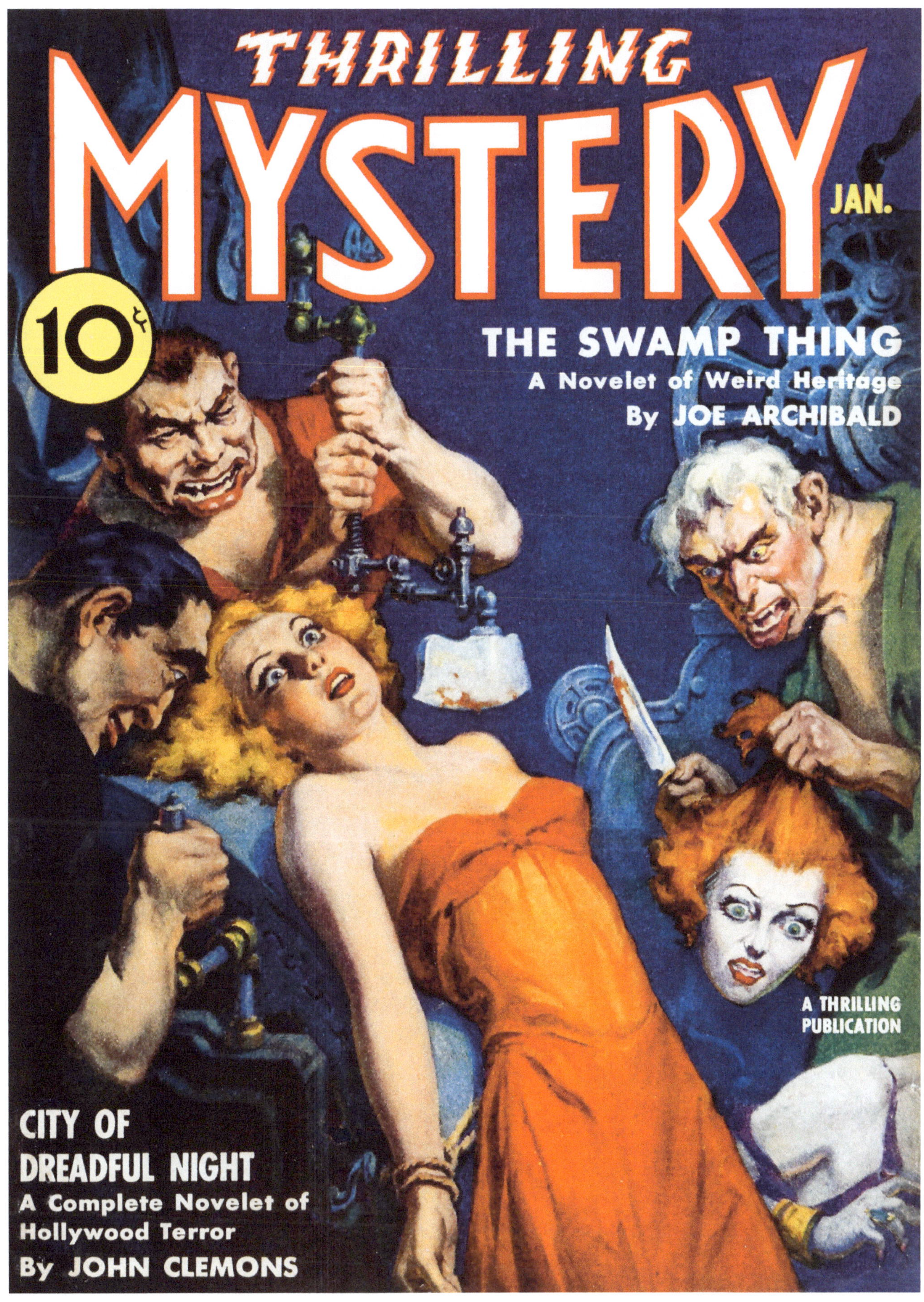
THRILLING
MYSTERY
JAN.
10¢
THE SWAMP THING
A Novelet of Weird Heritage
By JOE ARCHIBALD
A THRILLING PUBLICATION
CITY OF DREADFUL NIGHT
A Complete Novelet of Hollywood Terror
By JOHN CLEMONS

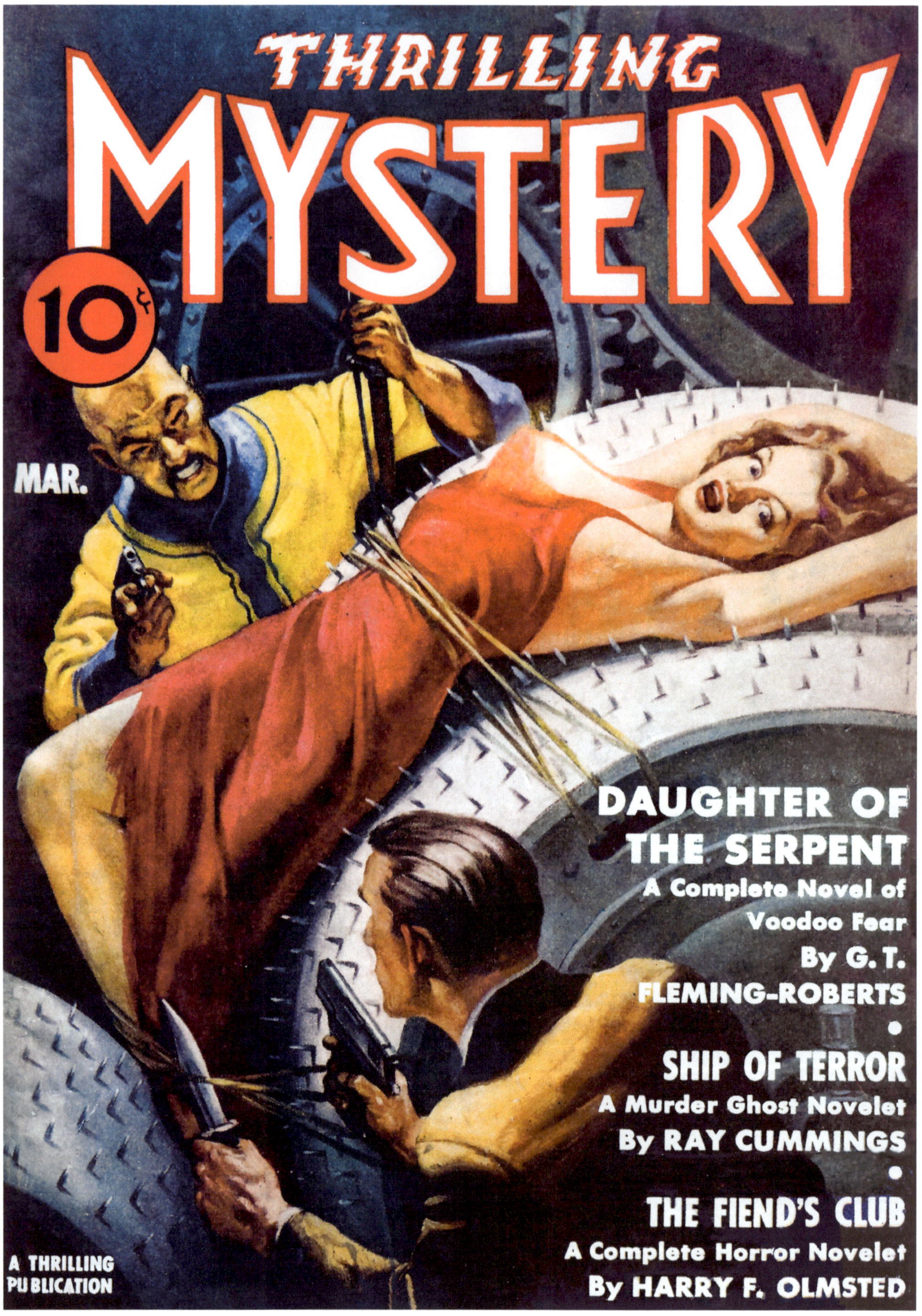

THRILLING
MYSTERY
10¢
MAR.
DAUGHTER OF
THE SERPENT
A Complete Novel of
Voodoo Fear
By G. T.
FLEMING-ROBERTS
SHIP OF TERROR
A Murder Ghost Novelet
By RAY CUMMINGS
THE FIEND'S CLUB
A Complete Horror Novelet
By HARRY F. OLMSTED
A THRILLING
PUBLICATION

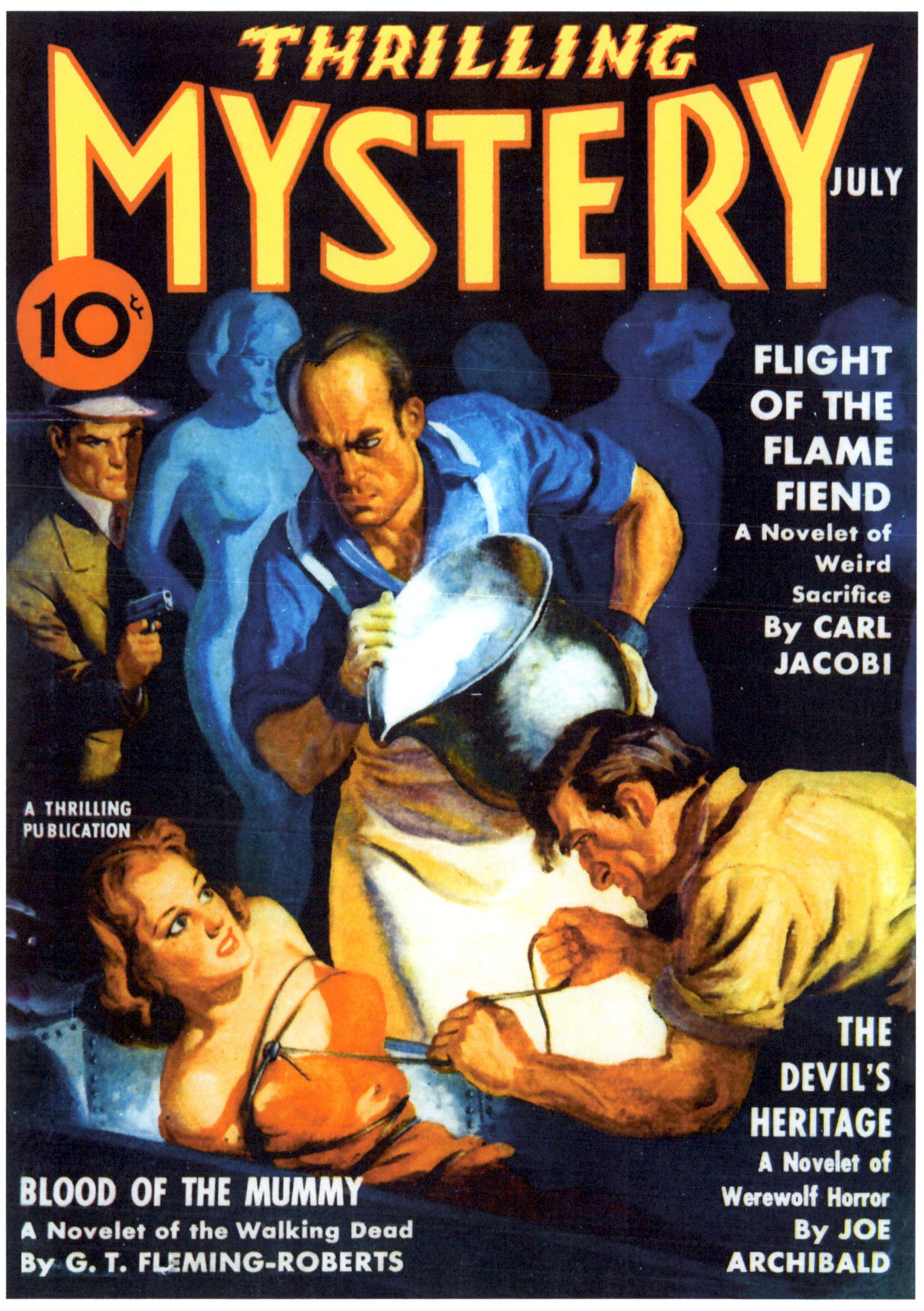

THRILLING
MYSTERY
JULY
10¢
FLIGHT OF THE FLAME FIEND
A Novelet of Weird Sacrifice
By CARL JACOBI
A THRILLING PUBLICATION
THE DEVIL'S HERITAGE
A Novelet of Werewolf Horror
By JOE ARCHIBALD
BLOOD OF THE MUMMY
A Novelet of the Walking Dead
By G. T. FLEMING-ROBERTS

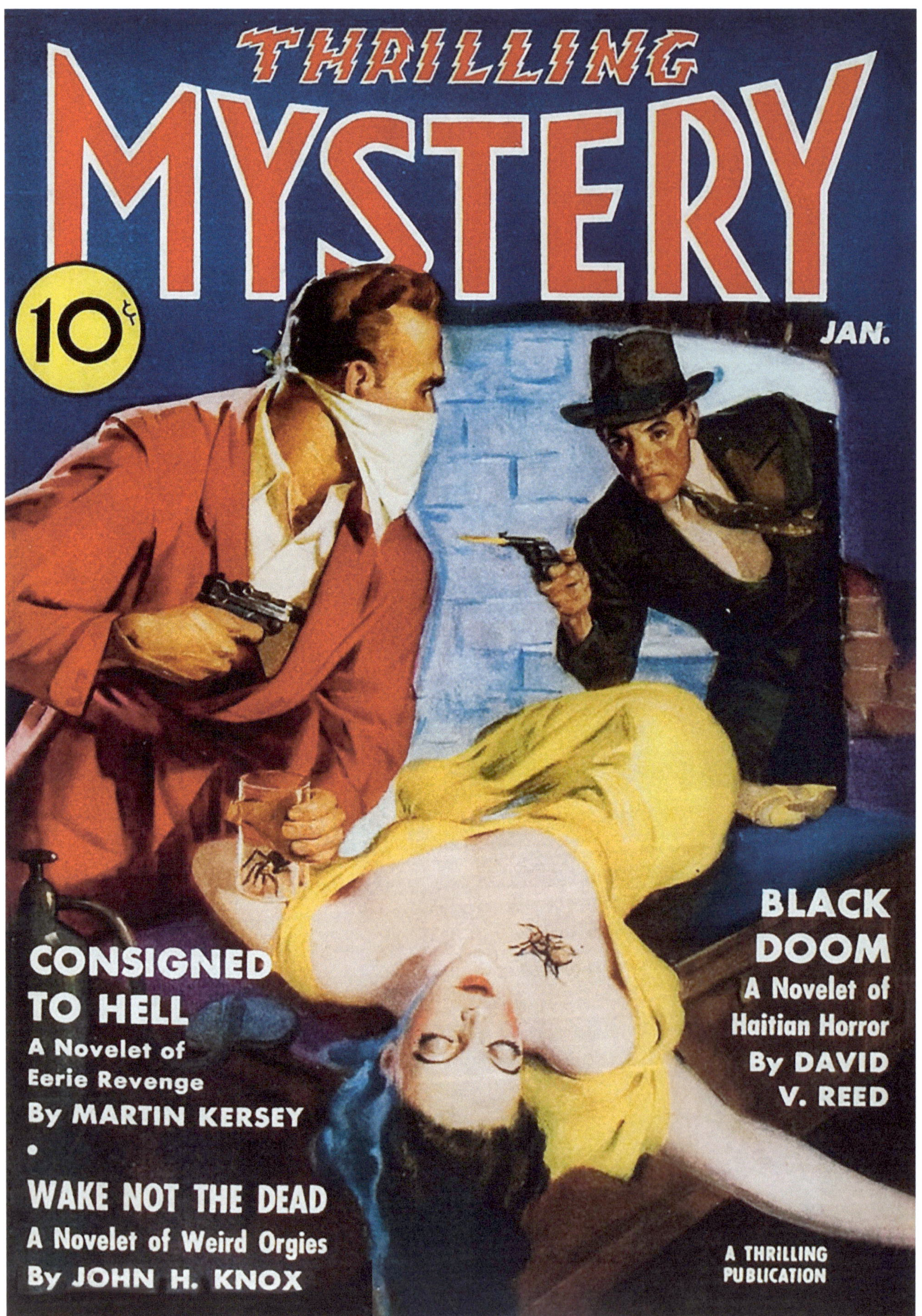

THRILLING MYSTERY

JANUARY 1940

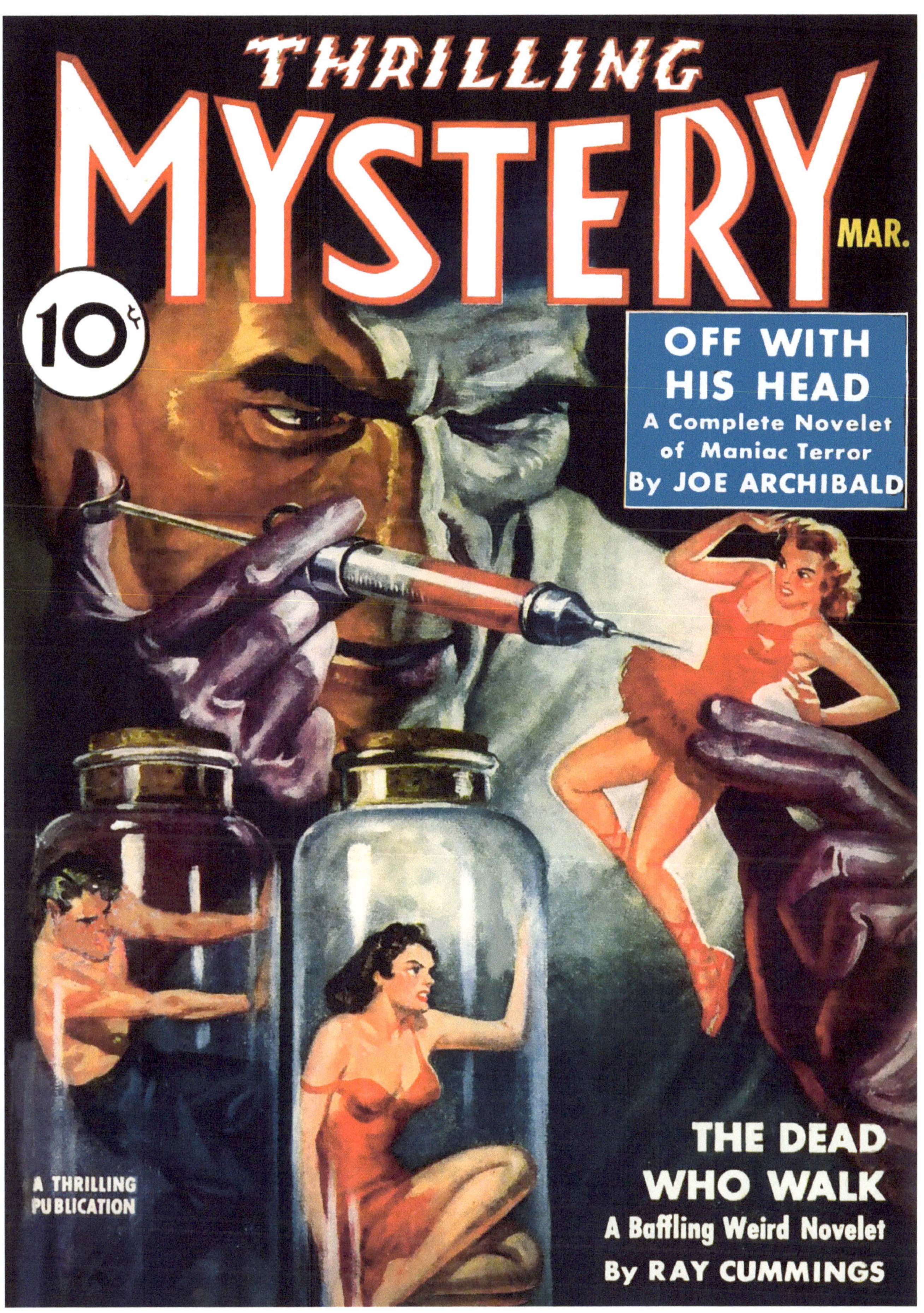
THRILLING
MYSTERY
MAR.
10¢
OFF WITH HIS HEAD
A Complete Novelet
of Maniac Terror
By JOE ARCHIBALD
A THRILLING
PUBLICATION
THE DEAD
WHO WALK
A Baffling Weird Novelet
By RAY CUMMINGS

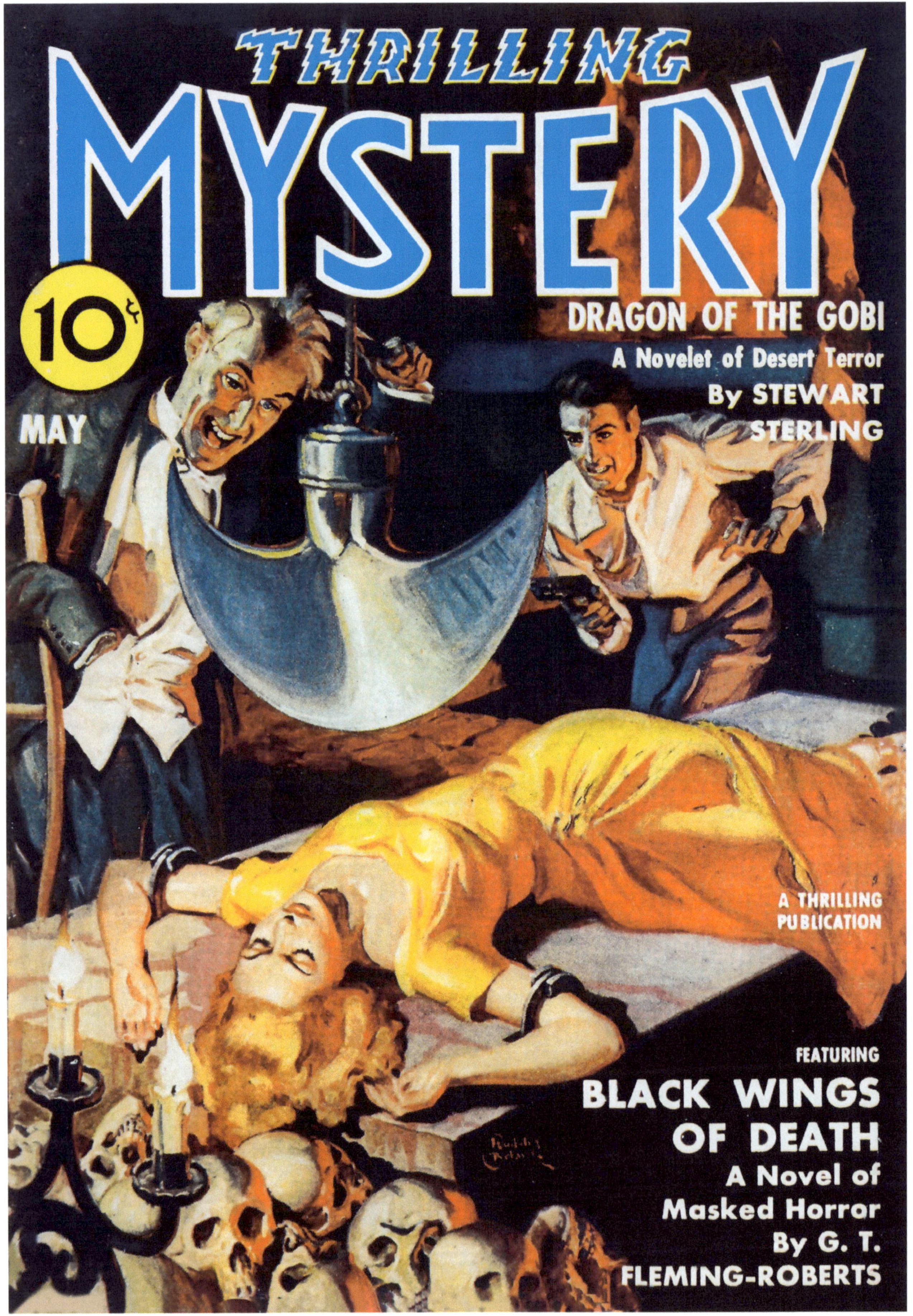

THRILLING
MYSTERY
10¢
MAY
DRAGON OF THE GOBI
A Novelet of Desert Terror
By STEWART STERLING
A THRILLING PUBLICATION
FEATURING
BLACK WINGS
OF DEATH
A Novel of
Masked Horror
By G. T.
FLEMING-ROBERTS

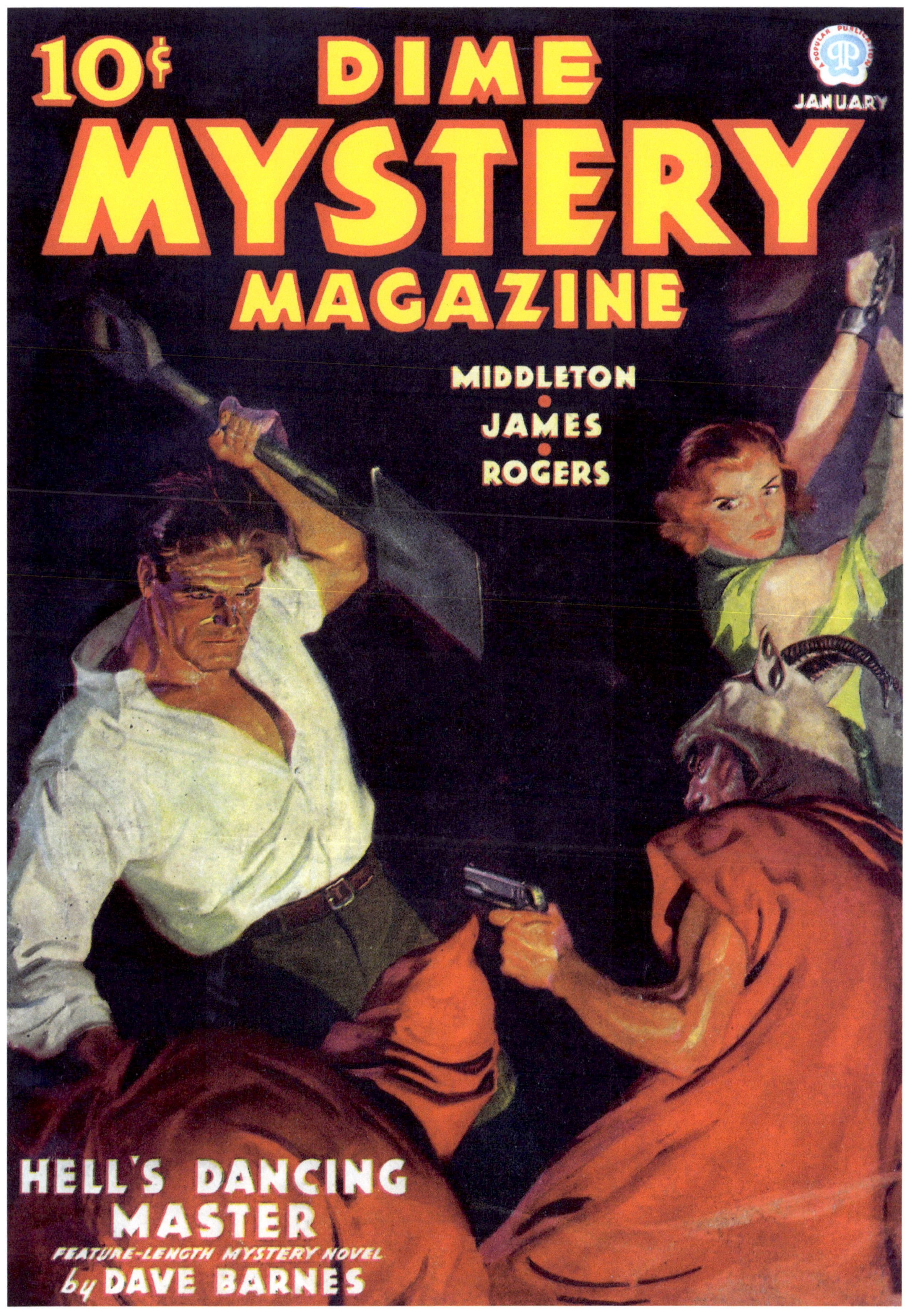

10¢
JANUARY
DIME MYSTERY MAGAZINE
MIDDLETON
JAMES
ROGERS
HELL'S DANCING MASTER
FEATURE-LENGTH MYSTERY NOVEL
by DAVE BARNES

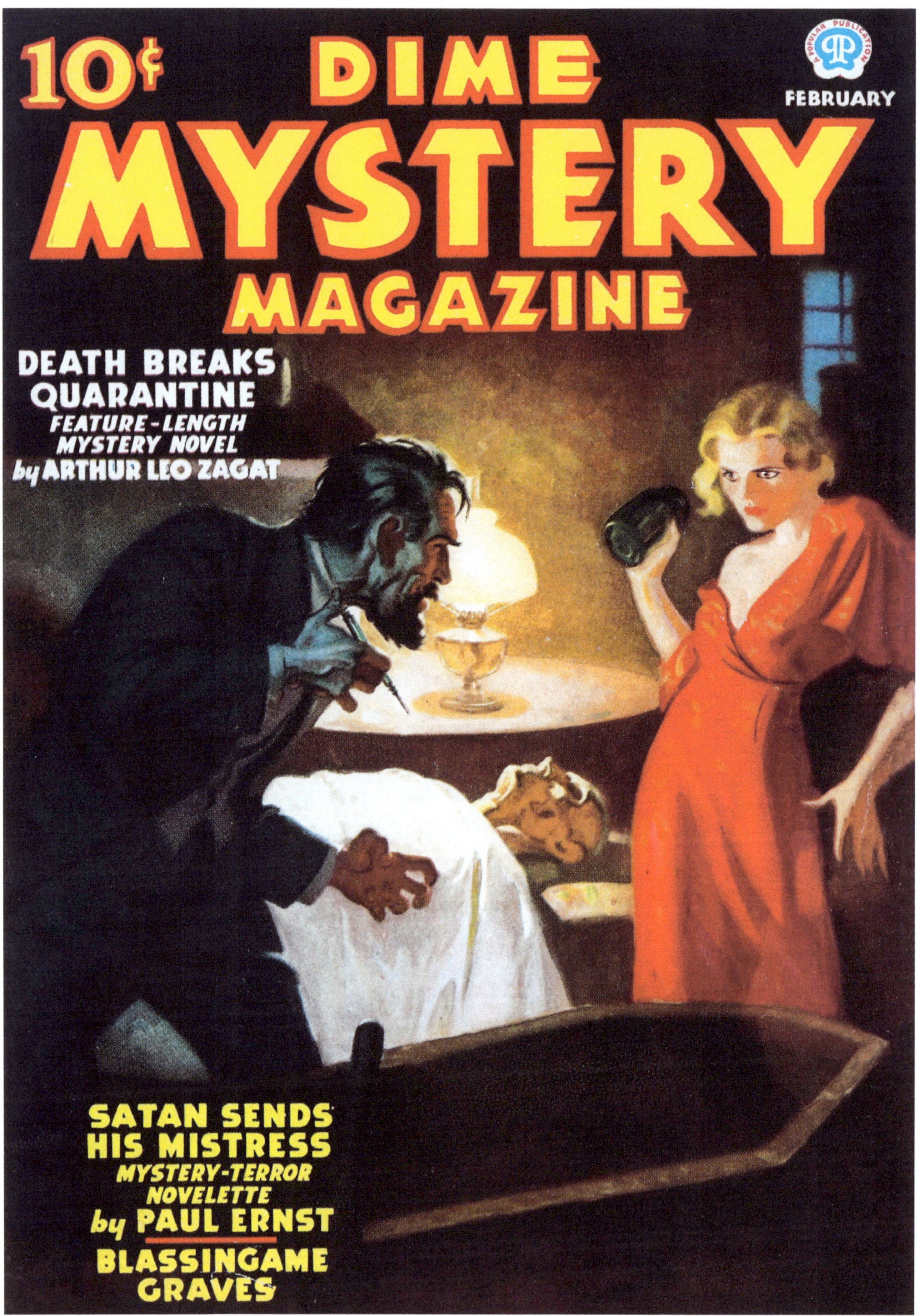

DIME MYSTERY MAGAZINE
FEBRUARY 1937

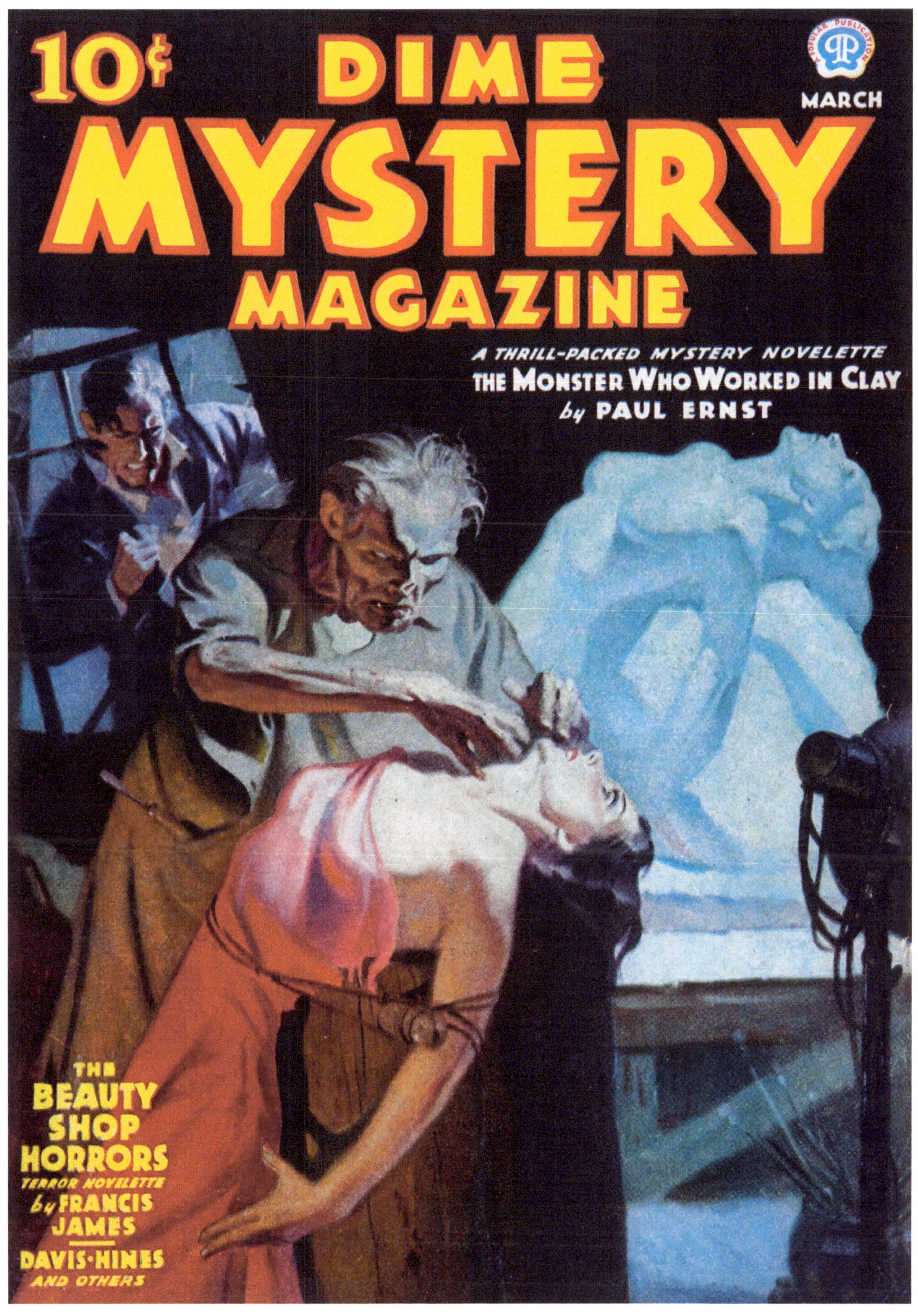

10¢
MARCH
DIME
MYSTERY
MAGAZINE
A THRILL-PACKED MYSTERY NOVELETTE
THE MONSTER WHO WORKED IN CLAY
by PAUL ERNST
THE BEAUTY SHOP HORRORS
TERROR NOVELETTE
by FRANCIS JAMES
DAVIS·HINES
AND OTHERS

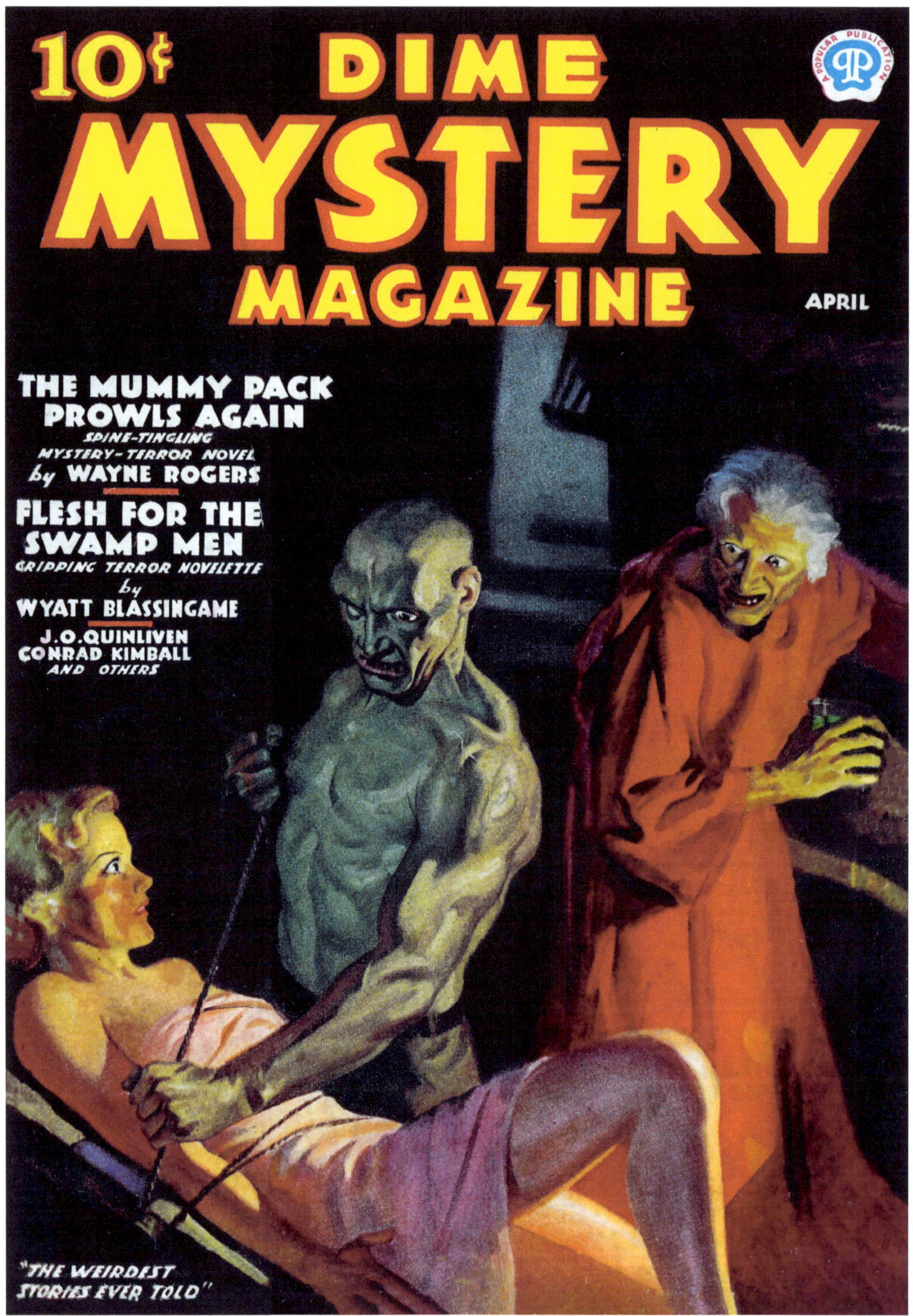

DIME MYSTERY MAGAZINE

APRIL 1937

84

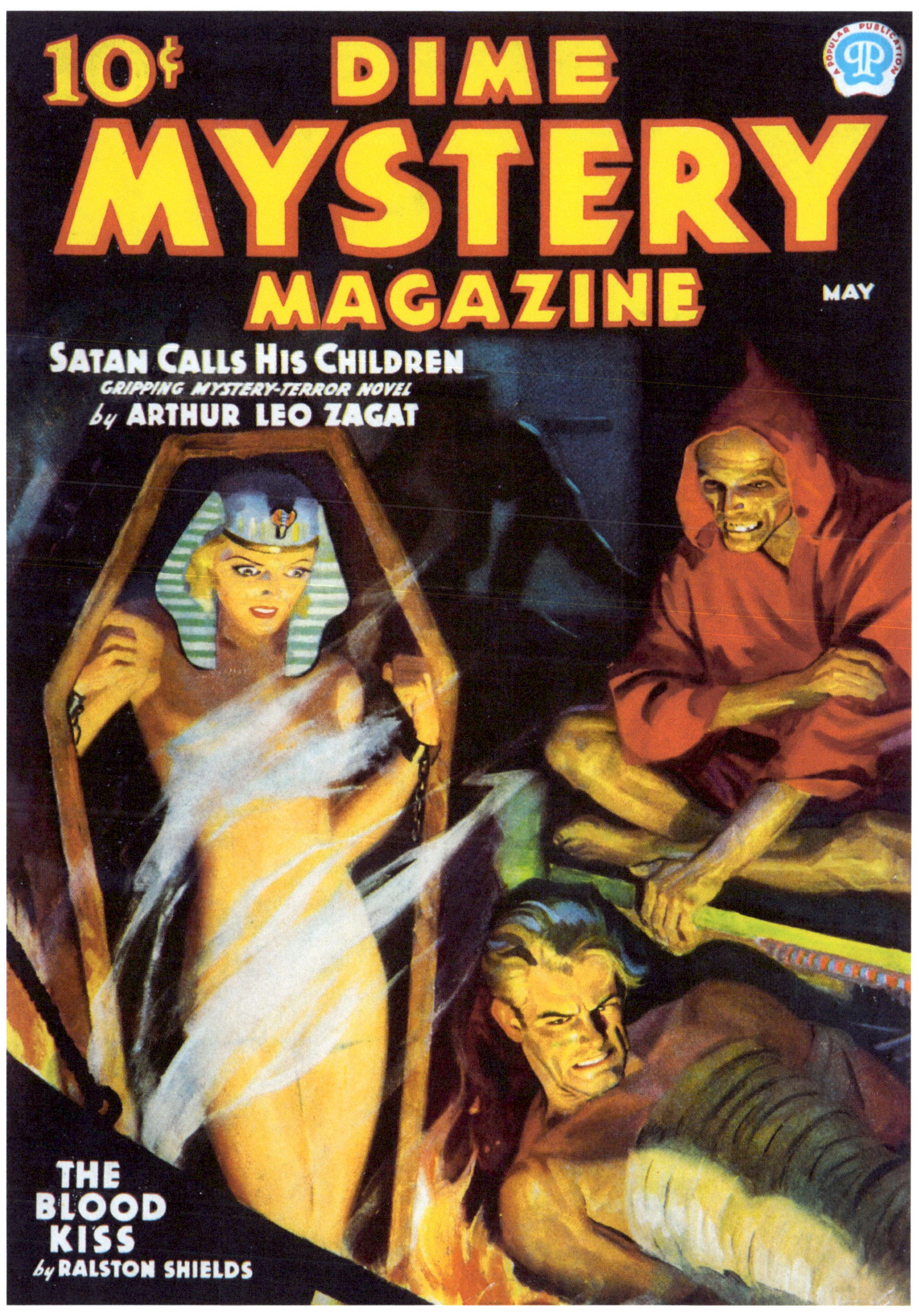

10¢
DIME MYSTERY MAGAZINE
MAY
SATAN CALLS HIS CHILDREN
GRIPPING MYSTERY-TERROR NOVEL
by ARTHUR LEO ZAGAT
THE BLOOD KISS
by RALSTON SHIELDS
A POPULAR PUBLICATION

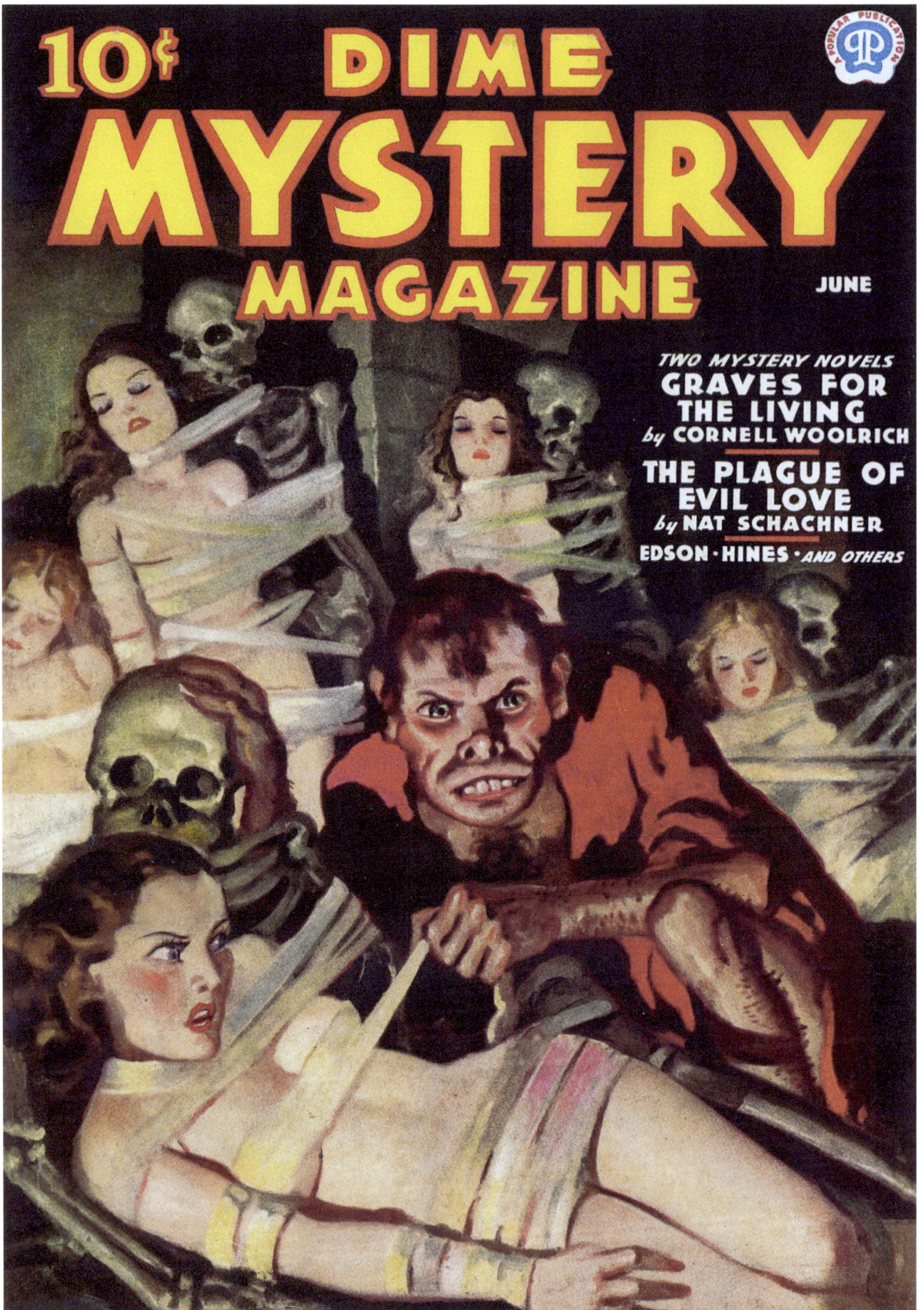

10¢
DIME MYSTERY MAGAZINE
JUNE
A POPULAR PUBLICATION
TWO MYSTERY NOVELS
GRAVES FOR THE LIVING
by CORNELL WOOLRICH
THE PLAGUE OF EVIL LOVE
by NAT SCHACHNER
EDSON · HINES · AND OTHERS

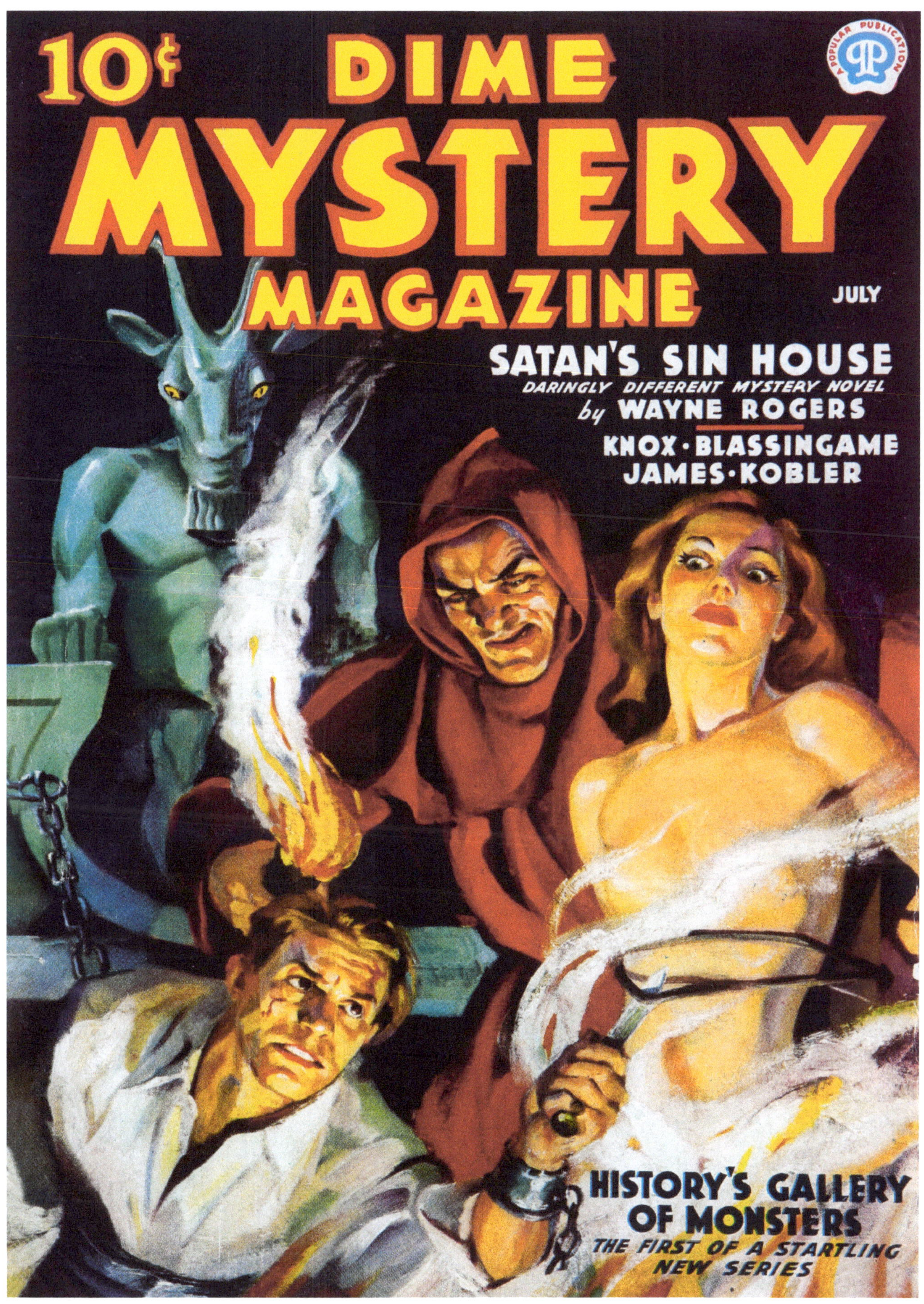

10¢
DIME
MYSTERY
MAGAZINE
JULY
SATAN'S SIN HOUSE
DARINGLY DIFFERENT MYSTERY NOVEL
by WAYNE ROGERS
KNOX·BLASSINGAME
JAMES·KOBLER
A POPULAR PUBLICATION
HISTORY'S GALLERY
OF MONSTERS
THE FIRST OF A STARTLING
NEW SERIES

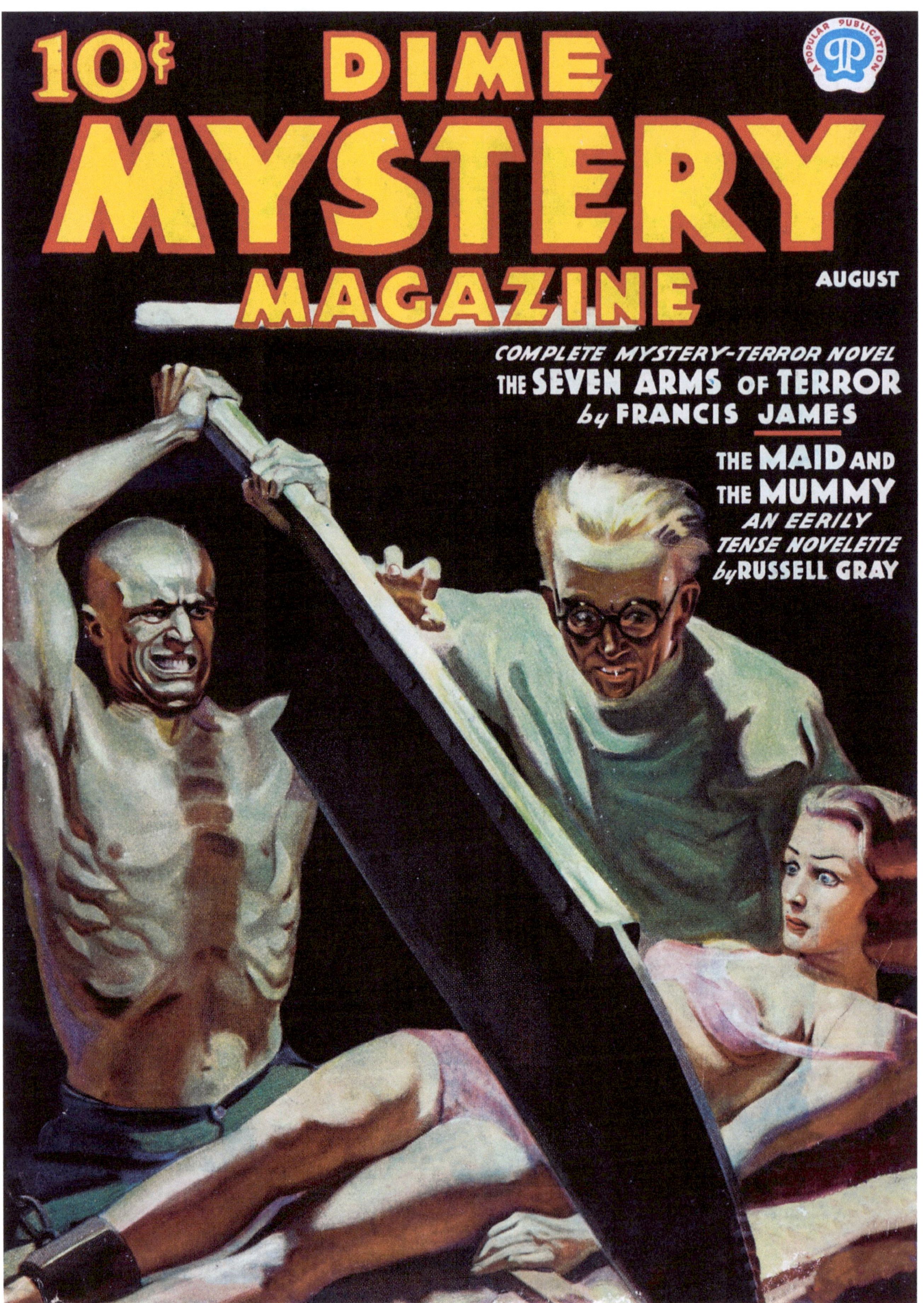

10¢
DIME MYSTERY MAGAZINE
AUGUST
COMPLETE MYSTERY-TERROR NOVEL
THE SEVEN ARMS OF TERROR
by FRANCIS JAMES
THE MAID AND THE MUMMY
AN EERILY TENSE NOVELETTE
by RUSSELL GRAY
A POPULAR PUBLICATION

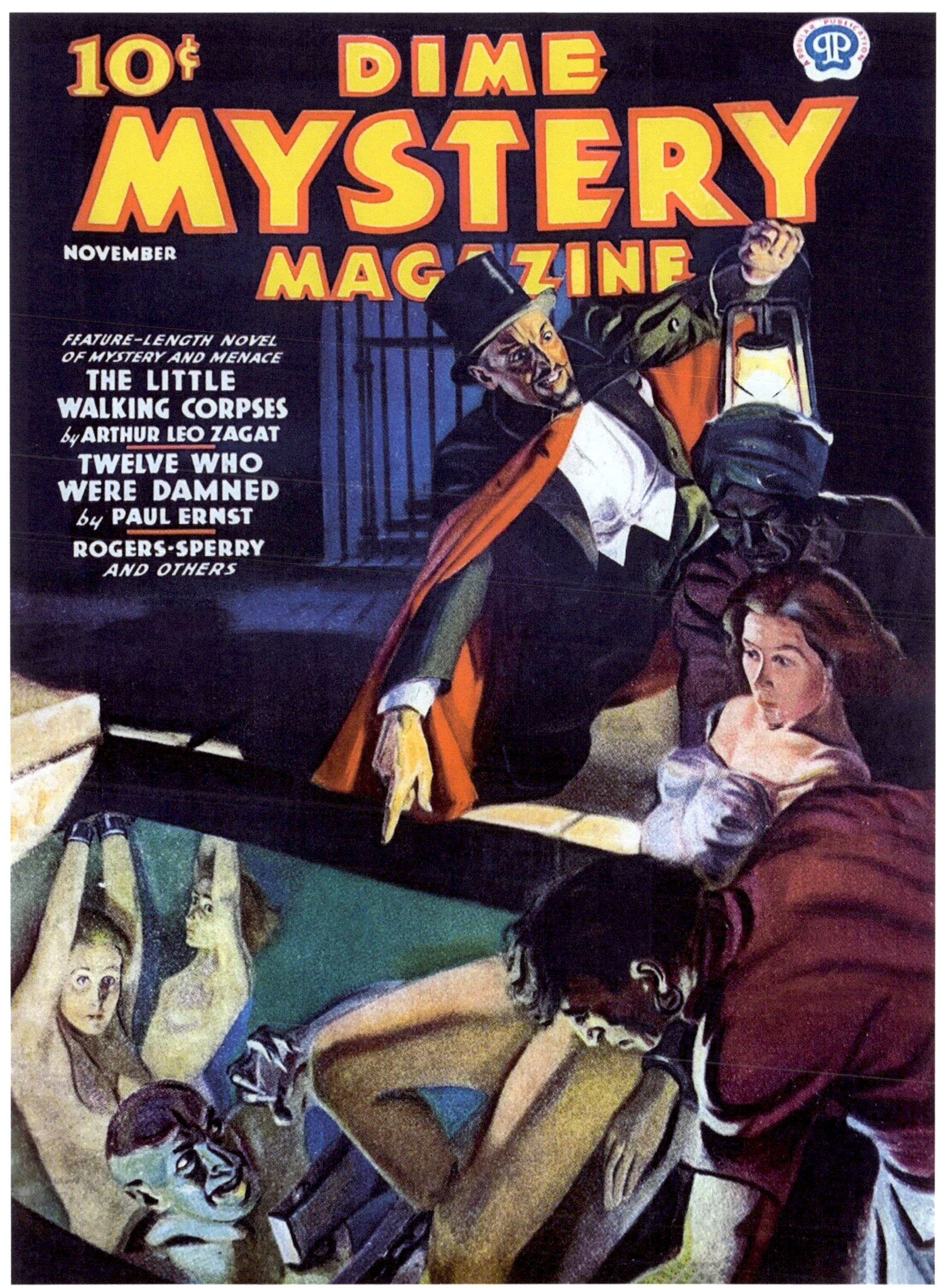

10¢
NOVEMBER
DIME MYSTERY MAGAZINE
FEATURE-LENGTH NOVEL OF MYSTERY AND MENACE
THE LITTLE WALKING CORPSES
by ARTHUR LEO ZAGAT
TWELVE WHO WERE DAMNED
by PAUL ERNST
ROGERS-SPERRY AND OTHERS

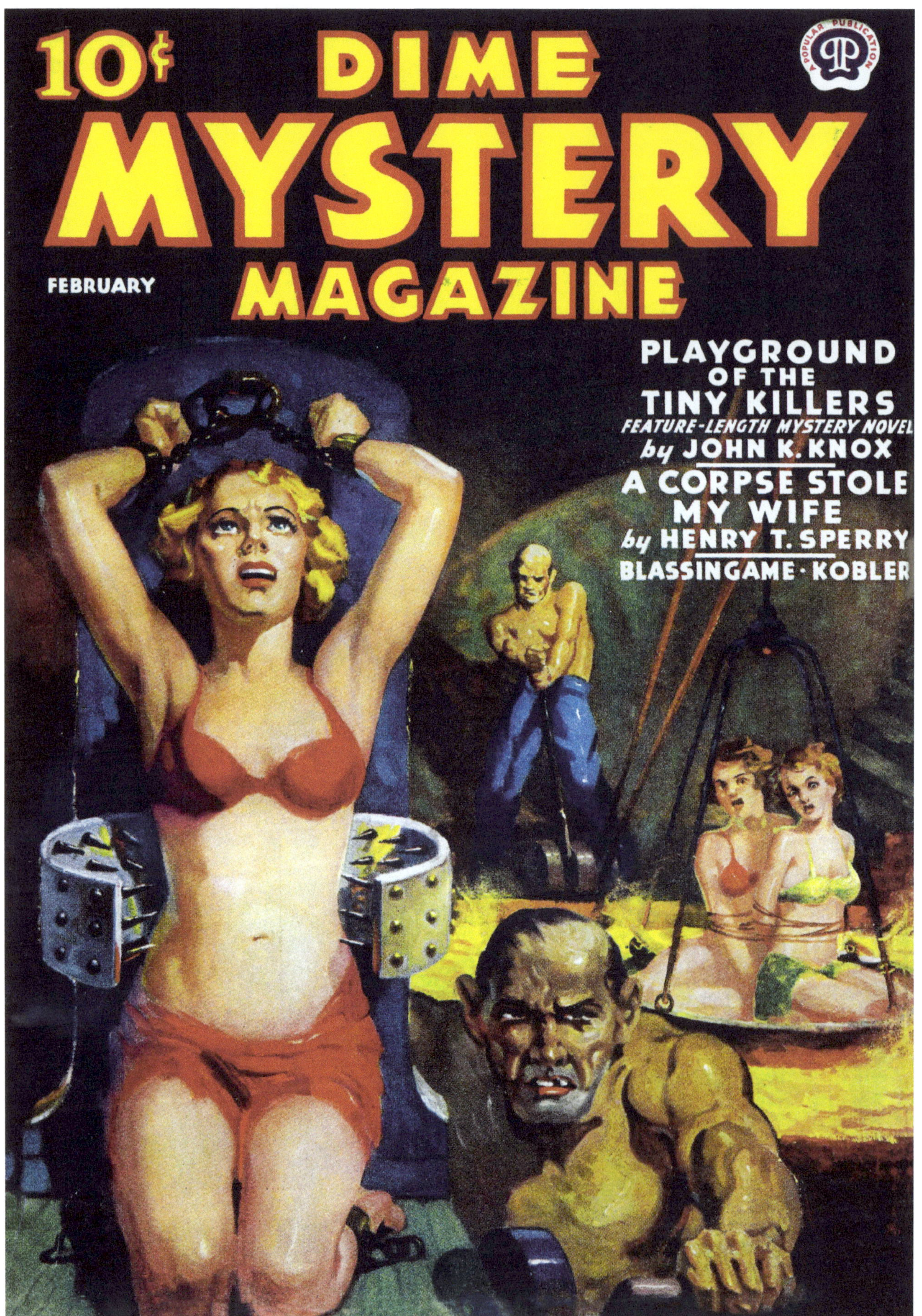

DIME MYSTERY MAGAZINE

FEBRUARY 1938

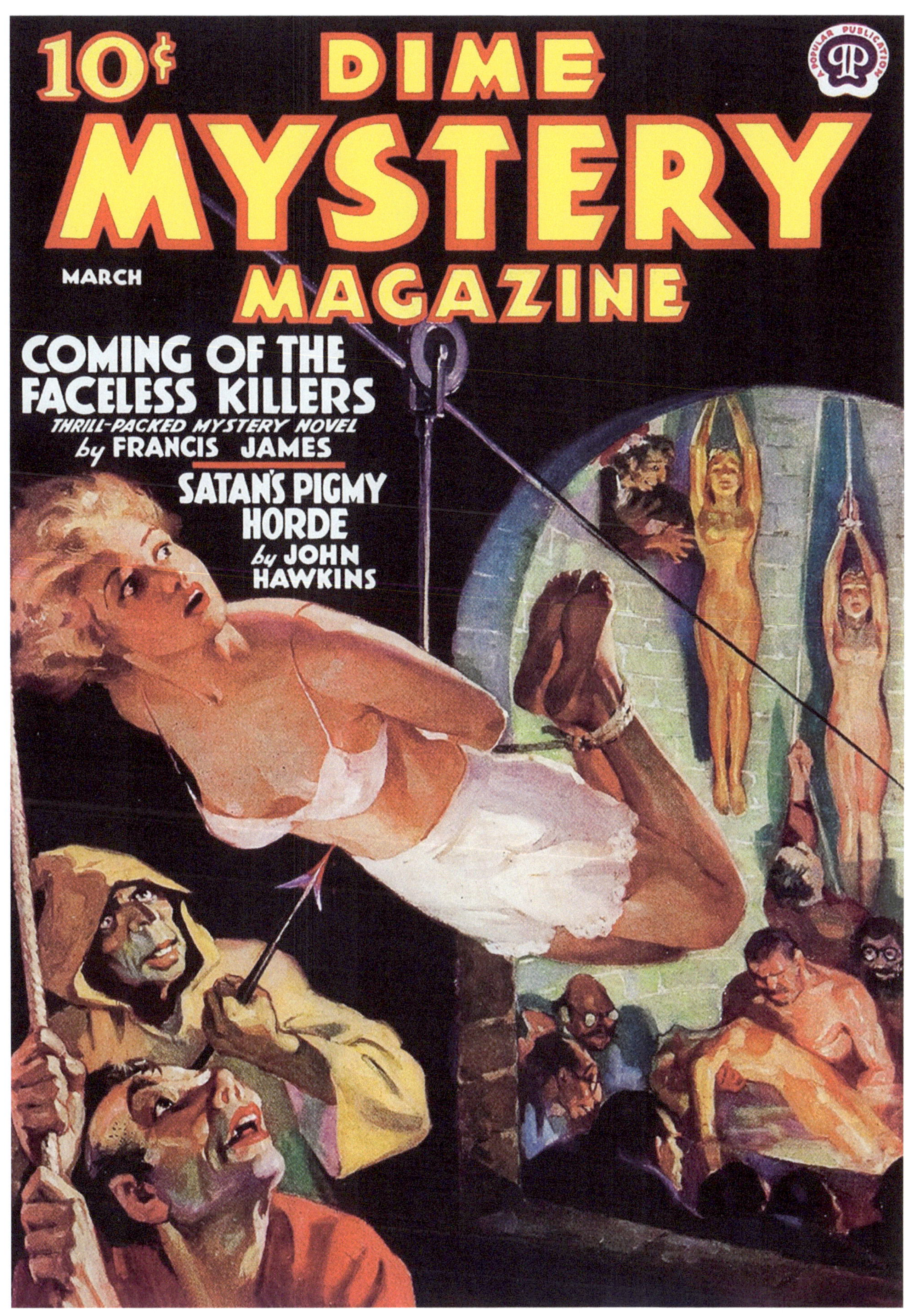

10¢
MARCH
DIME
MYSTERY
MAGAZINE
COMING OF THE FACELESS KILLERS
THRILL-PACKED MYSTERY NOVEL
by FRANCIS JAMES
SATAN'S PIGMY HORDE
by JOHN HAWKINS
A POPULAR PUBLICATION

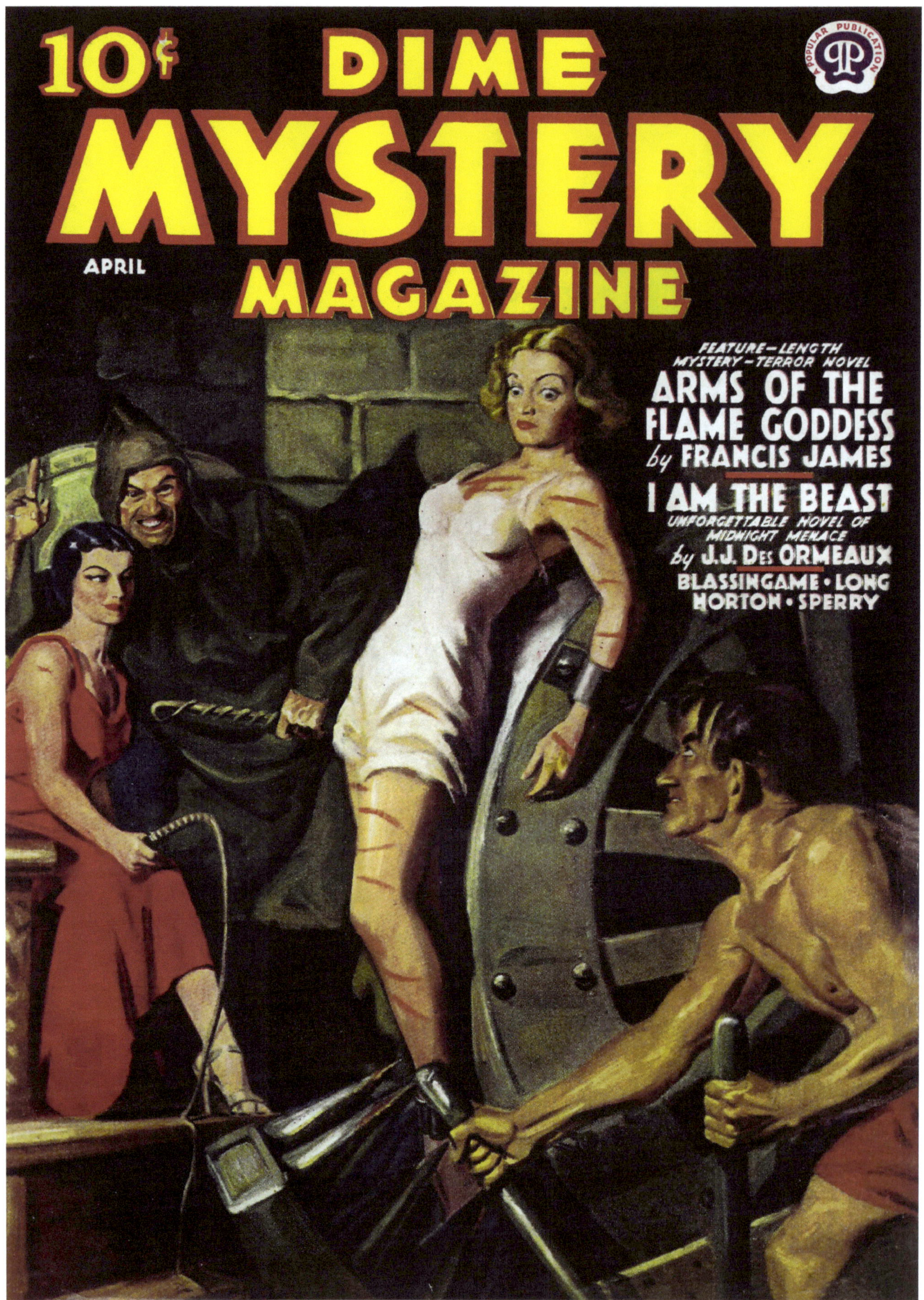

10¢
DIME
MYSTERY
MAGAZINE
APRIL
A POPULAR PUBLICATION
FEATURE—LENGTH
MYSTERY—TERROR NOVEL
ARMS OF THE FLAME GODDESS
by FRANCIS JAMES
I AM THE BEAST
UNFORGETTABLE NOVEL OF MIDNIGHT MENACE
by J.J. Des ORMEAUX
BLASSINGAME • LONG
HORTON • SPERRY

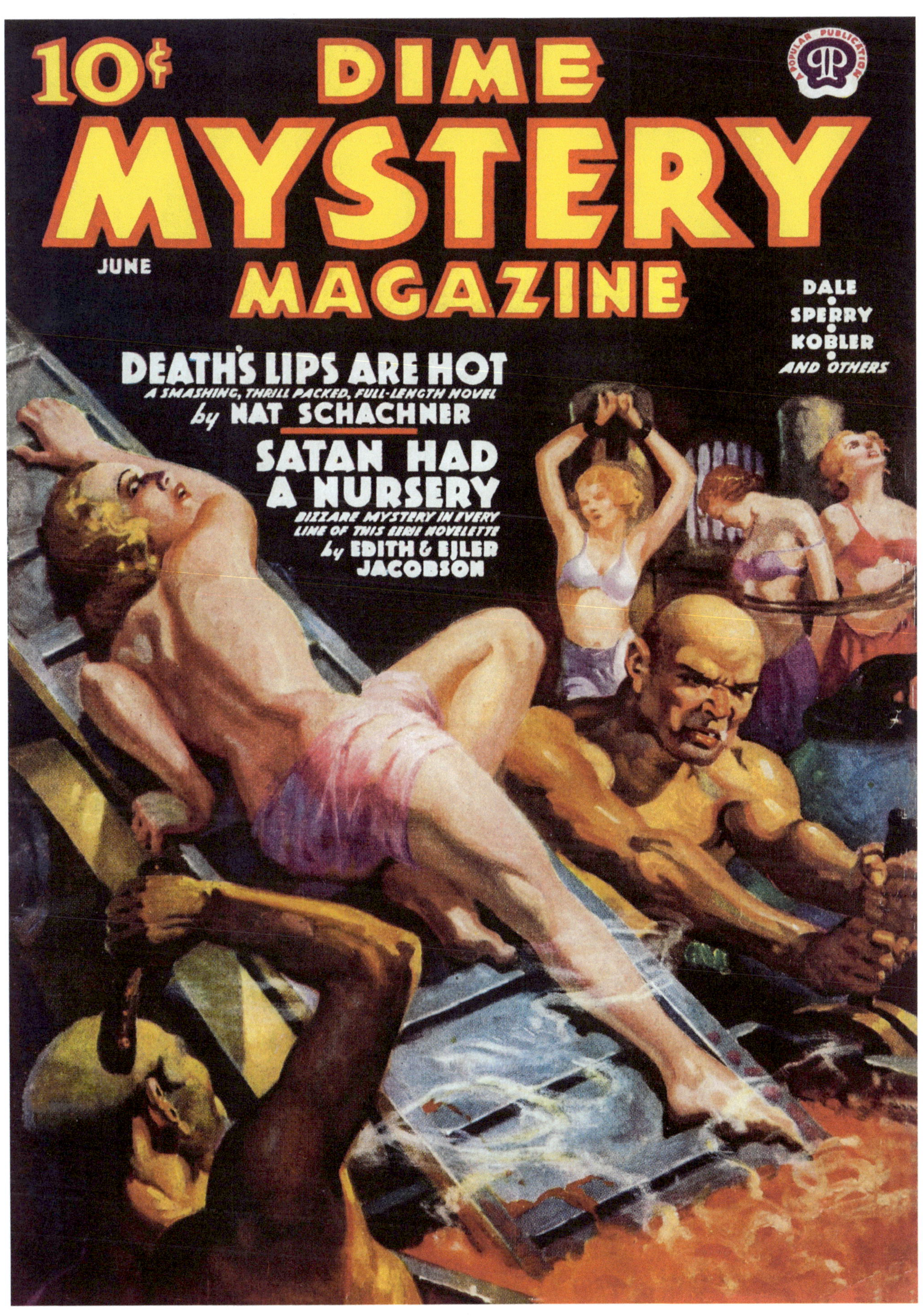

10¢
JUNE
DIME MYSTERY MAGAZINE
A POPULAR PUBLICATION
DALE • SPERRY • KOBLER AND OTHERS
DEATH'S LIPS ARE HOT
A SMASHING, THRILL PACKED, FULL-LENGTH NOVEL
by NAT SCHACHNER
SATAN HAD A NURSERY
BIZARRE MYSTERY IN EVERY LINE OF THIS EERIE NOVELETTE
by EDITH & EJLER JACOBSON

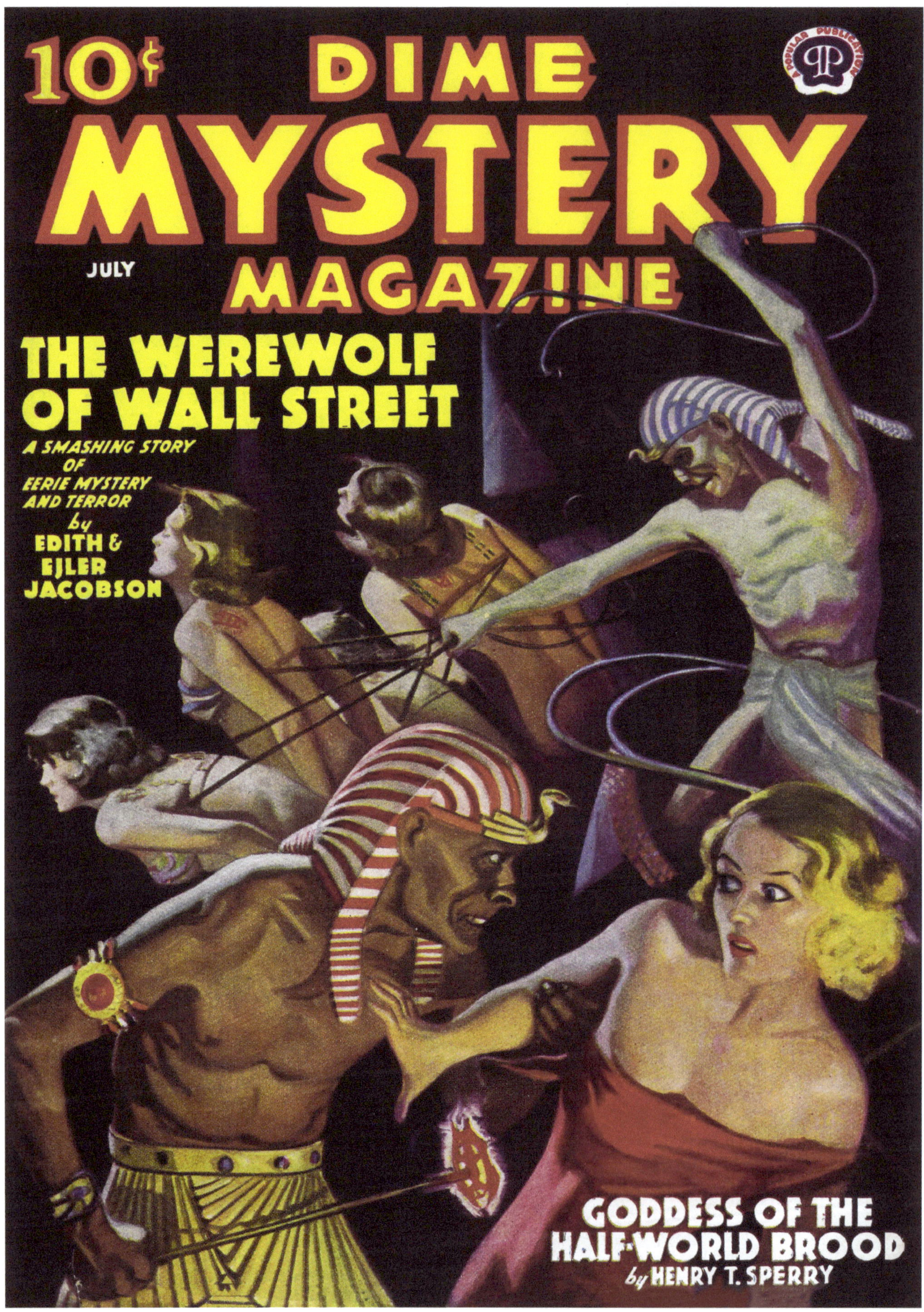

10¢
JULY
DIME MYSTERY MAGAZINE
THE WEREWOLF OF WALL STREET
A SMASHING STORY OF EERIE MYSTERY AND TERROR
by EDITH & EJLER JACOBSON
A POPULAR PUBLICATION
GODDESS OF THE HALF-WORLD BROOD
by HENRY T. SPERRY

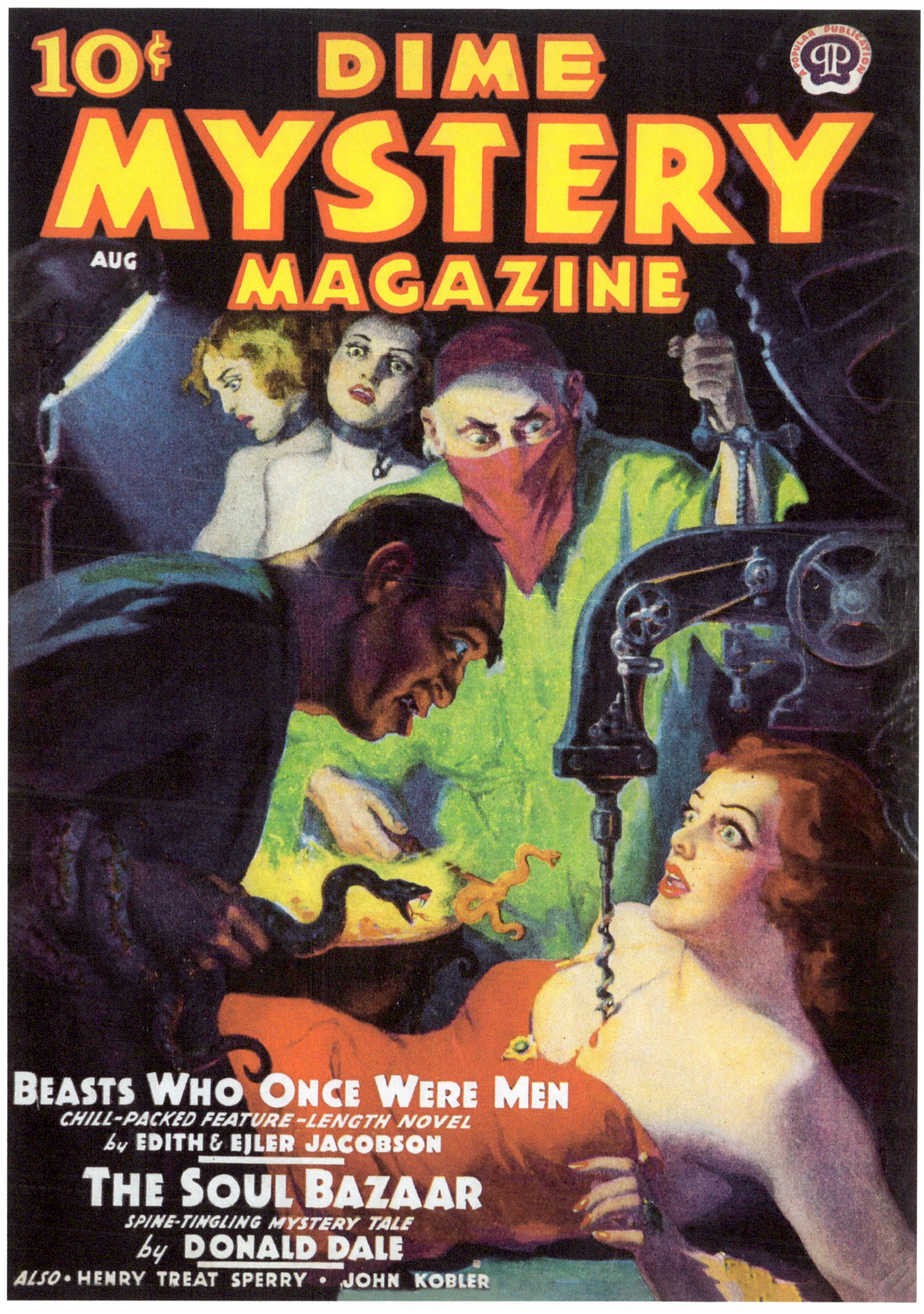

10¢
AUG
DIME MYSTERY MAGAZINE
BEASTS WHO ONCE WERE MEN
CHILL-PACKED FEATURE-LENGTH NOVEL
by EDITH & EJLER JACOBSON
THE SOUL BAZAAR
SPINE-TINGLING MYSTERY TALE
by DONALD DALE
ALSO • HENRY TREAT SPERRY • JOHN KOBLER

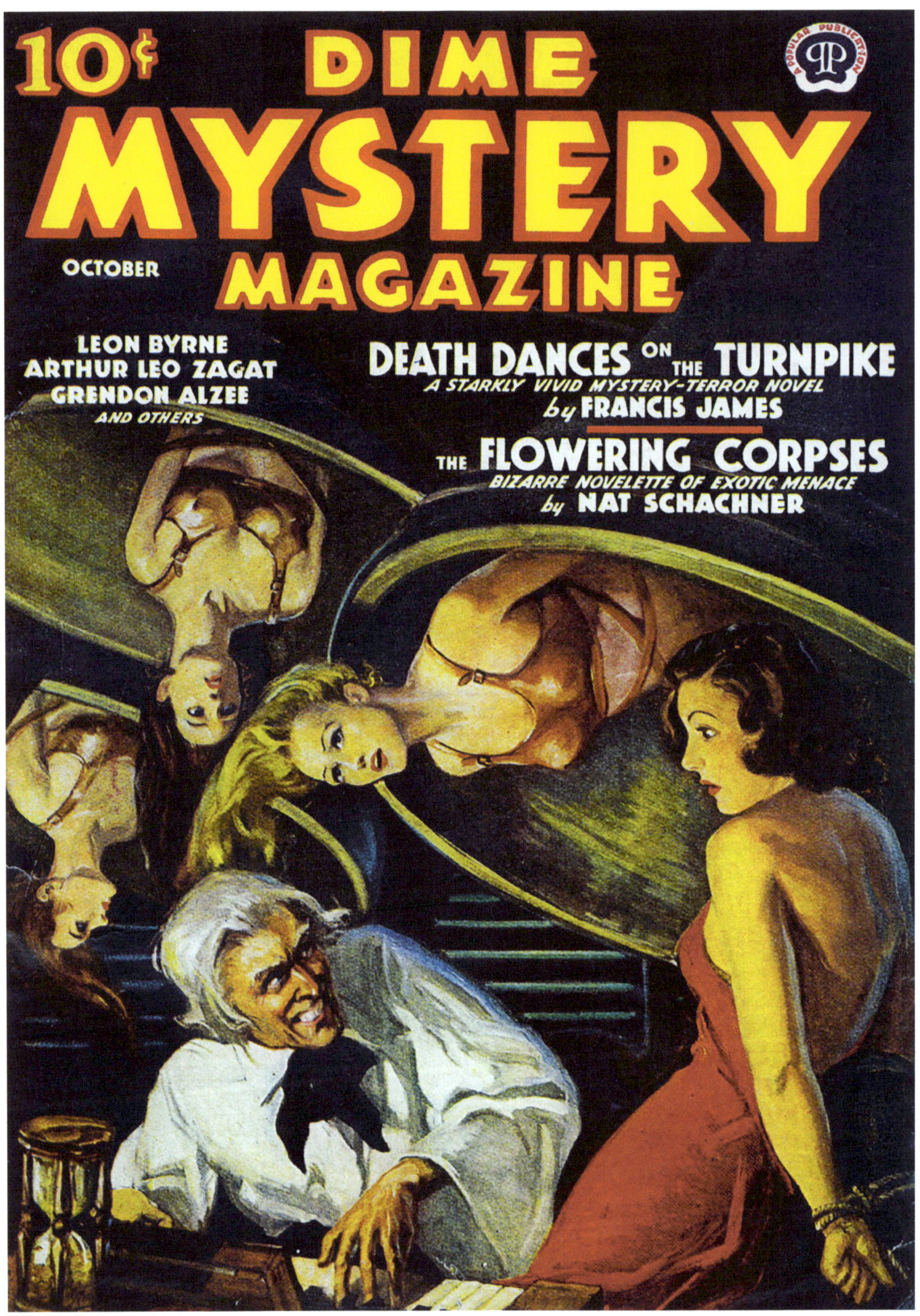

10¢
OCTOBER
DIME
MYSTERY
MAGAZINE
A POPULAR PUBLICATION
LEON BYRNE
ARTHUR LEO ZAGAT
GRENDON ALZEE
AND OTHERS
DEATH DANCES ON THE TURNPIKE
A STARKLY VIVID MYSTERY-TERROR NOVEL
by FRANCIS JAMES
THE FLOWERING CORPSES
BIZARRE NOVELETTE OF EXOTIC MENACE
by NAT SCHACHNER

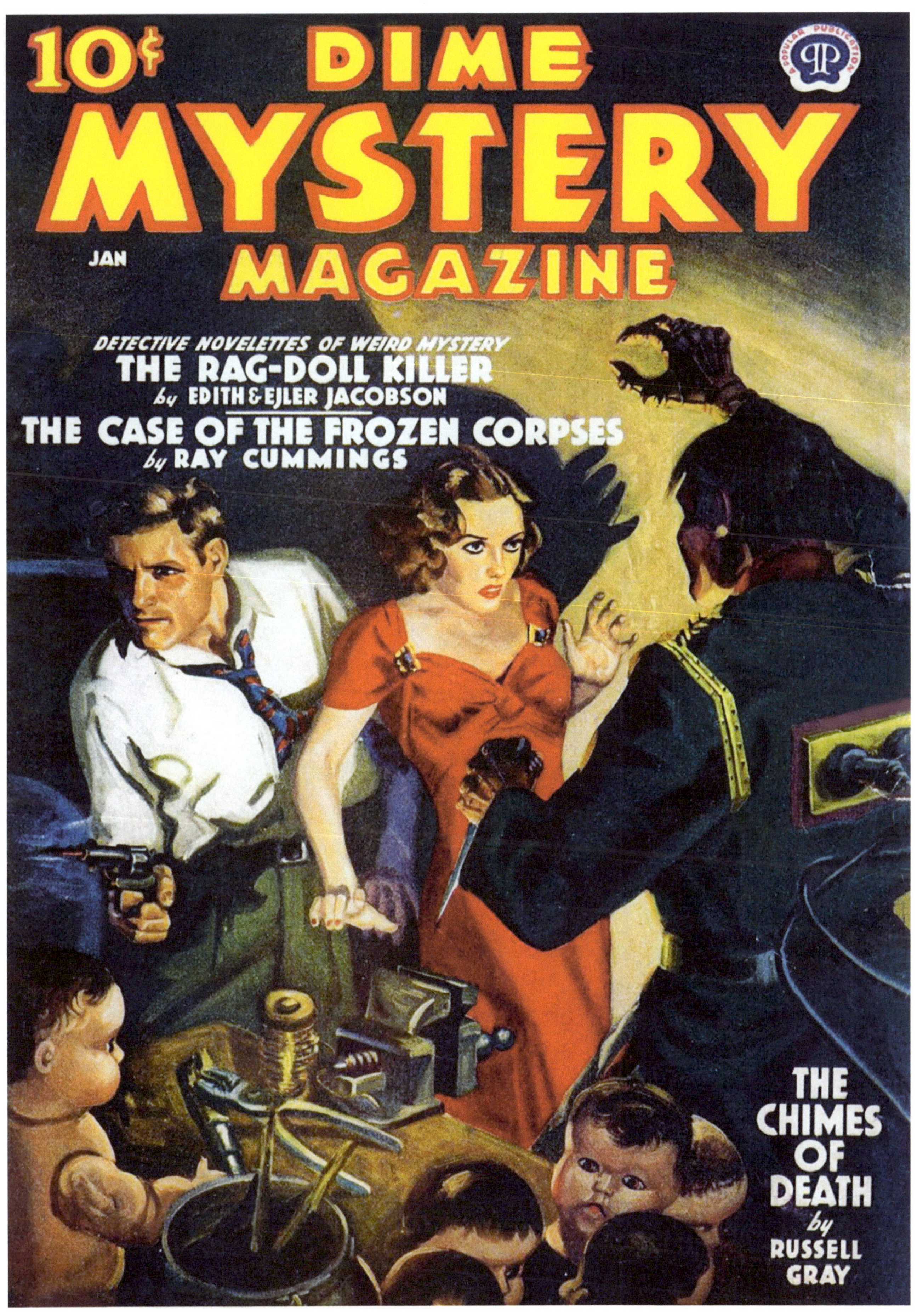

10¢
JAN
DIME MYSTERY MAGAZINE
DETECTIVE NOVELETTES OF WEIRD MYSTERY
THE RAG-DOLL KILLER
by EDITH & EJLER JACOBSON
THE CASE OF THE FROZEN CORPSES
by RAY CUMMINGS
THE CHIMES OF DEATH
by RUSSELL GRAY
A POPULAR PUBLICATION

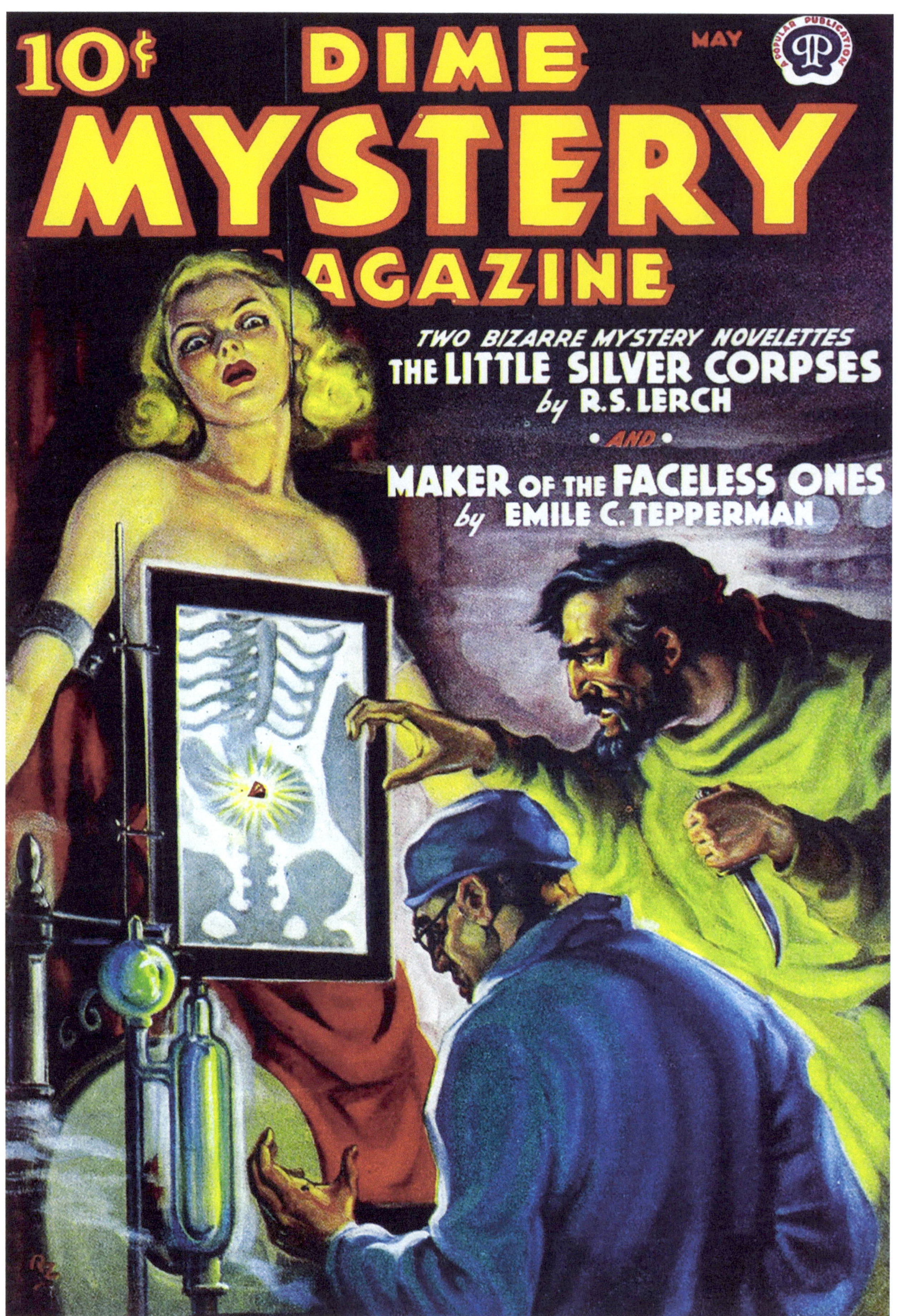

10¢
MAY
DIME MYSTERY MAGAZINE
TWO BIZARRE MYSTERY NOVELETTES
THE LITTLE SILVER CORPSES
by R. S. LERCH
AND
MAKER OF THE FACELESS ONES
by EMILE C. TEPPERMAN

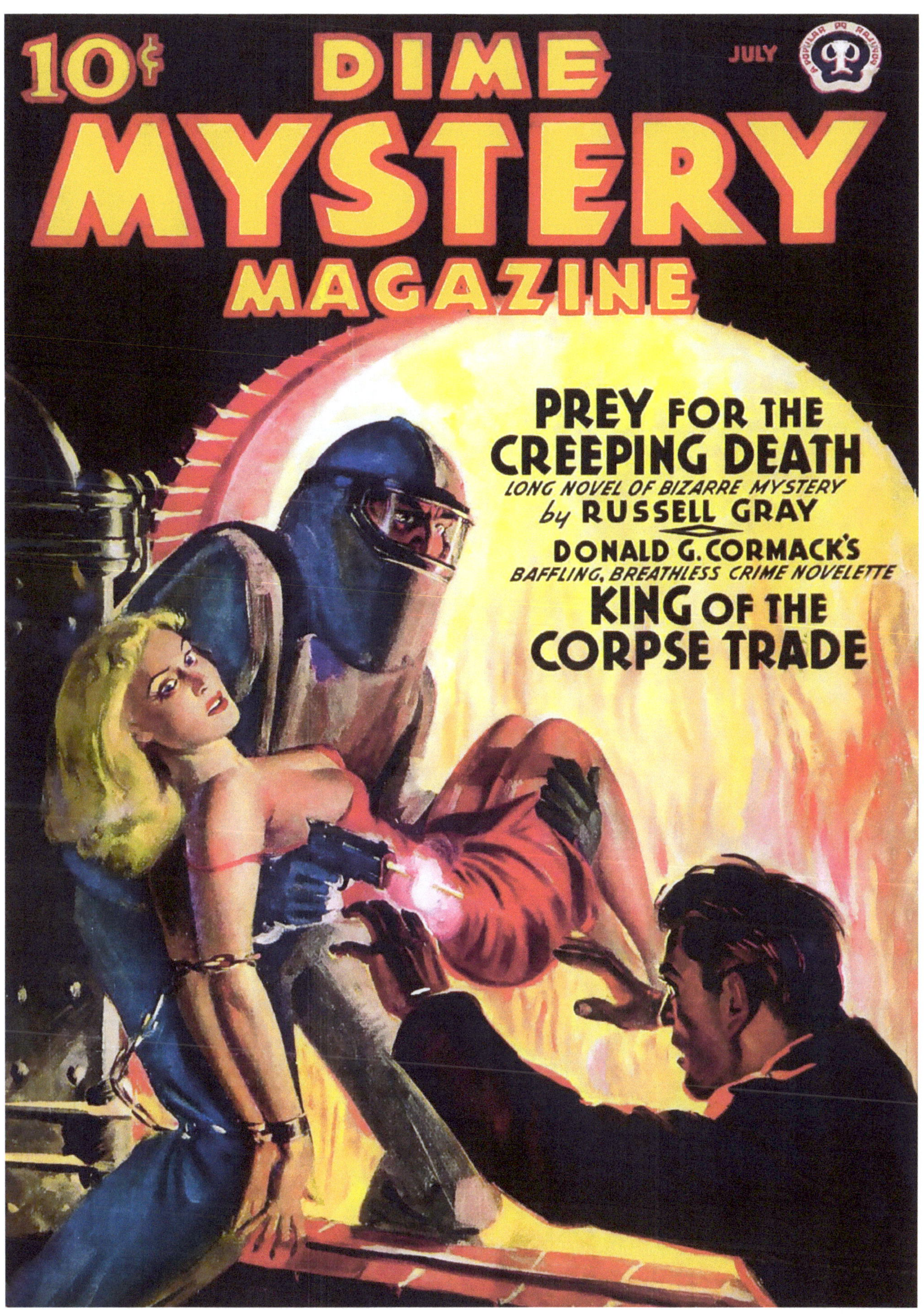

10¢
JULY
DIME MYSTERY MAGAZINE
PREY FOR THE CREEPING DEATH
LONG NOVEL OF BIZARRE MYSTERY
by RUSSELL GRAY
DONALD G. CORMACK'S
BAFFLING, BREATHLESS CRIME NOVELETTE
KING OF THE CORPSE TRADE

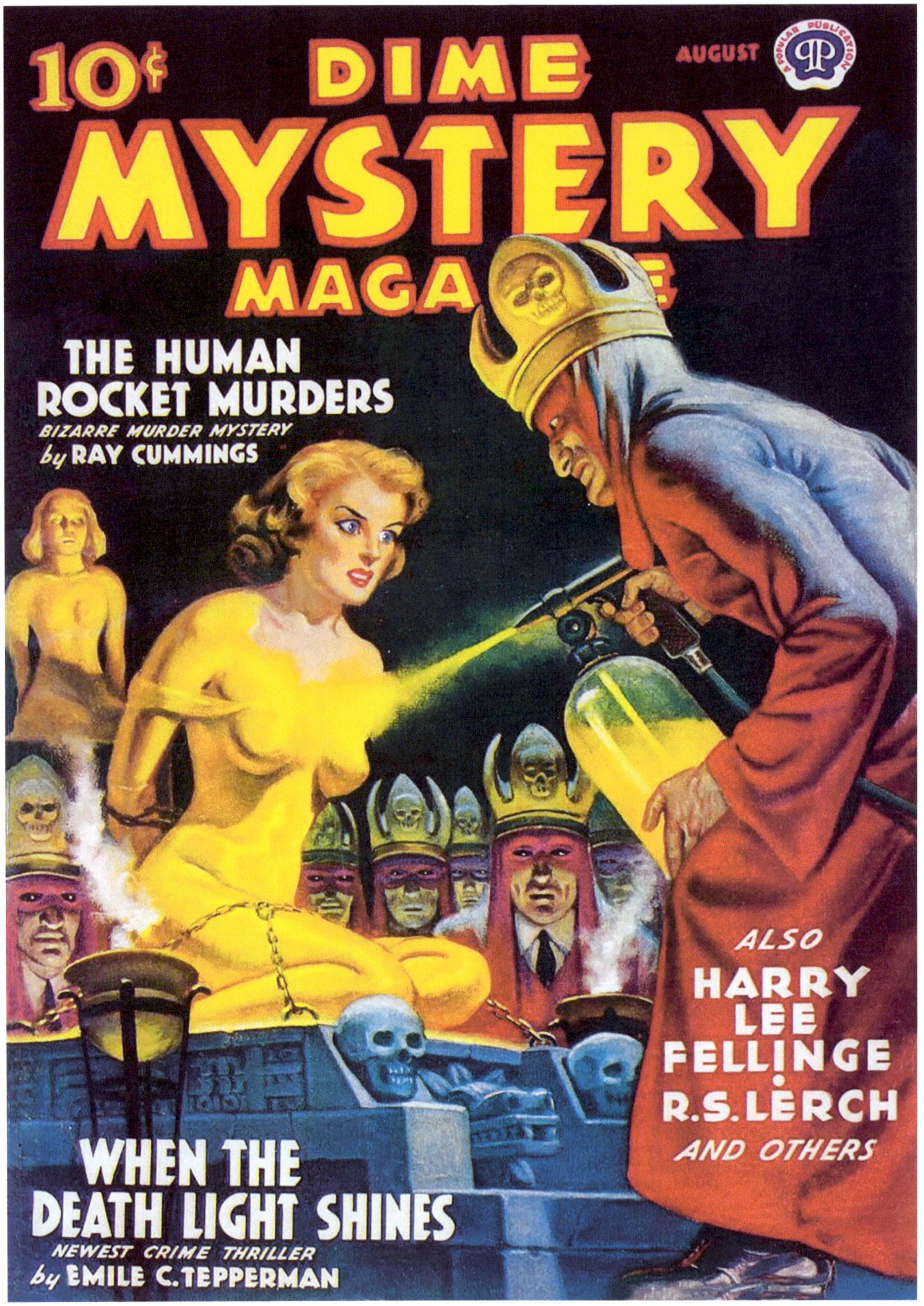

10¢
AUGUST
A POPULAR PUBLICATION
DIME MYSTERY MAGAZINE
THE HUMAN ROCKET MURDERS
BIZARRE MURDER MYSTERY
by RAY CUMMINGS
ALSO
HARRY LEE FELLINGE
R. S. LERCH
AND OTHERS
WHEN THE DEATH LIGHT SHINES
NEWEST CRIME THRILLER
by EMILE C. TEPPERMAN

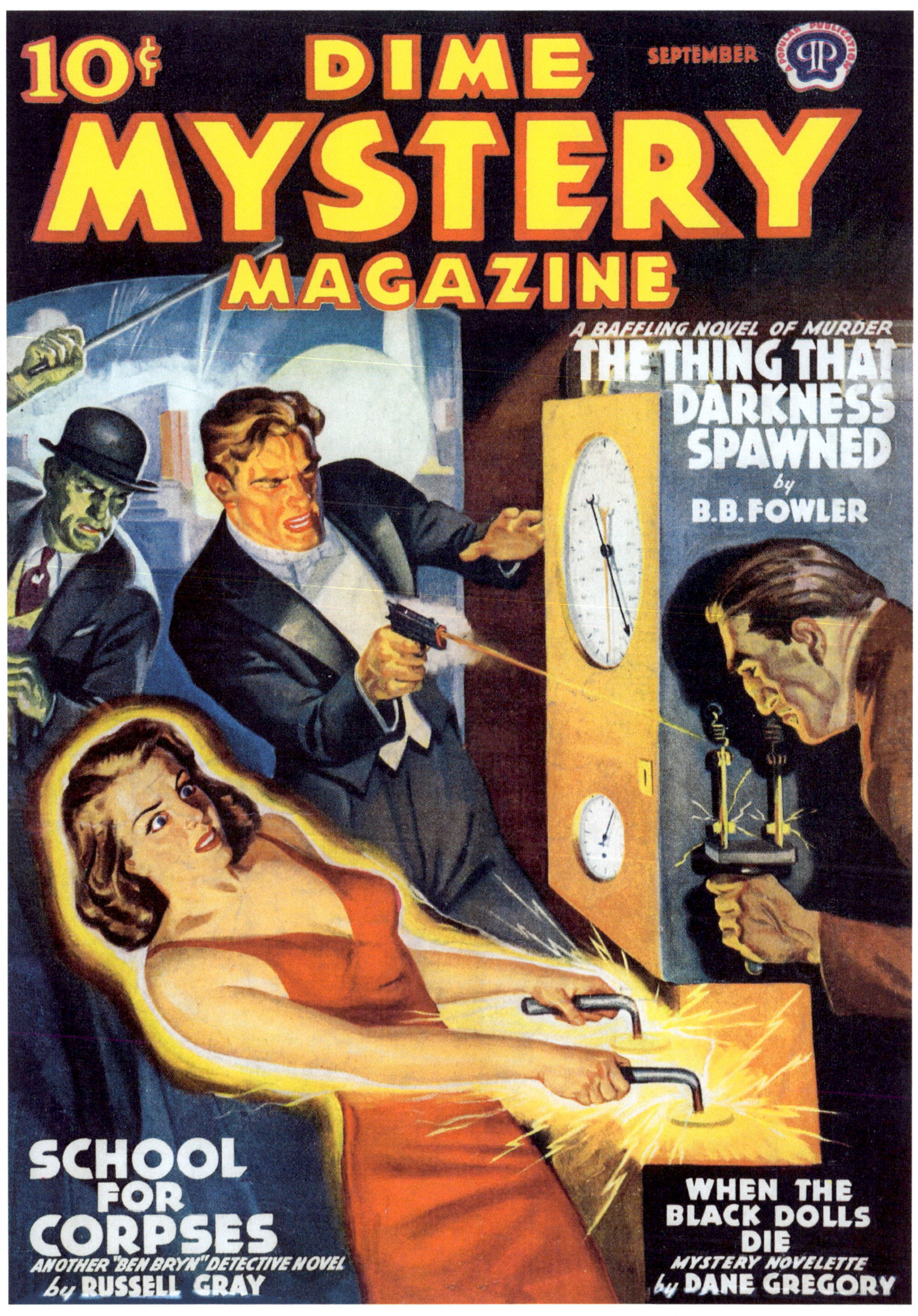

10¢
SEPTEMBER
DIME MYSTERY MAGAZINE
A BAFFLING NOVEL OF MURDER
THE THING THAT DARKNESS SPAWNED
by B.B. FOWLER
SCHOOL FOR CORPSES
ANOTHER "BEN BRYN" DETECTIVE NOVEL
by RUSSELL GRAY
WHEN THE BLACK DOLLS DIE
MYSTERY NOVELETTE
by DANE GREGORY

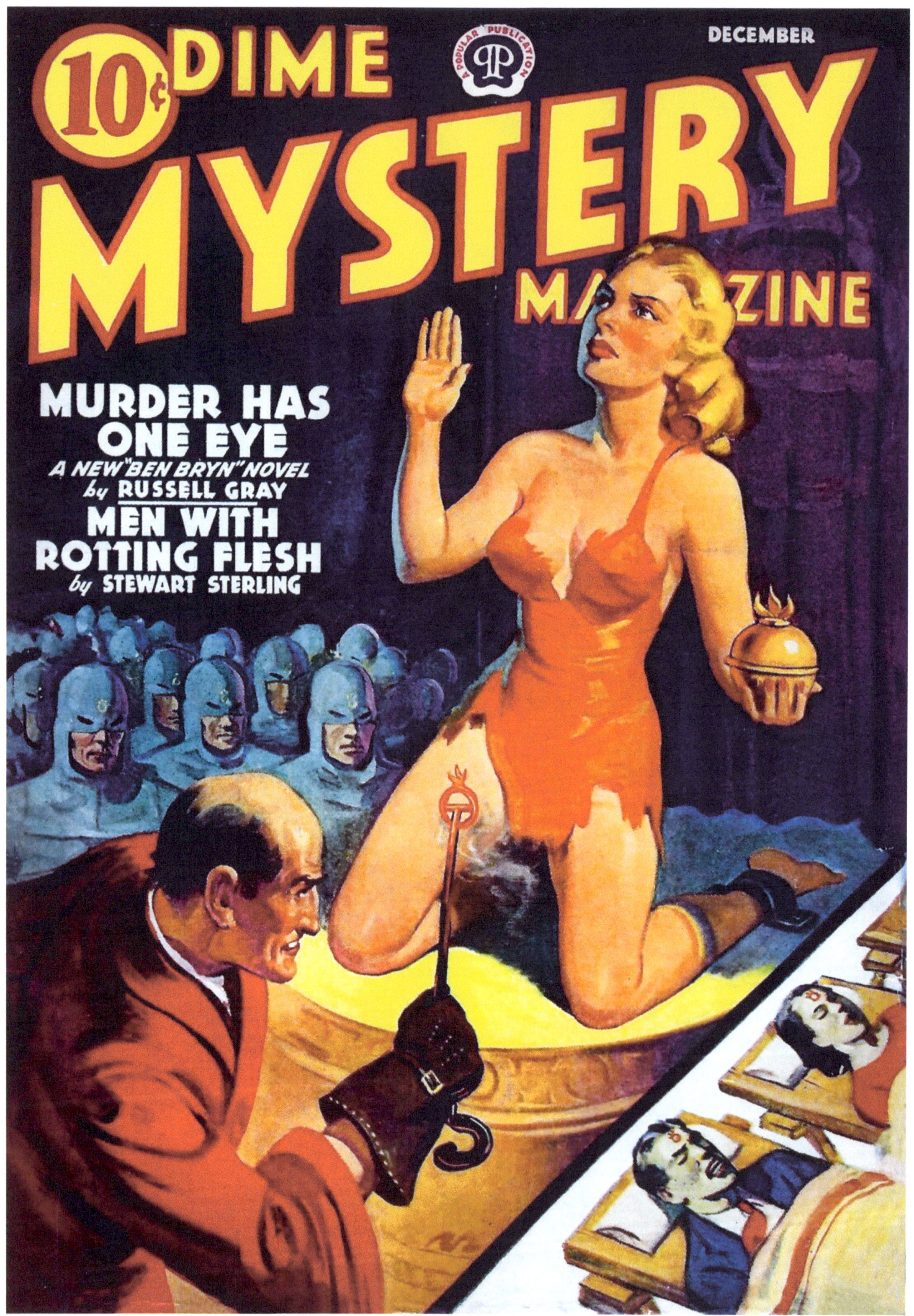

DIME MYSTERY MAGAZINE

DECEMBER 1939

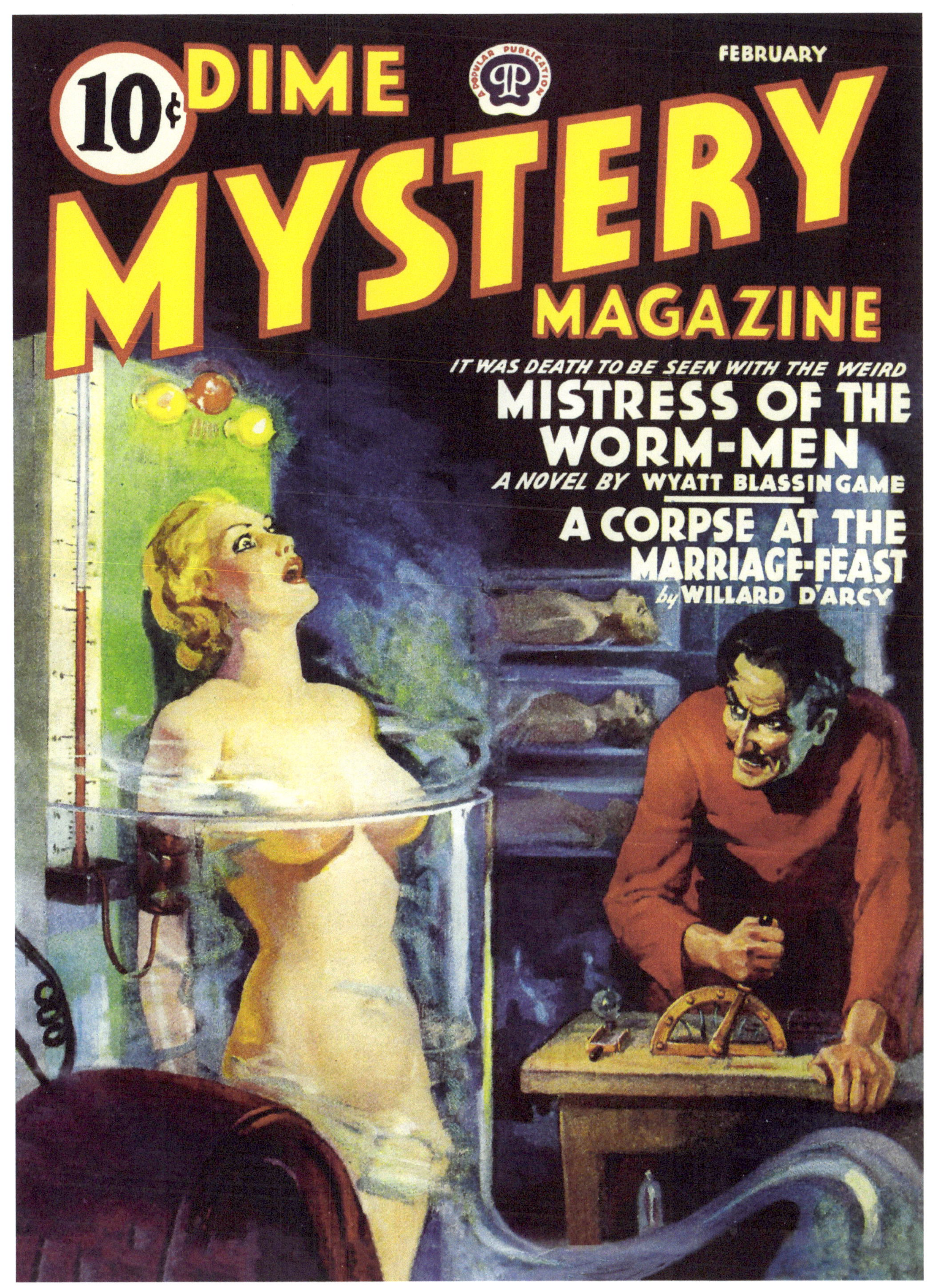

10¢
A POPULAR PUBLICATION
FEBRUARY
DIME MYSTERY MAGAZINE
IT WAS DEATH TO BE SEEN WITH THE WEIRD
MISTRESS OF THE WORM-MEN
A NOVEL BY WYATT BLASSINGAME
A CORPSE AT THE MARRIAGE-FEAST
by WILLARD D'ARCY

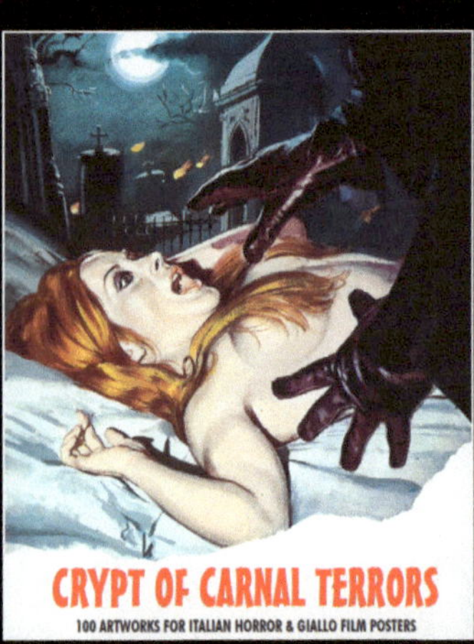
CRYPT OF CARNAL TERRORS
100 ARTWORKS FOR ITALIAN HORROR & GIALLO FILM POSTERS

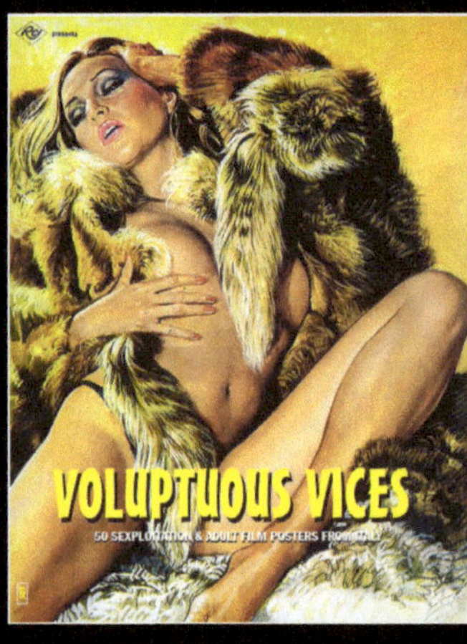
VOLUPTUOUS VICES
50 SEXPLOITATION & ADULT FILM POSTERS FROM ITALY

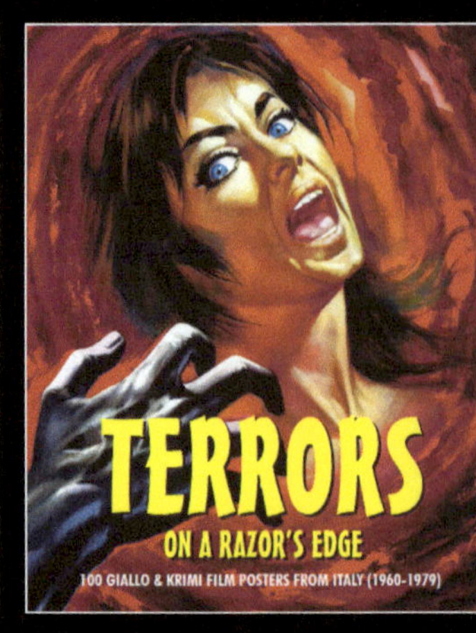
TERRORS
ON A RAZOR'S EDGE
100 GIALLO & KRIMI FILM POSTERS FROM ITALY (1960-1979)

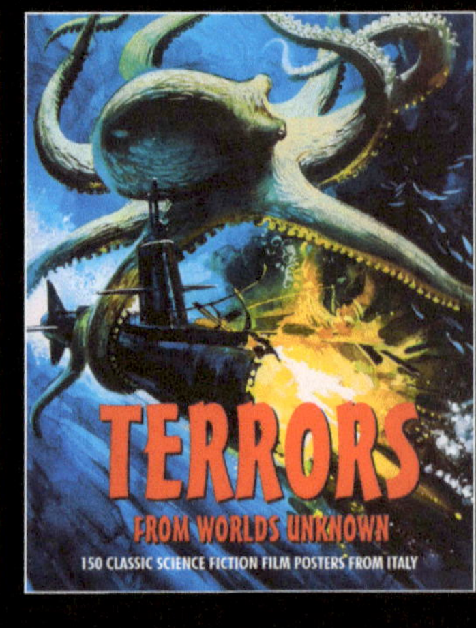
TERRORS
FROM WORLDS UNKNOWN
150 CLASSIC SCIENCE FICTION FILM POSTERS FROM ITALY

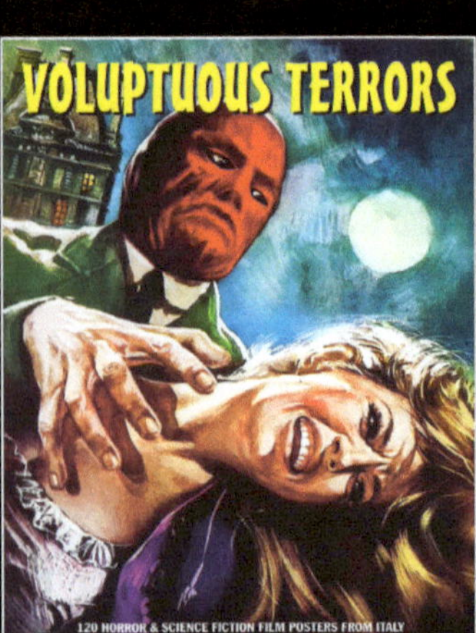
VOLUPTUOUS TERRORS
120 HORROR & SCIENCE FICTION FILM POSTERS FROM ITALY

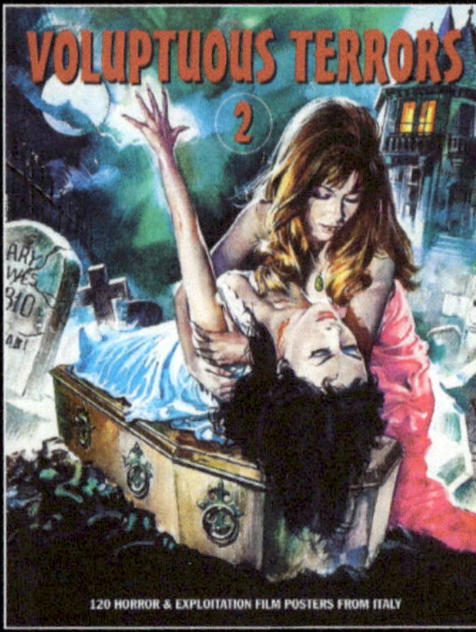
VOLUPTUOUS TERRORS
2
120 HORROR & EXPLOITATION FILM POSTERS FROM ITALY

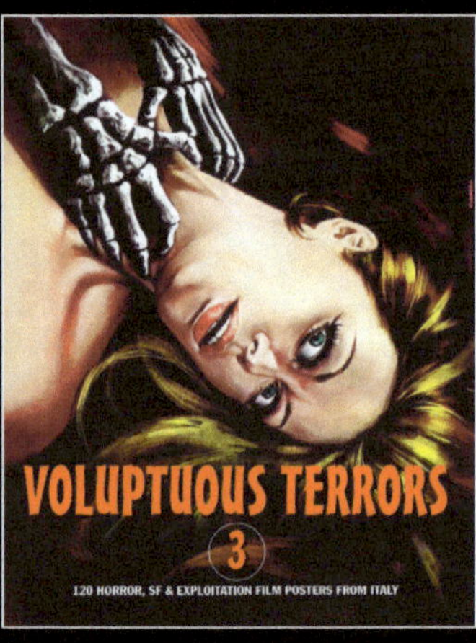
VOLUPTUOUS TERRORS
3
120 HORROR, SF & EXPLOITATION FILM POSTERS FROM ITALY

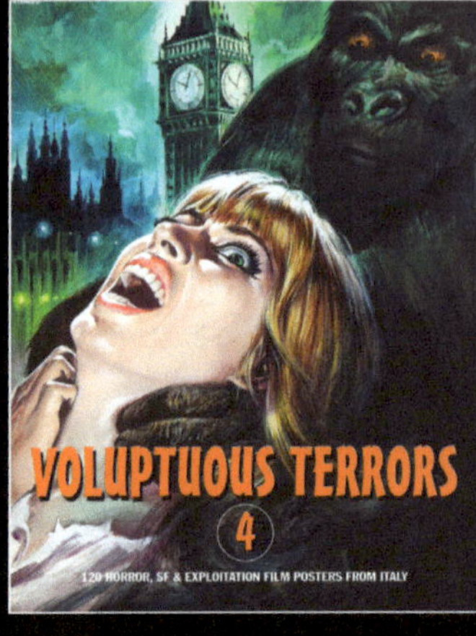
VOLUPTUOUS TERRORS
4
120 HORROR, SF & EXPLOITATION FILM POSTERS FROM ITALY

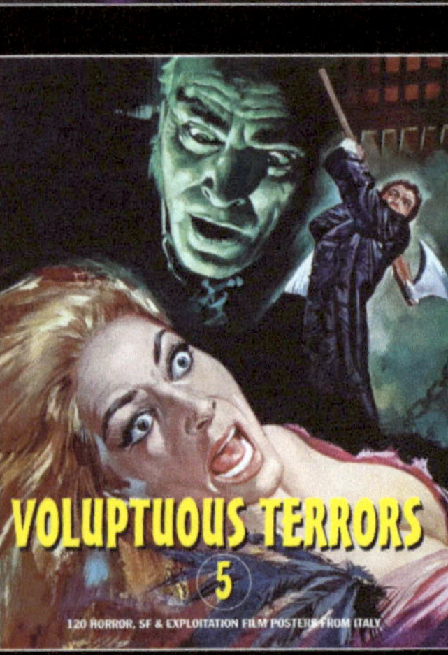
VOLUPTUOUS TERRORS
5
120 HORROR, SF & EXPLOITATION FILM POSTERS FROM ITALY

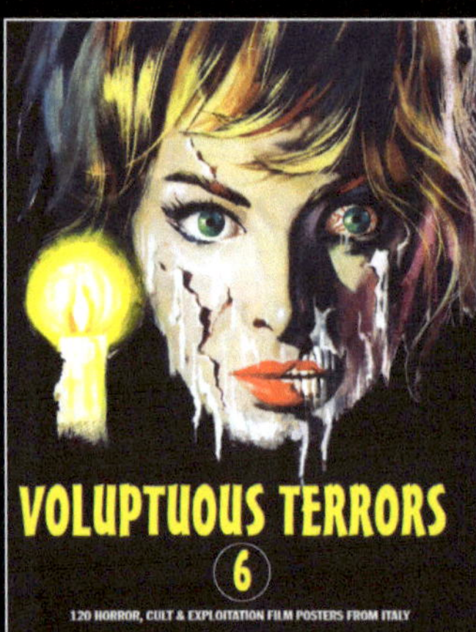
VOLUPTUOUS TERRORS
6
120 HORROR, CULT & EXPLOITATION FILM POSTERS FROM ITALY

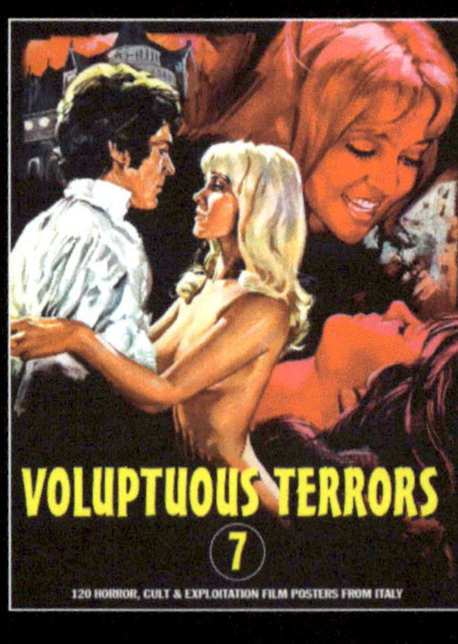
VOLUPTUOUS TERRORS
7
120 HORROR, CULT & EXPLOITATION FILM POSTERS FROM ITALY

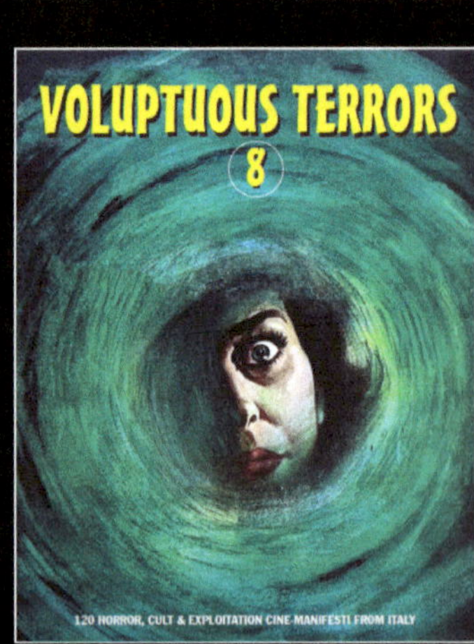
VOLUPTUOUS TERRORS
8
120 HORROR, CULT & EXPLOITATION CINE MANIFESTI FROM ITALY

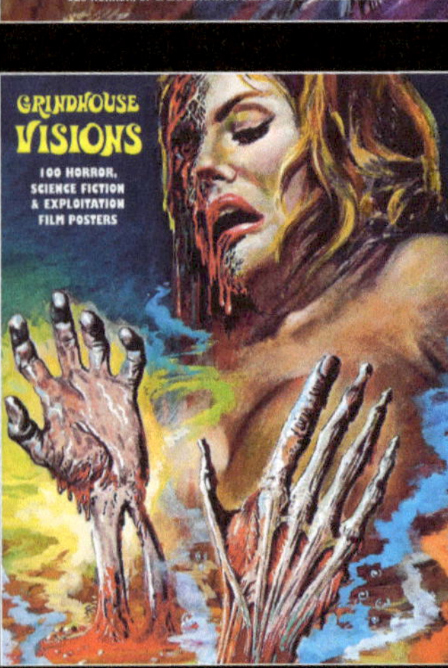
GRINDHOUSE
VISIONS
100 HORROR,
SCIENCE FICTION
& EXPLOITATION
FILM POSTERS

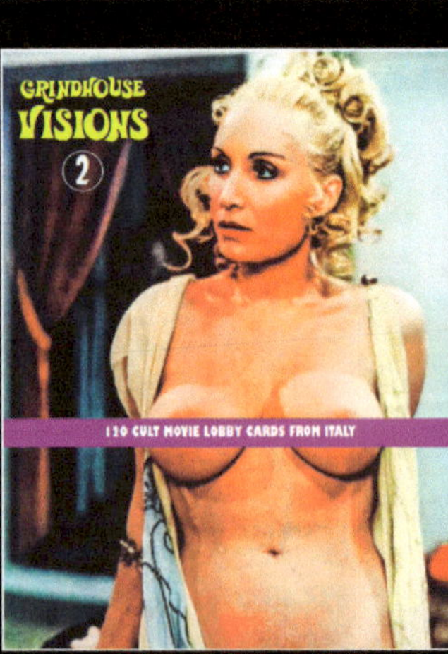
GRINDHOUSE
VISIONS
2
120 CULT MOVIE LOBBY CARDS FROM ITALY

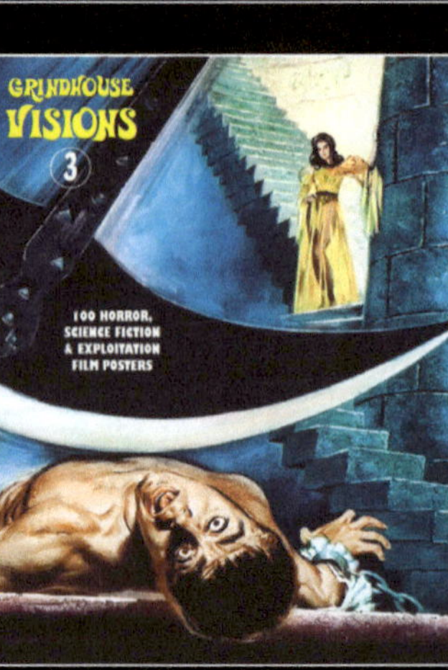
GRINDHOUSE
VISIONS
3
100 HORROR,
SCIENCE FICTION
& EXPLOITATION
FILM POSTERS

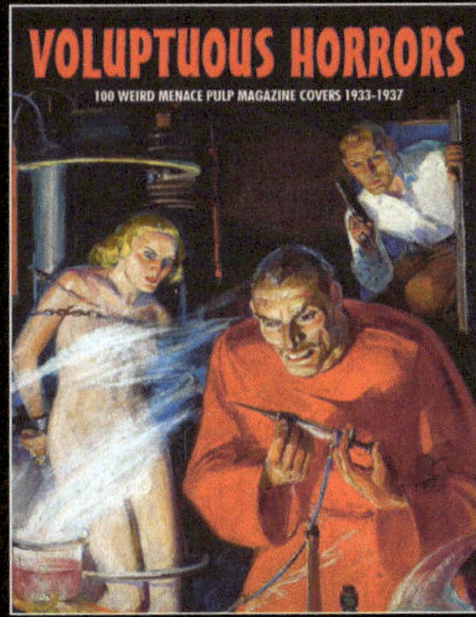

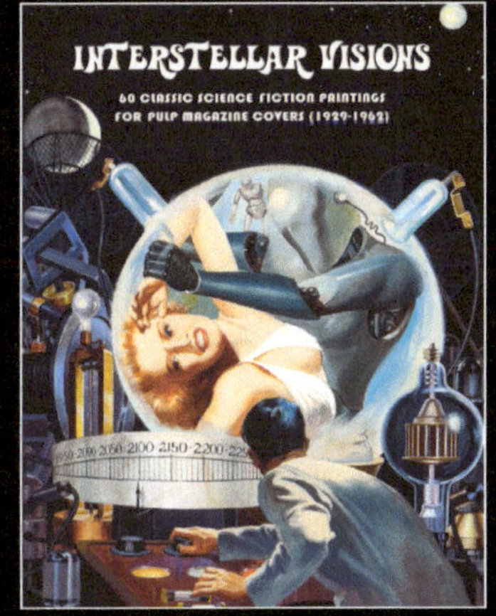

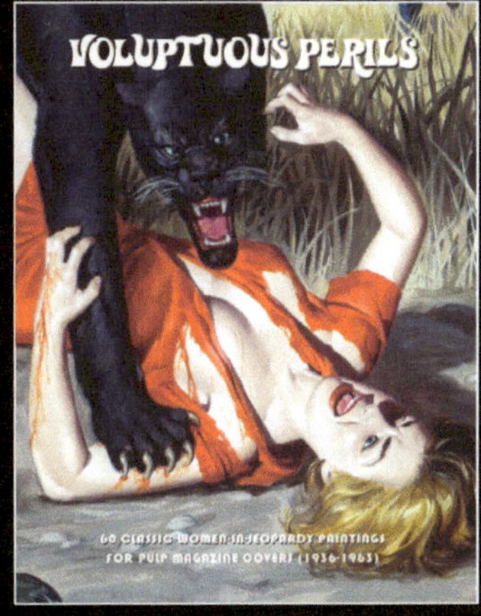

FILM HISTORY STUDIES FROM G.H. JANUS

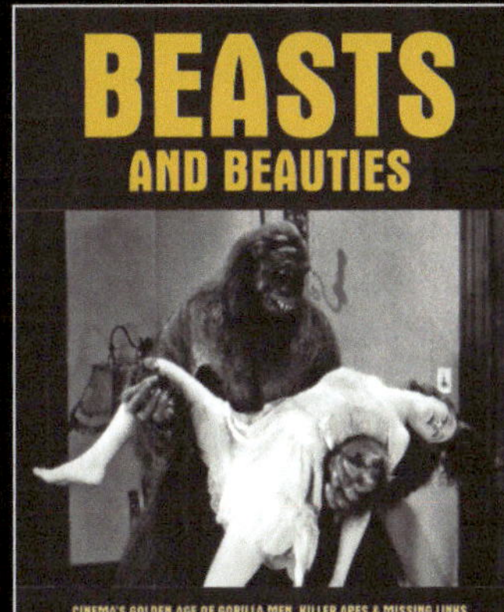

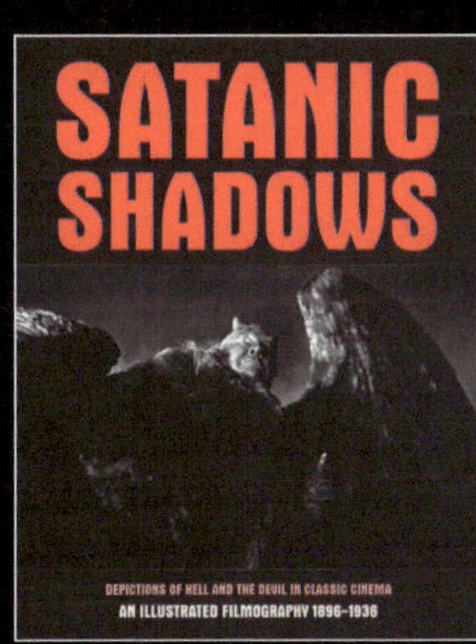

ALSO FROM BONEFYRE BOOKS

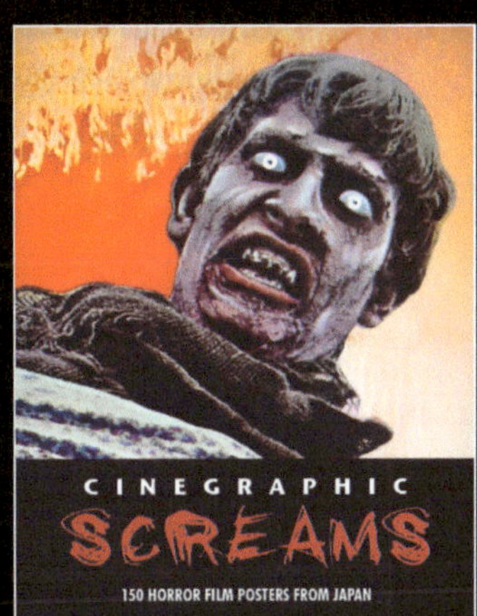

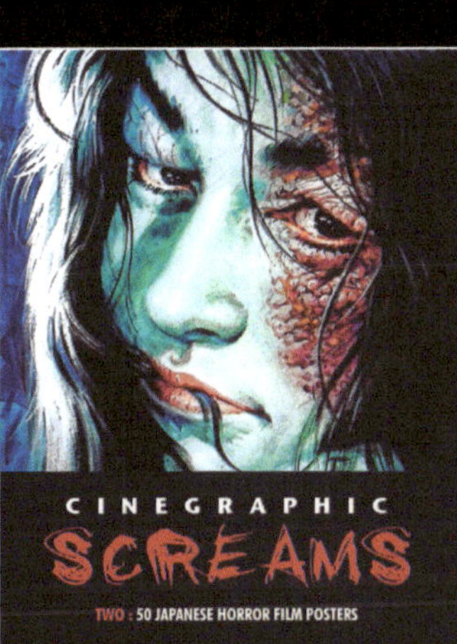